FEDERALISM
AND THE NEW WORLD ORDER

FEDERALISM
AND THE NEW WORLD ORDER

edited by

Stephen J. Randall

and

Roger Gibbins

University of Calgary Press

© 1994 Stephen J. Randall and Roger Gibbins. All rights reserved

University of Calgary Press
2500 University Drive N.W.
Calgary, Alberta, Canada T2N 1N4

Canadian Cataloguing in Publication Data

Main entry under title:
  Federalism and the new world order

  Papers from a conference held at the University of Calgary,
March 1993.
  Includes bibliographical references and index.
  ISBN 1-895176-56-5

  1. Federal government—Congresses. I. Randall, Stephen J.,
1944- II. Gibbins, Roger, 1947-
JC355.F42 1994   321.02   C94-910709-3

COMMITTED TO THE DEVELOPMENT OF CULTURE AND THE ARTS

All rights reserved. No part of this work covered by the copyrights hereon may be reproduced or used in any form or by any means—graphic, electronic or mechanical—without the prior permission of the publisher. Any request for photocopying, recording, taping or reproducing in information storage and retrieval systems of any part of this book shall be directed in writing to the Canadian Reprography Collective, 379 Adelaide Street West, Suite M1, Toronto, Ontario M5V 1S5.

Printed and bound in Canada by Hignell Printing Ltd.

∞ This book is printed on acid-free paper.

CONTENTS

Acknowledgements . . . . *ix*

Preface
Stephen J. Randall . . . . *xi*

I: REFLECTIONS ON FEDERALISM

On New Federalism
Mikhail S. Gorbachev 3

The Future of Federalism
James C. MacPherson 9

II: FEDERALIST REALITIES PAST AND PRESENT

The Challenge of New Politics and New Social Movements
to the Future of Federalism
Roger Gibbins 17

The Nation and the Future of Federalism
David G. Whitefield 43

Federalism: Russian Realities and Historical Experience
Yuri A. Krasin 57

COMMENTARY: States and Nations
Alan C. Cairns 71

III: ETHNICITY, NATIONALISM, AND FEDERALISM

Federalism and the Siamese Twins: Diversity and Entropy
in India's Domestic and Foreign Policy
Joyotpaul Chaudhuri 79

The Failure of Federalism: Yugoslavia
W. Harriet Critchley 99

The Future of Federalism:
Lessons from Canada and Québec
Alain-G. Gagnon and Guy Laforest 113

COMMENTARY: Ethnicity, Nationalism, and Federalism
Mathew Zachariah 133

IV: CONTEMPORARY CHALLENGES TO FEDERALISM

Federalism and the Environment: With Australia as a Case Study
Brian Galligan and Georgina Lynch 141

Ghosts of Federalism in the Soviet Successor States
Bohdan Harasymiw 165

Aboriginal Self-Government and Treaties:
A Discussion
Leroy Little Bear 183

COMMENTARY: Beyond Gloom and Doom—
Federalism, Citizenship, and Political Change
Linda Trimble 197

V: Transformations in Federal Structures

The European Community: Is it a Supranational State in the Making?
Gretchen M. MacMillan 215

Federalism and the Postsocialist Experience of Eastern Central Europe
Victor V. Kuvaldin 239

The Transformation of the Central and Eastern European Economies
Jan Adam 251

COMMENTARY: Whither Europe? Or, is There Life After the Bipolar World
Holger Herwig 275

Notes on Contributors 281

Index 287

Acknowledgements

Many individuals and institutions beyond the authors and editors have made this volume possible. For their work in helping to plan and implement the original symposium in Calgary at the time of Mikhail S. Gorbachev's national visit to Canada, we would like to express our appreciation to Dr Brenda Kennedy, Ashok Parmar, Monique Stadie and Reeta Padamsey of the International Centre. Dr. Kennedy and her staff were remarkably effective in organizing the event and facilitating the work of the other academics who participated in the conference. We are also very grateful to Mr. William T. Warden, Executive Director of the International Centre, for his commitment to making the national visit and the symposium a reality, as well as for providing a publication subsidy for the volume; to President Murray Fraser for his encouragement and active participation in the conference, and to Chancellor David Smith for his unfailing enthusiasm and commitment to the enterprise in which we were engaged.

Since the symposium was a joint venture between the University of Calgary, which initiated and organized the national visit by Mr Gorbachev, and the Gorbachev Foundation in Moscow, we would like especially to acknowledge the work of Yuri Krasin from the foundation. Not only did he contribute a paper to the volume, but he was a key actor in assembling the Russian members of the symposium.

Above all, this volume was made possible by the commitment which Mikhail S. Gorbachev brought to our attempt to understand the unfolding new world order of the post-Cold War era, in particular the future of federal systems of government within that new order. He brought deeply held personal convictions, the most significant experience of any contemporary world leader, and infectious warmth and enthusiasm to the enterprise. For that reason this volume is dedicated to him.

Finally, as on other occasions, we would like to acknowledge the remarkable work of our copyeditor Eileen Delman, who also prepared the index for the volume with her usual skill and expertise. At the University of

Calgary Press, Director Shirley Onn provided enthusiastic support for the project from the outset, as did University Press Production Editor John King. Press readers also rendered invaluable guidance for revision of an earlier version of the manuscript. To all of the above we are very grateful, although we alone of course are responsible for errors or omissions in the volume.

SR
RG

PREFACE

Stephen J. Randall

Like all books this one has a history. It is the product of remarkable and rapid changes in the international world order in the past three years; of the vision and humanity of one man—Mikhail Gorbachev; of the development of an institutional and personal link between the International Foundation for Socio-Economic and Political Studies in Moscow (the Gorbachev Foundation) and the University of Calgary. It is also the result of a coincidence of events in eastern and central Europe, Canada, and other areas of the world in the past decade, events which have made us more sensitive to our shared global problems.

On a grey, slushy afternoon in early March 1992, I travelled from the international airport in Moscow along the broad avenues that still distinguish Moscow to an imposing brick structure on Leningradsky Prospect, a guest—along with two colleagues from the University of Calgary and another from the London School of Slavonic and East European Studies—of the Gorbachev Foundation. That institution had just seen its first light of day, having been established by Mikhail Gorbachev and his advisers as he left the presidency of the Soviet Union at the end of December 1991. The symbolism of the imposing, yet largely empty, structure—which had previously housed the Communist Party training school—late on that Sunday afternoon was haunting. Was it really possible that the powerful empire and its leaders, institutions, and individuals who had dominated one half of the bipolar Cold War world for fifty years, had crumbled in a matter of months, with former Soviet republics tottering on the brink of open conflict with one another and the former central government?

The events surrounding the aborted coup of August 1991 in the Soviet Union captured the attention of the world, as did the erosion in the following months of the Soviet federal system, its institutions, and the power of its leaders. But the previous half-decade had also been remarkable. Mikhail Gorbachev stirred the imagination of the West in a way that no former Soviet leader had been able to achieve. His magnetic personal appeal and frequent appearances in the West; his strategic arms limitation talks with the Republican administration of Ronald Reagan in the United States; his contribution to the 'liberation' of eastern Europe; and his ability to unleash, if not always his capacity to contain, the forces of political and economic reform in the Soviet Union, all made him the central figure in the ending of the Cold War. The Berlin Wall, the most visible symbol of a world that had been too long polarized, too long incapable of achieving meaningful dialogue on issues of vital importance to humankind, finally came down.

Yet, Gorbachev himself was either unwilling or unable to control the forces of change in eastern and central Europe and of counterrevolution within the Soviet Union. And so, he fell from power, to be followed by political restructuring, political crisis in Russia and in its former republics, and a continued movement toward market economics and economic reform. For some, he had moved too quickly toward reform; for others, what he wrought was too little and too late. None questioned that he had had a dramatic impact in reshaping the Cold War world and contributing to its demise.

Our initial meeting with Mr Gorbachev and his staff at the Foundation produced the basis for the development of a collaborative relationship between the University of Calgary and the Gorbachev Foundation. The first fruits of that cooperative spirit was a conference at the University of Calgary in June 1992 on Civil Society. That conference, which included two members of the Gorbachev Foundation, Yuri Krasin and Georgy Shakhnazarov, explored in a preliminary way some of the topics and themes that are contained in this volume: social, economic, and political transitions in the world order and in the internal political order of states in various regions of the world, not least of which in the former Soviet Union and in Canada. A second phase of the relationship was a sequel conference in July 1992 in Moscow on aspects of the new world order, including health care as well as the political transitions occurring in both the eastern and western hemispheres. The third phase of the bilateral relationship was the organization of Mr Gorbachev's national visit to Canada in March 1993. The main academic event of Mr Gorbachev's activities at the University of Calgary, which inaugurated the national tour, was a jointly sponsored conference on the new world order and the future of federalism as a political structure. That conference generated the papers that are published in this volume.

The main international issue which attracted Mr Gorbachev and his staff was the political transition to a new world order, what he often referred to as the new civilization. It was evident that Gorbachev viewed the fate of federalism as a critical dimension of that system's transformation, a political system which was endangered by many of the developments that were occurring within the former Soviet Union, eastern Europe, and even the developed West. We accordingly considered it essential that the authors of these papers address federalism within the context of broader international challenges and that it be done so in a comparative manner, avoiding an exclusive concern with Canada or the former Soviet Union. Indeed, one of the objectives of this volume is to attempt to heighten the understanding of Canadians that the issues that bedevil federalism within Canada are not unique to the Canadian experience and must be understood in a comparative and international context.

Thus, the essays which follow range widely over the former Soviet Union, eastern and central Europe, the European Community, India, Australia, and Canada, with passing discussion of the United States. Although the essays in the volume are disparate, and perhaps seem disconnected at times, the overarching theme is social, political, and economic change and their challenge to the world we have shared since World War II. The essays were chosen to address thematic issues perceived to be critical in the current developments: the importance of the division of powers within federal states; the challenge to federalism of what is referred to in this volume as the "new social movements": feminism, environmentalism, aboriginal rights; the role of ethnicity and nationalism; the relationship between nation states and supranational federations, such as the European Community or the Commonwealth of Independent States; economic restructuring in central and eastern Europe. What the essays do not deal with are foreign and defense policy and national security issues, which, it might be suggested, could certainly be considered as forces influencing federal arrangements as well as world order.

At the heart of debate is whether federalism can cope with the strains that have been placed on it in recent years. Designers of federal systems, whether in the United States, where the debate was inaugurated and refined in *The Federalist Papers* in the late eighteenth century, or in Canada, Russia, or elsewhere, have been consistent in their concerns about power: who holds it; how it is divided; how it is limited; what safeguards exist for minorities within the system. The essence of federalism is a constitutional sharing of political power and jurisdiction among two or more defined orders of government (see James MacPherson's observations in this volume), although, as

Brian Galligan and Georgian Lynch are careful to stress, the division of powers need not involve a hierarchy of powers. The papers in general suggested that the issue of how to divide power was in itself only one of a broad range of challenges to federal states and that new challenges to federal systems— such as the environment, ethnicity, and gender—have been added to more traditional, historical issues. An international tendency toward the establishment of regional trading blocs—including the North American Free Trade Agreement among Canada, the United States, and Mexico—and the entrenchment of such supranational federations as the European Community, raised further questions about the capacity of the traditional federations to survive.

An element of pessimism pervaded the discussions of federalism's future, largely because of the concern that regional governments within larger federal systems would not be able to contend with the broader, often international, challenges which face governments today, including the Third World challenges of massive poverty, ethnic and religious fervour, migration, and crime, that have led various analysts, including political scientist Samuel P. Huntington, to warn of an impending "clash of civilizations," in which cultural conflict will replace traditional nation-state conflict (1993; see also Kaplan 1994; Homer-Dixon 1991).

Not all of the following papers present a pessimistic view of federalism's future—Linda Trimble, Brian Galligan and Georgina Lynch, and Joyotpaul Chaudhuri are important departures from that approach. David Whitefield, in his analysis of the very concept and historical development of the "nation," concludes that federations will continue to play a "dominant role" in European political organization. Nonetheless, there remains considerable concern that federalism may not be able to survive the challenges which now face it.

Canada and the former Soviet Union are logically at the core of the papers in this volume. In both areas, federalism is beleaguered, challenged by forces old and new. The Soviet Union collapsed under the weight of its own history and contradictions to be replaced by a makeshift Commonwealth of Independent States (CIS), and the continuation of the Russian Federation. But the future of both the Russian Federation and the CIS remains uncertain, as both Yuri Krasin and Victor Kuvaldin effectively demonstrate in their essays. The problems confronting the former Soviet republics in 1994 seem almost overwhelming. In addition to the dislocation occasioned by the faltering transition to market economies, there are a wide range of traditional problems: an historical legacy of fear and distrust among the former republics; struggles for political and economic power in the republics; traditional tensions among ethnic groups within the former Soviet Union; historical Russian imperialist ambitions, and the anxieties of former Soviet Republics faced with that ambition; the desire of elite groups within the former republics jealous of their newfound autonomy. Such dynamics underline the difficulties that confront the region—as evidenced in the papers by Mikhail Gorbachev, Yuri Krasin, Victor Kuvaldin, Jan Adam, Bohdan Harasymiw, and David Whitefield.

Such problems have not been limited to the former Soviet Republics, but have also exploded in the former Soviet sphere of influence in central-eastern Europe. The Soviet Union's demise created a vacuum of power in eastern and central Europe, as well as in the larger East-West balance. Gorbachev's more liberal approach to Soviet satellites made reform, even rebellion, inevitable within the Soviet sphere. East and West Germany achieved reunification after half a century of division, although not without continuing major adjustment problems. Elsewhere in central Europe, stability was even more fragile with the removal of the stabilizing influence of the Union of Soviet Socialist Republics and the East-West conflict. As Harriet Critchley so effectively chronicles in this volume, one of the major flashpoints of Europe remained the Balkans, which succumbed to the ethnic, religious, and territorial strains that had been kept in uneasy check since World War II. Ethnic exclusiveness made a resurgence that was especially pronounced in, but not limited to, the case of Yugoslavia, where civil war and the disintegration of the country involved genocide and publicly espoused "ethnic cleansing," as Christian battled Muslim. Yuri Krasin and Victor Kuvaldin both suggest that ethnic/nationality divisiveness was also frequently at the heart of conflict in the former Soviet Union and within Russia itself, as former republics began to chart their own independent courses, free of their previous dominance from Moscow.

Ethnic nationalism was only one, albeit a powerful and emotive, force that threatened established political structures and economic ties. So many major forces seemed less relevant within the traditional boundaries of the state. Environmental concerns, and certainly the effects of environmental damage and crises, were international as well as national and local problems, but their solutions were rarely attainable with local attention alone. Brian Galligan and Georgina Lynch, in their thorough analysis of the "new federalism" in Australia, nonetheless indicate that there is room for optimism that environmental issues can be addressed through cooperation among international, national, and local governments.

Nothing could have more dramatically underlined the international nature of the environmental crisis, as well as the nationalist impediments to cooperation, than the effort of the United Nations to focus the attention of the world on the environment at a conference held in Rio de Janeiro in June 1992. The world watched with misgivings, which at times gave way to dismay, as the delegates to the United Nations Conference on Environment and Development struggled to overcome differing national priorities in identifying environmental problems. Clearly, all nations—industrial and preindustrial—faced massive environmental hurdles in their quest either for development in what was once known as the third world, or for sustained growth in the developed nations. Although multinational solutions remained elusive, environmental problems were clearly ones that could not be faced and resolved by single nations alone.

By the 1990s, the world was confronted with apparently contradictory tendencies toward, on the one hand, heightened nationalism, with ethnic, linguistic, and religious considerations paramount; and, on the other, the growing importance of supranational organizations. The European Community was the most successful model of the latter, politically and economically; but in the area of trade, regional economic groupings and free trade areas gained increasing momentum, whether the Association of Southeast Asian Nations (ASEAN) group in countries in Asia, Mercosur in Southern Latin America, the United States-Canada Free Trade Agreement, or the emerging North American Free Trade Agreement (NAFTA). The realities of modern international trade and investment also served to threaten traditional state structures and jurisdictions. Provincial and state impediments to the movement of goods, capital, and services within and among nations had become anachronistic. The emerging new world order in the post-Cold War era was one in which narrow national and local exclusiveness seemed to have no legitimate place, but in which that quest for exclusiveness was as vigorous as ever. It is difficult to determine whether there was a cause-and-effect relationship between the intensification of nationalism and the emphasis on capitalist globalism. Without doubt, many traditional groups and their values were threatened by the quest for global economic integration. Yet, as Victor Kuvaldin of the Gorbachev Foundation suggests, many of those eastern European nations wracked by ethnic conflicts, in these early post-Soviet and post-Cold War years, have promptly sought to draw closer to the western

European Community in an effort to achieve economic advantage and modernization after decades within the Soviet system.

Another tension, or even contradiction, between the forces that stress nationalism and reform on the one side, and internationalism and capitalist globalism on the other, is that the former tend to be perceived as democratic, liberal, even radical, while the latter are considered by many as decidedly conservative in nature. As Roger Gibbins demonstrates in his analysis of the new social movements, those movements, whether feminism or environmentalism, are highly interventionist and statist in nature, even though they are also inclined to be critical of traditional elites, left-libertarian in political orientation, and seek greater democratization of the political process. Moreover, as Gibbins suggests, the Canadian political left has tended to be antifederalist, with the result that the new social movements challenge existing federalist structures.

Such an orientation is not surprising. Even a cursory reading of the classic document on early federalism, the United States *Federalist Papers*, written by John Jay, James Madison, and Alexander Hamilton in the course of the debate over the ratification of the American Constitution, reveals that the central issue at the heart of all political systems has been power and its control. Power struggles between traditional and new elites, between minorities with and majorities without power are the essence of politics and will remain so whether a political system is federal in nature or not. The critical distinction that Gibbins makes, however, is that while federal systems tend to protect a cultural diversity and pluralism, they protect pluralism that is "manifested in territorial communities, interests, and identities," and the new social movements tend to transcend those territorial boundaries.

Joyotpaul Chaudhuri, in his analysis of the evolving Indian system, suggests that the Indian political structure itself tends to foster religious, ethnic, and regional conflicts, as well as weaken Indian economic development and the articulation of an effective foreign policy. For Chaudhuri, the most effective means of alleviating the present difficulties is to seek a process of gradual greater decentralization of the political system. As Chaudhuri notes, India is an essentially unitary state, adopted from the British legal model; but Indian culture is more pluralistic than that unitary state in the legal realm might imply. The diversity and conflictual nature of Indian culture, including political culture, is especially embodied in the area of religion, with the often violent clash between Hinduism and fundamentalist Islam. The Indian central government has historically been unable to resolve, in any permanent way, the tensions that exist between the centre and the periphery, especially in Kashmir, Punjab, and the northern Hindu area. In India, as in parts of the eastern European crises, it has been difficult to separate religion and ethnicity as the roots of conflict. Mathew Zachariah, in his summary analysis of the papers on ethnicity and nationalism, shares the concerns of other authors that the nation-state needs to come to terms with the ethnic, religious, and other cultural tensions that have placed such intense strains on the fabric of federal societies.

For David Whitefield, the problems of state structures and organizations transcend the question of federalism. Drawing and elaborating upon the work of British Marxist historian Eric Hobsbawm, Whitefield expresses little surprise, and perhaps less anxiety, about the current state of flux in federal states. To Whitefield, and of course to Hobsbawm, a "nation" is a fluid, dynamic entity and concept, and not entirely a desirable one, flowing out of the interests and machinations of politicians rather than being the natural product of popular desire and creation. It is thus not surprising that with the resurgence of nationalism in its various guises, as the twentieth century draws to a rather chaotic close, federalism and other forms of political order should be in question.

For Canadians, the crises facing federal states elsewhere in the world seemed ominous. Canada had for decades been engaged in a difficult and often bitter debate over the nature and future of Canadian federalism. The place of the province of Québec was, for many people, the critical issue in that constitutional debate, as Guy Laforest and Alain-G. Gagnon discuss in their paper on the future of federalism in the Québec-Canada relationship. What Laforest and Gagnon emphasize in their paper is the basic tension between federal practices and Québec's "search for nationhood." Here, Gagnon and Laforest's support for asymmetry in Canadian federalism may find an ally in Brian Galligan's view that divisions of power within federal systems do not require a hierarchy of power. Gagnon and Laforest's contention that at the heart of the Canadian dilemma is the "failure of political elites to recognize competing visions" parallels Yuri Krasin's analysis of the situation in the former Soviet Republics, the CIS, and Russian Federation, although in those instances it is not a "failure" to recognize competing visions but the vested interest of those elites not to do so. What Gagnon and Laforest appear not to accept was the evidence in the course of both the Meech Lake and Charlottetown federal-provincial negotiations that the political dynamic and agenda in the country had altered. New issues arose or at least moved closer to centre stage in the federal and constitutional discussions. How did one incorporate into a constitutional arrangement concerns over native rights or over the status of women, to mention only two major areas in which debate was intense? For Gagnon and Laforest, the effort to incorporate into the Charlottetown package an aboriginal government as a "third order" of federalism in Canada was a "political strategy" developed by the federal government and the anglophone provinces to "short circuit Québec's ambitions." Leroy Little Bear provides a different perspective on the issue of aboriginal rights within the Canadian confederation, underlining the failure of English and French Canadians to come to terms with the legitimacy of the political agenda of Canada's first peoples.

Certainly other regional problems intruded into the negotiations. Canada was no more a static society than was the Soviet Union, and the regional balance of economic power and population had changed dramatically with the rise of western Canada in the post-1945 years, and the continued stagnation and decline in eastern Canada. For many westerners, a constitutional arrangement that was based on a traditional view of Canadian confederation, one tied more to the historical dominance by Ontario and Québec, seemed an anachronism in the 1990s. The result of these conflicting visions was that two major constitutional packages—the Meech Lake constitutional reforms and those concluded at Charlottetown—had failed by the fall of 1992, both rejected by shifting coalitions of political interests within Canadian society.

Linda Trimble of the University of Alberta observes in her essay in this volume that there is considerable value in attempting to view the Canadian federal dilemma in a broader perspective. Noting that non-Canadian specialists, whether Canadians concerned with eastern Europe, an American who studies India, or an Australian who studies the environment, appear to be more optimistic about the capacity of federalism to cope with modern challenges, Professor Trimble suggests that an international and thematic comparative perspective is essential to those Canadian purveyors of "gloom and doom" in their analyses of the Canadian federal experience and prospects. As she observes, Canadian political scientists have for years been predicting the demise of Canadian federalism as a political system because Canada allegedly lacks the necessary degree of integration and cohesion to make the system workable. Yet she, like Brian Galligan and Georgina Lynch, remains optimistic, at least about the Canadian case.

Alan Cairns of the University of British Columbia notes in his discussion that all of the authors in the collection are able to identify negative forces, powers that are laying siege to the viability of existing political, economic, and cultural institutions; few, however, are able to identify forces that may play a positive role in bringing about the stability which is essential to a new world order. Ironically, the individual who has witnessed and participated most directly in the political and international changes of the past decades—Mikhail Gorbachev—articulates the most optimism. Mr Gorbachev is able to echo Roger Gibbins's exhortation that we not panic in the face of seemingly insurmountable odds. At the same time, Mr Gorbachev appeals to us all to think globally and internationally as we engage in a critical reassessment of values along the route to a "new civilization." It is difficult for readers aware of the violent and tragic clashes in Bosnia-Herzogovina, where the United Nations has striven in vain to bring a resolution of conflict, to share Mr. Gorbachev's hope that we are beginning to witness, in the post-Cold War world, "global thinking and planetary consciousness." Yet, few of us could quarrel with his conclusion that we may pay an excessive cost if we, globally, are not able to come to terms effectively with change and the challenges that confront us. We pay the price of both complacency and intransigence.

One of the critical sessions of the conference dealt with the issue and future of broader federations, whether the European Community (EC) or the relationship of eastern and central Europe to other nations within the region and to the European Community. As Holger Herwig notes in his concluding synthesis, here, as elsewhere, there was debate and disagreement. One significant dimension of the discussion of "supranational federations" by Jan Adam, Gretchen MacMillan, and Victor Kuvaldin was their effort to link federalism in Europe to the question of economic structure and reforms. Here, as Professor Herwig observes, Victor Kuvaldin's suggestion of the need to distinguish among several tiers of European states is especially instructive, with the first tier occupied by Poland, Czechoslovakia and Hungary, a second to the south involving Slovakia, Romania, Bulgaria, and Serbia. In the former, which Kuvaldin sees as having passed the crisis, he approved of the "shock treatment" economic approach employed for reforms in Poland, Czechoslovakia, and Hungary. Jan Adam concludes in his examination of the course of economic reform in the same countries that, with the demise of the Soviet Union and the Council of Mutual Economic Assistance (COMECON), a gradualist approach to economic reform would have been preferable to the shock treatment favoured by many economists. Further, Kuvaldin expresses an optimism about federalism in the region shared by few of the authors, identifying possible regional subgroupings of cooperation, such as a Balkan Community, on the road to a broader European integration, which might involve alternatives to the EC.

Gretchen MacMillan finds little basis for the suggestion of alternatives to the EC, and is optimistic that the EC will be able to resolve its economic, citizenship, and political differences; however, she shares with others at the conference the view that there is generally a gap between the roles and views of the political elites and the general populace. For Professor MacMillan, the transition of the EC from an elite to a more broadly based, and hence democratic and representative body, lies at the core of future development in the EC. She thus leaves the debate where it began, with questions and dilemmas rather than solutions.

It is hoped that Canadian-Russian friendship, the University of Calgary-Gorbachev Foundation relationship, and the personal ties that have emerged in the course of developing institutional linkages in the post-Cold War and post-Soviet eras will provide the basis for a more effective understanding of the forces that shape our national histories and the emergence of the "new civilization" to which Mr. Gorbachev and his generation have contributed, frequently at a very high personal cost to themselves.

In the final analysis, federalism, as with all political systems, is fundamentally about power—who holds it, how it is divided and shared, and how responsibly and effectively it is administered. The future challenge remains as it has in the past—to achieve an effective and delicate balance between individual and collective rights, between national and local, between international and national power and interests. That challenge may prove no easier to attain for future generations than it has in the past, but the cessation of the Cold War provides a window of opportunity to achieve a degree of multinational cooperation that has been missing for much of this century on an international level.

References

Homer-Dixon, Thomas Fraser. 1991. "On the Threshold: Environmental Changes as Causes of Acute Conflict," *International Security* 15 (Fall): 76-116.
Huntington, Samuel P. 1993. "The Clash of Civilizations?" *Foreign Affairs* 72, No. 2 (Summer).
Kaplan, Robert D. 1994. "The Coming Anarchy," *Atlantic* 273, No. 2 (February): 44-76.

I: REFLECTIONS ON FEDERALISM

On New Federalism

Mikhail S. Gorbachev

The subject of federalism is a focal point of my reflections on the years of *perestroika* and the present time. I would like to begin with an important methodological proposition. In my view, it would be impossible to correctly assess the processes going on today in federal states without attempting to understand them in the context of current profound changes in the world. We must not be confused as we face new challenges in international relations, in the world economy, and in federalism.

We are involved in a great reappraisal of values. Such a reappraisal is a natural stage along the road to a new civilization. It is good that we understand this now, though, in many ways, we are already late.

The process of internationalization is gaining momentum. Thus we need planetary thinking, global consciousness, and above all, we urgently need to find mechanisms to manage this process rather than relying on spontaneous responses.

I know from my own bitter experience the price one sometimes has to pay for being too slow in politics. I am repeatedly asked what I would have done if I were able to return to the year 1985. My answer is very definite: I would make the same choices; however, the tactics that I might use and the politics I might employ would need to be altered in an effort to produce a different course of events, not only in the Union of Soviet Socialist Republics (USSR), but in Europe and the world as a whole.

We were all somewhat euphoric when the Cold War ended, when the walls that had long separated us came down, when the Berlin Wall was destroyed. We realized that, despite all our differences, we shared one civilization, and that those differences were a great advantage, not a disadvantage. It seemed events would take their own course, and the main thing had been done.

Then came Yugoslavia. How did the international community act in the face of events taking place there? It was both theoretically and politically unprepared for this new situation. Its reaction was similar to that of 'the good old times.' The Yugoslavs themselves barely understood the situation, but to us, outsiders, everything seemed clear.

Let us turn to the situation after the USSR's abolition. Foreign ministers of various countries, as if competing, started travelling across the former Soviet territory. It was as if they were afraid of being late to shake hands with the leaders of the republics that had declared their sovereignty.

We now know what this has led to in Yugoslavia, and we also know what is going on in the former Soviet Union. We are paying for our arrogance and slowness in working out topical political issues. And these mistakes are very costly indeed. That is why I value the efforts being aimed at comprehending these problems theoretically.

While reflecting on the essence and consequences of one drama that occurred in the Soviet Union after the August coup and the Belovezh meeting, we cannot help seeing that those events were objectively conditioned by the contradictions that had accumulated in the country. Yet, on the other hand, we understand how strong the influence of the subjective factor was on those processes.

A discussion on federalism should take into consideration three trends operating simultaneously in today's world. First, the current powerful economic integration reveals great potentialities for production growth essential for the well being of people. Secondly, nations and ethnic groups—and sometimes the smaller the group, the more vigorously its goals are sought—want to preserve their own identity. Both scholars and politicians have to identify mechanisms to reconcile these two trends in the best way. Thirdly, the desire of nations and ethnic groups to preserve their identity is being widely exploited by ruling elites to attain their political ambitions. This particular aspect had often been overlooked. But much of the current process has been shaped by the behaviour of ruling elites. This tendency has been witnessed in the former Soviet Union. Not only people committed to democratic reforms, but also political adventurers, exploited the ideas of sovereignty, independence, preservation of national identity, and revival of nations and ethnic groups as the totalitarian system came to an end.

This leaves us with a question. Was the USSR's dissolution inevitable, or could the self-liquidation of that great state have been avoided? Our country, a huge and complex state, took centuries to evolve. It was a classic empire in which the component parts were loosely connected with one another, or even located on different continents. Our country's most distinctive feature was that it had been taking shape around a strong Slavic nucleus. It expanded in a kind of concentric circle, and masses of people migrated as part of that process. As those masses settled the vast territory of our country, there were contradictions and collisions on the one hand, and cooperation on the other hand. As a result, a certain diverse and complex community was formed.

Twenty percent of Soviet citizens lived outside the territories of their national communities. Twenty-five million of those people are Russians. Inside the Soviet Union, there were no state frontiers; there were only administrative boundaries. The economy was based on a division of economic and production functions whose degree of cooperation was higher than that in the European Economic Community. The Soviet Union included a common defense, a common railroad system, a common energy system, a common system of functioning and development of sciences. Thirty million people entered into interethnic marriages.

Aware of all this, two years before the August coup, I said publicly that we would not be able to separate and should not do so, that we had to redistribute powers. And, we were close to achieving that goal through the negotiation of an important treaty which would have created a union of all the sovereign states, a document interesting not only theoretically, but also practically and politically.

This kind of union, by the way, used to be Lenin's view. Following the revolution of October 1917, all of the peoples of the Russian Empire declared their independence, even administrative territorial entities. Inside the Stravropol region, from which I come, there was an independent Soviet republic with its own government—the Council of People's Commissars.

Most of Lenin's associates were not ready to meet that challenge. Prior to the October Revolution, Lenin himself was a convinced unitarist. But, when he saw what was actually happening, he accepted the notion of a federative union, and saved Russia from collapse. Later, Stalin, while preserving the name of the federation, essentially created a unitary state. Thus, he suppressed the new approach that emerged from the revolution.

When we began *perestroika*, and the society embarked on the road toward democracy, the striving for sovereignty reemerged in politics and turned into a powerful public movement. My forebodings and predictions about the detrimental consequences of the USSR's disintegration have quickly been realized. Everything that is happening in Russia and the other republics resulted from economic, political, social, and human disintegration which is the consequence of the breakup of the country.

One other question is also natural. Is it possible to restore the USSR? There are some political groups supporting the idea. I believe that such a notion is a reactionary one. There are new realities we need to identify (indeed, we are already doing so), new means to establish cooperation among the former Soviet republics. Recent public opinion polls conducted in the republics indicate that even more people than during the 1991 referendum now favour a new association of the republics, and they are placing considerable popular pressure on the politicians to move in that direction. I think that necessity and experience will reassert themselves; they will answer the question of what kind of new union the future should hold.

In general, after the USSR's breakup, the problem of federalism is as important to us today as it was earlier. It used to be an issue within the Soviet Union, but now it has become a domestic problem for some of the republics. Furthermore, it is not simply federalism, but a new federalism that is now on the agenda.

Russia is a complicated federation, a very complex national and interethnic entity. For the new Russia, federalism is an issue of great importance, as are economic and social problems. A new kind of Russian federalism must take into consideration not only the variety of ethnic entities, but also large regions with predominant Russian populations, which wish to have a status that would not be less than the status of the autonomous republics of Russia. For example, the problem of federalism is being hotly debated in the Ukraine where eleven to twelve million Russians live in highly concentrated areas, especially in the Donetsky region and in the Crimea. These two regions are now claiming the status of independent sovereignties of the Russian Federation. This wish is quite natural and legitimate. A federation is in no way restricted to ethnic relations. The world experience demonstrates it is a form of statehood that ensures the most effective way of relations between a part and a whole in the interests of the entire social organism's normal functioning.

Federalism also implies a broader perspective—as a universal principle for the building of new international relations within a new world order. Mankind has found itself in a principally new situation in which the whole paradigm of relations within states, between states, and between nationalities is undergoing transformations. We must not ignore the desire of people of any nation to seek to preserve their own identity. The question remains, how can we find the best way toward this aim? Do we solve the problem by separating ethnic groups from their former states, or can we accomplish the objective through developing new federal relations including wide autonomies of regions? The first way is fraught with dangerous consequences and can plunge the world into collapse. The situation in Yugoslavia gives an obvious warning against this. But there is another experience in history, for example, the settlement of the ethnic problem in Switzerland, Belgium, and some other countries.

A total sovereignization of ethnolinguistic communities would lead not only to a painful breakup of many states, but also to a total revision of state borders, resulting, in turn, in a drastic change of the world geopolitical situation. According to different estimates, there are from 3,500 to 7,000 ethnic groups and tribes on our planet. If all of them are constitutionalized as states, the coordination of international economic and political activity in the world would be practically impossible. Most of newly established states would be weak and unstable entities in need of permanent assistance. Their domestic crises and conflicts with neighbours would continuously poison the international climate.

Breaking with the former state entails plenty of problems pertaining to separation, division of property, or changing configurations of borders. At the same time, the issue of ethnic minorities would remain unresolved, for there are practically no homogeneous ethnic territories in the world. Newly established states would have their own ethnic minorities which would, in turn, put forward their sovereignty demands.

All this will inevitably affect foreign policy. The irredentist movement of minorities will receive support and understanding from outside, both at the public and state levels. Weak countries unable to regulate their relations with their ethnic minorities may tempt neighbouring states to use the situation for selfish purposes. Xenophobia provoked by militant nationalism will also create problems, especially if directed against a relatively large group of ethnically foreign citizens who are permanent residents in a given territory.

The subject of federalism is relevant not only to the former Soviet republics and the Balkans, but also to North America, Europe, India, and China. So, the phenomenon of federalism affects the interests of the entire global community. Here I see the grounds for the joining of efforts, not only intellectual, but also political, to comprehend these topical issues. I can also visualize a new role for the United Nations in this endeavour.

We need to use instruments of international law to encourage the will to achieve self-determination through federalism, not separatism. A truly democratic federalism can readily allow diverse forms of realizing the quest for sovereignty and self-expression among ethnic communities and groups. I believe the potential of autonomous statehood is far from being exhausted; it enables nationalities and ethnolinguistic groups to preserve their identity without breaking federal ties.

Mechanisms of concrete stimuli which make federalism more attractive and better than separatism still need a thorough analysis. One thing is clear: these stimuli should be both positive (grants from international organizations, preferential credits and trade) and negative (various sanctions in case of nonconstructive positions). The world community's total spending for those stimuli will most probably be lower than those needed to put down the fire of numerous conflicts.

Life is always richer than any sophisticated models and patterns that we could propose. The separation of an ethnic community may become inevitable. For such cases we should develop an international code of behaviour that would regulate the process of the formation of new state entities, in line with recognized international procedures that would envisage the following measures: (1) a referendum on separation with a regional differentiation in order to avoid any encroachments on the rights of ethnolinguistic groups; (2) settlement through agreement of all disputable issues and reciprocal claims with the remaining part of a state (or other separating parts); (3) settlement of unresolved issue by the International Court of Justice; (4) a newly independent state's acceptance of previous treaty commitments; and (5) a trial period is needed to check up on the fulfillment of the above terms by a newly independent state.

The formal recognition of newly independent states by other countries should be possible only after the United Nation's positive decision based on the results of the trial period. When I say this, I mean the errors made in recent years (for example, in the USSR and Yugoslavia).

We also need to study the principles of the best organized federation, based on a comprehensive analysis of the world experience of federalism, and work out a federal model which would be more acceptable than separation for interested ethnic groups. As can be seen, those who support federalism have a lot of work ahead.

The Future of Federalism

James C. MacPherson

Introduction

In the history of ideas and forms of government, federalism is a relatively recent experiment, going back just over two hundred years to its utilization in the U.S. Constitution. Today, federalism—which I define as a form of government in which public authority is divided between two or more constitutionally defined orders of government—is an important, but by no means pervasive or dominant, form of government on the world stage. Moreover, its fate has been quite mixed in recent years. In some countries, it thrives and is a central and unchallenged feature of government. The United States, Australia, Germany, and Switzerland are examples. In other countries federalism does not so much thrive as survive; its continuation is often challenged and always fragile. Canada probably comes within this category. In a third group of countries, federalism fails and a federal nation disintegrates, sometimes peacefully, as in Czechoslovakia, and, other times, with great bloodshed, as in Yugoslavia. In a fourth group of countries, some form of federalism is tried as something new to overcome serious problems in government or society (or both) in a nation. In different ways, Belgium, Spain, and Italy are all modern experimenters with federalism.

The purpose of this conference on civil society, according to the conference programme, is "to explore the evolving nature of federalism and its viability as a political structure in comparative international perspective." Some would say that this is not an important question, that forms of government are irrelevant, as, for example, Alexander Pope, in *An Essay on Man*, wrote:

> For forms of government let fools contest:
> Whate'er is best administered is best. (n.d.: 209)

I do not agree with Pope. Forms of government are relevant. They can contribute to violence and disintegration or to peace and progress. What about federalism as a form of government? Although its origins are in simpler times (two centuries ago, rural societies), and in western-style democracies, is it nevertheless a form of government that can be useful in a complex modern world and in nations with different histories of government? I will attempt to answer this question by mentioning a few of the advantages and problems of federalism and then providing my personal conclusion about the title of this conference—"The Future of Federalism."

Advantages of Federalism

I would suggest that federalism as a form of government has at least three strong advantages. First, because federalism is a system of government premised on divided powers, it is consistent with the very essence of modern constitutionalism—limited government operating under the rule of law.

Secondly, the actual operation of government in some federal nations has been, in my view, quite good. Canada is a worthy example. Federalism can help to reconcile historical tensions. (Surely in terms of Canadian history, it has been a better response to English-French conflict than the centuries-long battles from Louisbourg to The Plains of Abraham, or the solution of assimilation of the French minority proposed in the famous *Durham Report*.) Federalism is a useful way to attempt to reconcile the competing strains of economic globalization and social localization; and, federalism is an effective means of stimulating innovation in a nation (in Canada, treating the provinces as "laboratories of innovation or experimentation," from Saskatchewan and medicare in the 1940s to, perhaps, New Brunswick and secondary education in the 1990s, is an important component of our progress as a nation).

Thirdly, I believe that there is a symmetry between the underlying values of federalism and the values that all successful and peaceful societies must display. Federalism is not just about form—constitutional form or institutional form. It is also about societies and the people who inhabit them. Just as the essence of the federal form of government is the notion of divided governmental authority, so the essence of a federal society is one in which the people in the society possess and exhibit divided loyalties. This, in turn, compels them to recognize that others in the society also possess divided loyalties. The result, I believe, is the flowering of such values as humility, sharing, tolerance, trust, respect—in a word, *balance*. In a society with strong elements of diversity and even conflict, there is a greater chance of reconciliation if these values are present. Federalism is deeply rooted in these values and, therefore, is a form of government that can help overcome conflict and promote reconciliation and shared progress.

Problems of Federalism

There are many problems with federalism, especially in a complex world with many forms of governments. Some problems are indigenous to an individual federal nation. However, I would like to mention two that seem to be particularly difficult to resolve and which tend to manifest themselves in many modern federations.

First, federalism is closely linked with the notions of geography and territory. It has demonstrated that it is a form of government that can help resolve conflicts if the differences or cleavages in a society can be defined in territorial terms, as is the case in Canada with the English/French dichotomy. Often, however, as Professor Richard Simeon has discussed (1992), federalism has not been effective if the differences in a society cannot be captured in territorial terms, and federalism is not representative of the interests of nonterritorially defined groups.

The obvious example in the modern world is ethnic nationalism. Federalism premised on territorial considerations has not been adequate to save federal nations where the ethnic configurations did not follow clear territorial boundaries. Professor Simeon provides the clearest, and most tragic, example, that of eastern Europe, where the creation of new states is, in turn, creating new minorities, which may become isolated from their previous ties outside the states, thus leaving them open to possible exploitation. The consequence may be that these new minorities will also demand their autonomy, creating a cascading effect which is inherently destabilizing.

A similar cascade is not unimaginable if Québec separated from Canada. It is clear that the aboriginal people of Québec do not feel that their first loyalty would be to a new independent nation called Québec. If Québec separated from Canada, a subsequent partition of Québec into a French-speaking south and an aboriginal north would be a possibility.

The second problem with federalism arises if governments in the federation concentrate too much on accommodating differences and ignore building on those traditions, values, and aspirations which a people share. When that happens, the differences can become the core values. In marriages, that can lead to divorce; in nations, it can lead to disintegration of the old nation and the creation of new national entities. This happened a year ago in Czechoslovakia, when a failure to think in terms of shared history, values, and aspirations for the future (all of which were strong enough to create the Velvet Revolution overthrowing fifty years of Soviet-imposed Communist rule), led to the quiet dissolution of an attractive and viable nation (The Velvet Divorce).

A similar Velvet Divorce is possible in Canada, which constantly seems preoccupied with distinctiveness and entitlements rather than with cohesion and responsibilities. In other long-standing federations—the United States, Australia, Germany, and Switzerland—there is only the remotest chance of disintegration because in those countries there is a powerful thread of collective concentration on unifying values.

The great Canadian teacher and author, Professor Northrop Frye, has spoken of the "imaginative patterns" of nations. Federalism poses the risk that the imaginative pattern in a country will focus on differences, diversity, and grievances rather than on nourishing a comprehensive shared sense of identification and belonging. If that happens then a federal nation can die.

Conclusion

I am a Canadian. My knowledge of other countries and their systems of government—even other federal countries—is imperfect. I am inclined, therefore, to agree with Professor Alan Cairns who has written:

> Canada, with one of the oldest uninterrupted constitutional regimes in the world, is not a pure type, the understanding of which will generate insights readily transferable to other lands and climes where constitutional forms and ethnic forces interact. (n.d.: 2)

Nevertheless, I am optimistic about federalism as a form of government, in Canada and in the world community of nations. I believe that its fidelity to constitutionalism, its flexibility and adaptability (for example, in Canada, federalism has accommodated the constitutional protection for individual and group rights mandated by the *Canadian Charter of Rights and Freedoms*, and, in Belgium, federalism has been recently modified to permit a dissolution of powers on a nonterritorial basis in such areas as language, culture, social life and education), and its roots in such values as tolerance, respect, and balance should make federalism an attractive form of government for many nations, including Canada, in the twenty-first century.

Let me conclude on this note. At this conference, the focus has been on federalism as a form of government. Although, as I said earlier, forms of government are important, it is nevertheless difficult to predict whether federalism or any other system of government will be relevant and useful in the twenty-first century. I am certain, however, that in the twenty-first century, as in all previous centuries, the progress of the human race will depend as much on the personal qualities of our leaders as on any structural considerations. Leaders who display compassion, integrity, vision, and wisdom will make the world a better place. We can only hope that the twenty-first century will produce such leaders.

In the twentieth century, we have had a few great statesmen who have possessed the qualities of compassion, integrity, vision, and wisdom. Mr Gorbachev was, and is today, such a statesman. He has made the world a much better place. He has earned our gratitude and respect.

References

Cairns, Alan. n.d. "Constitutional Government and the Two Faces of Ethnicity: Federalism is not Enough." In *Rethinking Federalism: Citizens, Markers and Governments in a Changing World*, edited by Karen Knop, et al. Mimeo. Vancouver, UBC Press (forthcoming).

Pope, Alexander. n.d. *An Essay on Man.* New York: R. Worthington.

Simeon, Richard. 1992. Paper presented at the Federalism and the Nation State conference. Centre for International Studies and the International Business and Trade Law Programme, Toronto (June 4-6).

II: *Federalist Realities Past and Present*

The Challenge of New Politics and New Social Movements to the Future of Federalism

Roger Gibbins

Federalism is often seen as the best way to accommodate two of the most pervasive forces shaping the contemporary political landscape. The first of these is the globalization of the economy and the elimination of barriers to trade; the second is the struggle to protect cultural diversity in the face of economic globalization. Historically, federalism has provided an institutional balance between these competing forces. In the Canadian case, for example, the federal system established in 1867 facilitated the emergence of a transcontinental economy, while at the same time protecting important cultural, linguistic, and religious differences among provincial communities. It is not surprising, then, that federalism is seen as an appropriate institutional response to more contemporary, but not dissimilar challenges.

However, this faith in federalism often fails to take into account a third force of change swirling through the political landscape. The social movements associated with what has been termed the "new politics," movements including but by no means restricted to environmentalism and feminism,[1] pose a growing challenge to the institutional status quo in western industrialized states. This challenge, furthermore, may be particularly problematic for federal states because, unlike the challenges posed by economic globalization and the protection of cultural diversity, it is less easily accommodated by federalism. Indeed, it can be argued that the new politics is as likely to corrode existing federal systems as it is to support the broader application of federal principles to the new world order. To make this argument, I begin with a brief conceptual description of the new politics and the associated new social movements. The discussion then turns to the general new politics

---

1. "New social movements" also include the animal liberation movement, the peace movement, protest against the military and civilian use of nuclear energy, and support for gay rights.

challenge to contemporary federal states, and to a more detailed case study of environmentalism. The discussion continues by exploring the potential role of federalism in environmental governance, and concludes by returning to the more general impact of the new politics on both contemporary federal states and the future potential of federalism.

It should be noted at the outset that the use throughout the analysis of words such as "corrode" and "erode" does not imply that the new politics challenge to federal values and institutions is unfortunate or pernicious; this terminology is meant more to capture the moderate pace and intensity of the challenge. Thus, no argument will be made that the supporters of the new politics are about to confront federalism in the streets. Rather, the argument is that the challenge to federalism is embedded within the logic of the new politics, and that it will come to have a gradual yet significant impact as the new politics transforms the political landscape. Hence the notion of corrosion or erosion—change that may occur gradually, even imperceptibly over the short run, but which nonetheless has a transformative potential.

It should also be noted that I am not predicting the demise of federal states or federalism. As Krasner has explained, there is a great deal of institutional inertia within the existing state system: "historical developments are path dependent; once certain choices are made, they constrain future possibilities." Krasner goes on to emphasis that "institutional arrangements perpetuate themselves across time, even in situations where utilitarian calculations would suggest that they are dysfunctional" (1988: 67, 72). His argument, I would suggest, applies with equal force to federalism and federal states; the fact that federal arrangements might be dysfunctional with respect to some aspects of the new political agenda will not necessarily lead to the demise of such arrangements.[2] However, we can identify important points of institutional and political tension that federal states will confront as they move to address the new political agenda. Their success in this respect could well determine federalism's shape and potential in the next century.

New Politics and New Social Movements

New politics occur at the intersection of new social issues and new forms of political participation. The social movements associated with the new politics

---

2. For an insightful discussion of institutional inertia within the Australian federal system, see Galligan and Walsh (1991); for a discussion of the Canadian case, see Cairns (1977).

tend to form around nonterritorial interests and communities, a characteristic of particular importance to the present discussion. They are, moreover, transformative movements which often seek to rebuild rather than reform the social order. But what exactly is new? Nonterritorial politics *per se* are not new, and neither are many of the so-called new issues. Feminism, for example, has much deeper roots than the new politics label would suggest, and Goodin points out that conservation societies and associations for the prevention of cruelty to animals emerged well before the twentieth century (1992a: 1). What may be new are not the issues themselves but their enhanced placement on the political agenda, a change which is associated in turn with a more wide-ranging shift in political and social values.[3] Therefore, the new politics cannot be simply equated with public support for specific issues. For instance, public support for many of the policy initiatives supported by feminists may extend well beyond the feminist movement *per se*; an individual may support pay equity without identifying herself or himself as a feminist. Thus, the new politics generally, and new social movements specifically, can be identified by a number of characteristics quite apart from stances taken on specific policy issues.

First, new social movements are emphatically political, and in this sense have transformed issues with deeper historical roots. For example, the phrase "the personal is political" sets the contemporary feminist movement apart from its earlier roots by stressing that if the constraints on women's lives are to be reduced, such change will require "collective action in the political arena, not individual action in each person's private life" (Adamson et al. 1988: 201). The new emphasis on political action among environmentalists comes, in part, from the conclusion that the natural sciences alone cannot provide solutions to dilemmas inherent in managing the environmental commons for the public good (Hardin and Baden 1977). Goodin argues that the contemporary environmental movement "carves out a much larger role for politics—both nationally and internationally—than previous understandings, which saw much more scope for individual initiatives making all the difference" (1992a: 4). Perhaps McKibben's essay best captures the point:

> A purely personal effort is, of course, just a gesture—a good gesture, but a gesture. The greenhouse effect is the first environmental problem

---

3. This shift in political priorities, and the underlying change in social values which it reflects, is captured by the term "postmaterialism" (Inglehart, 1977; 1990).

we can't escape by moving to the woods. *There are no personal solutions.* There is no time to just decide we'll raise enlightened children and they'll slowly change the world. (1989: 204, emphasis added)

New social movements are also political in that they are interventionist, emphasizing the need to change existing patterns and behaviours. As Chiras argues, from the environmentalist perspective, "given the built-in flaws of governments and economies, it is unlikely that a desirable (sustainable) future can evolve by default" (1992: 140). In a similar fashion, feminists argue for state intervention to break long-standing patterns of patriarchal dominance, discrimination, and exploitation.

Secondly, the new politics is different in both substance and style. It is associated with left-libertarian support for greater democratization, including direct democracy, and suuport for more decentralized political decision-making (Kitschelt 1988: 127), the latter being of immediate relevance for any discussion of federalism. The social movements associated with the new politics embrace elite-challenging political behavior (Dalton 1988; Inglehart 1990), a characteristic which also has significant implications for federal forms of government. In the past, the politics of class and religion were largely fought out within the territorial containers of nation states; the containers themselves were not challenged, apart from the radical left. In a similar fashion, the subcontainers within federal states—the provinces and states—were not challenged and, in some cases, were reinforced by class and religious conflict.[4] Now, the new politics challenges the federal containers; the general lack of confidence expressed in the institutional status quo extends to its federal aspects. In federal states, moreover, the most salient elites are often those identified with federal institutions and structures. Therefore we might expect that the elite-challenging behaviour of the new politics will extend to territorial forms of political organization and to their associated political elites.

Thirdly, Goodin suggests that what is new in the new politics is an expanded scope (1992a: 4). Environmentalists, for example, expand the political agenda in two ways: by discussing the so-called rights of nonhuman species and even landscapes, and by stressing problems—ozone depletion, global

---

4. Again, the exception comes from the left. Historically, the Canadian left has been less than enthusiastic about federalism, and the Labor party in Australia, until the early 1970s, formally advocated the abolition of federalism.

warming, acid rain, deforestation, and species extinction—which are planetary in scope. Moreover, they seek solutions which reach beyond the scope of conventional political organizations and action:

> Concerted action on the part of all—or virtually all—nations of the world will be required if catastrophic changes in the ozone layer or in the global climate are reliably to be averted. This is not to say that individual nations and individual households will not still have a role to play. It is merely to say that, to play their role efficaciously, they will have to play it in league with others, according to some properly elaborated plan of joint action. The sphere within which such coordination of joint plans of action takes place is, of course, the sphere of politics. (1992:4)

The contemporary feminist movement is also marked by the increased scope of its analysis and field of action. Writers such as Kate Millett (1969) dramatically expanded our definition of the political to include the most intimate human relationships. The phrase "the personal is political" captures this increased scope and the push for a radically expanded political agenda.

Fourthly, the politics associated with new social movements are at times the intense and uncompromising politics of secular fundamentalism (Goodin 1992b: 12-13; Offe 1983). The manifesto of the British Ecology Party, for example, begins with a quote from Schumacher, one with which most fundamentalist groups would be comfortable:

> We must do what we conceive to be the right thing and not bother our heads or burden our souls with whether we're going to be successful. Because if we don't do the right thing, we'll just be part of the disease and not part of the cure. (cited in Young 1990: 194)

In the motto of the American environmentalist organization Earth First!— "No compromise in defence of Mother Earth"—one can hear echoes of Barry Goldwater, in 1964: "extremism in the defence of liberty is no vice." To say this, however, is not to criticize such movements but rather to draw a distinction with the complex and nuanced tradeoffs of federal politics. Whereas federal politics is inherently flexible and relatively unprincipled, the new politics is principled and less flexible—how can one compromise when the fate of the planet is at stake, or when discussing the rights of more than half the population? As Offe notes, "the causes for their lack of tolerance and willingness to compromise are neither individual nor institutional, but rather themes and problems which are, by their very nature, ill-suited to compromise" (1983: 49-50).

Finally, the new politics is often identified with values which reach beyond specific territorial or even national communities, values which may be expressed in universal terms. Hence the prominence of "rights" in the political discourse of the new politics. While new social movements do not gloss over cultural differences,[5] they do bring into focus a very real tension between such differences and the universal values embedded within the new politics. This tension, central to the challenge that the new politics poses to federal values and institutions, emerges in debates over the desirability of national standards or objectives.

While the above does not provide an exhaustive description of the new politics or new social movements, it does set the stage for a discussion of the more specific challenge that the new politics poses to contemporary federal states. This challenge can be sketched, first, in general terms, and, secondly, with respect to a more specific but hopefully still broadly illustrative thread of the new politics.

The New Politics Challenge to Federal Values and Institutions

The particular vulnerability of federal states to the new politics challenge can be traced to two basic characteristics of federalism. First, federal systems protect cultural diversity, or social pluralism. Secondly, they protect a particular form of pluralism, and that is pluralism manifested in territorial communities, interests, and identities. This is not to say that the protection of territorial diversity *per se* is the *raison d'être* of federalism, for cultural, linguistic, and religious pluralisms also lie at the foundation of such federal states as Canada and Switzerland. However, the protection of these latter pluralisms is operationalized in territorial terms; the pluralist communities that are best protected are those which can be spatially defined. Pluralism which lacks territorial definition, or which slops over territorial boundaries, is particularly problematic for federal states. Thus, while federal states may have been established to protect a variety of pluralisms, the protection of ter-

---

5. For example, contemporary feminist theory is very concerned with issues of difference and diversity.

ritorial diversity is the characteristic feature of contemporary federal states, even in those cases where such protection is a means to other ends.

Contemporary federal states have a number of features which arise from their territorial organization and normative commitment to diversity, and which are directly related to the corrosive challenge posed by the new politics and new social movements. First, territorial identifications are of considerable political salience for citizens in federal states. However, the new politics challenges this salience by promoting alternative political identities based on nonterritorial communities (for example, gender) or on policy concerns (for example, environmentalism) that transcend or crosscut the territorial communities making up federal states.

Secondly, the jurisdictional "lines-on-maps" which delineate states and provinces within federal systems, and the constitutional division of powers among such units, are of primary importance in federal states. However, jurisdiction boundaries are often seen as irrelevant and even dysfunctional to the new politics agenda. Thirdly, while federal systems place considerable emphasis on political sovereignty, new social movements challenge the integrity of political sovereignty as it applies both within the divided jurisdictions of federal states and within the international community.

And finally, federal systems promote territorial diversity and differentiation with respect to the design and implementation of public policies. The new politics, however, is relatively intolerant of territorial diversity and differentiation; the idiosyncratic values of territorial communities are challenged by more universalistic values. In general, the new politics poses a challenge to federal states that extends both from and across these four features. Environmentalism provides a specific illustration.

The Challenge of Environmentalism to Federal States

The tension between the logic of environmentalism and federalism emerges from the four features of contemporary federal states identified above. The degree of tension is in turn related to the form of environmentalism at issue, for there is an important distinction between deep or "dark green" environmentalism and reformist or "light green" environmentalism. The distinction is nicely captured by McKibben, who notes that "environmentally sound is not the same as natural" (1989: 209): light green environmentalists pursue the environmentally sound, while dark green environmentalists seek to protect nature for its own sake. The light greens are thus more prepared to work within and to build upon existing institutions, and, on this front, have been attacked by the deep greens for trying to repair a system which the latter feel should be left to collapse (Young 1990: 149). Although both reformist and deep environmentalists challenge existing political frameworks, the deep green critique is more radical and, thus, potentially more problematic for federal states. However, the deep greens also draw upon a much narrower spectrum of political support than do reformist environmentalists, and as a consequence it is the latter who pose the more immediate corrosive challenge to federal states.

Salience of Territorial Identifications. Environmentalism challenges the political salience of territorial identifications by promoting an alternative form of political consciousness. A growing environmental consciousness threatens to overshadow the territorial loyalties, or at least the politicization of those loyalties, embedded within and sustained by federal states. Deep ecology is particularly associated with a transcendent or "transpersonal" environmental identification that values nature for its own sake, and which is not easily reconciled with the politicized territorial loyalties common to federal states (Devall and Sessions 1985). This transcendent identification is dramatically captured by deep ecologist Warwick Fox (1989: 32-36), who argues that we strive:

> not to identify ourselves exclusively with our leaf (our personal, biographic self), our twig (our family), the leaves (our friends), our minor sub-branch (our race), our branch (our species), and so on, but rather to identify ourselves with the tree. This necessarily leads, at the limit, to an impartial (but deeply felt) identification with *all* particulars (all leaves on the tree).

Rifkin's notion of biosphere politics, which "envisions the earth as a living organism, and the human species as a partner and participant, dependent upon the proper functioning of the biosphere and at the same time responsible for its well-being" (1991: 3), also draws from this new environmental consciousness. A transcendent environmental identity has been linked by others to the emergence of a global ethical code which "transcends the particular moral codes which have developed to serve the needs of classes, ethnic groups, nations or religious traditions" (Young 1990: 170). In summary, the biocentric—as opposed to anthropocentric—world views associated with deep ecology strike "at the root of our identities" (McKibben 1989: 175), and there is no reason to assume that the politicized territorial identities associated with federal states will be immune. To the extent that a new environmental consciousness succeeds in transforming our political values and identities, it will erode the territorial foundations of federal states.

Importance of "Lines-on-Maps." Jurisdictional boundaries, both international and domestic, are often seen as irrelevant and even dysfunctional to the concerns addressed by environmentalists. In large part, this view stems from the disregard shown to political boundaries by environmental problems. In this respect, the Brundtland Report implicitly challenged the constitutional order of federal states by conceptualizing the environment as "a cohesive unity which renders political boundaries mere legal fictions," and by arguing that "ecosystems do not respect national boundaries" (World Commission on Environment and Development 1987, 38). For the report's authors, the lack of fit between ecological and political boundaries has real and unfortunate consequences for the protection of common environmental interests (47). This point is picked up by Walters, who points out that "as fictional as boundaries may be, in a physical sense they do create political constituencies, they determine which people will manage which natural resources, and, having been drawn over the face of the world in disregard for the patterns of ecosystems which sustain life, political boundaries create problems" (1991: 422).[6] Rifkin maintains that existing political boundaries (he does not address, as most environmentalists do not address, federal boundaries *per se*) are incompatible with new patterns of environmental thought:

> While the geospheric politics of the nation-state and multi-national was designed to enclose and commodify the global commons, the biospheric politics of the new age is designed to *eliminate the arbitrary political and commercial barriers* that have clogged the biospheric arteries and make whole the planetary organism. The political challenge of the new biospheric politics is to *tear down the walls of enclosure* and reopen the global commons, to treat the planet as a single unified organism. (1991: 287, emphasis added)

Some of the barriers to be torn down would undoubtedly be those integral to federal states. Thus, the logic of environmentalism, by challenging the rel-

---

6. For example, jurisdictional boundaries in the United States have been identified as a major impediment to the development of effective recycling programs (Chiras 1992: 149).

Some of the barriers to be torn down would undoubtedly be those integral to federal states. Thus, the logic of environmentalism, by challenging the relevance of jurisdictional boundaries, also challenges federalism and the constitutional framework of contemporary federal states.

The underlying logic of environmentalism and federalism become further entangled when environmental problems spill over from one political jurisdiction to the next, or when the economic benefits and environmental costs of projects fall into different jurisdictions. As Simeon notes, spillover effects, in general, promote the centralization of power in federal states, and environmental spillover effects create strong pressures for the centralization of jurisdictional control and the establishment of national standards (1983: 144). This tendency to shift jurisdictional control upwards, and thus to corrode the constitutional division of powers, may be further reinforced by the tactics adopted by environmentalists. Their use of the courts, a political forum that is particularly amenable to the erosion of federal values and institutions, has created upward pressure on the constitutional division of powers in federal states.[7]

Importance of Sovereignty. Just as the logic of environmentalism contributes to the erosion of jurisdictional and political boundaries, so too does it constitute an assault on sovereignty, broadly defined. However, this assault is particularly germane to federal states which are often preoccupied with the divided sovereignty reflected in the constitutional division of powers, and with the mechanics and preservation of that division. It has a potential impact on the internal constitutional structures of federal states and on the limited jurisdictional sovereignty enjoyed by the constituent units of federal states.

The environmental critique of sovereignty comes from a number of directions. Environmentalism is rooted in the values of the natural sciences (Paehlke 1989: 273), and those values deprecate the importance of national

---

7. All of this depends on how the courts position themselves with respect to federal values. While the American Supreme Court and the Judicial Committee of the Privy Council (as it affected the evolution of Canadian constitutional law) were defenders of federal values in the past, this has been less evident in recent years. Derthick, for example, argues that in the United States, "government by judges is government at the expense of the states" (1992: 672). Bzdera's comprehensive comparative study of high courts in federal and quasi-federal states (1993) offers compelling evidence that such courts have a centralist impact on the constitutional division of powers and a nationalist influence on the definition of social values.

sovereignty. If sovereignty comes into conflict with environmental protection, if, for example, the developmental strategies of Brazil threaten the ecological diversity of rain forest habitats, then environmentalists argue that the preservation of national sovereignty is too high a price to pay.[8] Rifkin joins the attack on national sovereignty by calling for a new biospheric politics which will "transcend national boundaries," and by arguing that the emergence of this new biospheric politics and a new "biospheric culture" will mark the end of the nation state as the dominant political institution (1991: 319, 5). The critique of sovereignty is further expanded by changing conceptions of security in the new world order. Environmentalists argue that national security requires global and not just national environmental protection. Hence, and paradoxically, so-called national interests are best served by a diminution of territorial sovereignty. Note, for example, the following passage from Chiras:

> International cooperation is thwarted by a reluctance on behalf of governments to relinquish sovereign rights for the sake of the whole. As they see it, international accords to control pollution or reduce environmental destruction give outsiders an unprecedented say in internal government policy, obstructing the right to self rule. While most of us recognize that giving up a little control to save the planet is a small price to pay for our common future, not all countries agree.
> (1992: 167)

To the extent that this assault on sovereignty is successful, there is no reason to assume that subsystem sovereignty within federal states will escape unscathed.

Territorial Diversity with Respect to Public Policy. At one level, environmentalists are very supportive of diversity; the preservation of biological diversity is central to the environmental creed. Nevertheless, the political challenge is to protect diversity at one level while imposing more global standards at another, as Rifkin notes:

> An Earth-oriented politics will be as diverse as the ecosystems that make up the planet and as unified as the biospheric process that unites

---

8. Sovereignty is particularly problematic when environmental concerns such as global warming and ozone depletion extend beyond the reach of national governments.

it into a single organism. 'Thinking globally and acting locally' means participating deeply in the local community and bioregion and sharing responsibility internationally for the ecological well-being of the planet. (1991: 312)

Initially federalism might seem to be the appropriate mechanism for balancing the competing needs for local diversity and global protection; after all, the preservation of local diversity is what federalism is all about. Yet environmentalists tend to be relatively intolerant of the territorial differentiation with respect to the design, implementation, and application of environmental policies and standards that is implicit to federal states. Kara argues that their goal is "environmental convergence," and it is difficult to reconcile convergence with the policy differentiation inherent in and promoted by federal forms of government (1992: 192). This intolerance, coupled with the transboundary problems inherent in many environmental issues, has led to progressive pressure on federal systems to strengthen the authority of national governments with respect to environmental policy and regulation (Crotty 1987; Kamieniecki and Ferral 1991; Pierce et al. 1986; Rabe 1991; Regens 1989; Welborn 1988).

To this point, the discussion has distinguished a number of tensions between the logic of federalism and environmentalism in contemporary federal states. Environmentalism challenges the territorial identifications, internal jurisdictional boundaries, subsystem autonomy, and policy differentiation characteristic of contemporary federal states. However, there are also significant areas of complementarity; the support among environmentalists for decentralization, their respect for diversity, and their acceptance of interdependence as a core principle of life all suggest ways in which environmentalism and federalism might be mutually reinforcing. These somewhat contradictory expectations about tension and complementarity can be brought into focus by exploring how environmentalists approach matters of political governance.

Environmental Governance

Questions of governance are central to the environmental movement. In the public choice literature, for example, it is recognized that the environmental commons may not be coterminous with existing political jurisdictions, and that effective management of the commons may require new political structures which transcend those jurisdictions (Hardin and Baden 1977: 177).

towards new international structures with coercive powers (Boardman 1991: 451; Newsom 1988-89: 29). There is, thus, a general recognition among environmentalists that a change in existing patterns of governance is required if environmental problems are to be effectively addressed.

However, there is much greater consensus on the nature of the problem than there is on the nature of the solution. To the extent that alternative models of governance have begun to emerge, they are based on two quite different and not easily reconciled strategies. First, there is an emphasis on greater decentralization in order to create a better fit between governance and ecosystems. This emphasis is linked to a desire expressed by most new social movements for greater grass-roots participation in political decision making. Secondly, there is an emphasis on new global standards and practices, and thus for new global institutions charged with the protection of the environmental commons. As Commoner argues, action at the level of the nation state is not enough:

> What the United States—or indeed any one country—does will not in itself end the war against nature. It is a global war and only global action will end it. (1990: 236)

There is, then, a desire to move decision-making power down to local communities more in touch with their immediate ecologies, and up to the global community where planetary concerns could be more effectively addressed. Not surprisingly, federalism appears to offer a potential means of reconciling these competing ambitions. However, before turning to a discussion of federalism per se we must first explore the decentralization option in greater detail.

Support for Decentralization

Environmentalists in general, and deep ecologists in particular, support decentralized, nonhierarchical forms of governance (Goldsmith 1972; Porritt 1984: 166; Roszak 1978; Young 1990: 187-88); decentralization is the core environmental political principle. Goodin, for example, concludes that greens "are decidedly of the view that decentralized, egalitarian political mechanisms are to be preferred to centralized, hierarchical ones" (1992*b*: 15).⁹ Young makes a similar case:

> For deep ecologists the moves towards centralization sweeping the globe are profoundly worrying. For them, the growth of multinationals, centralized governments and bigger organizations are moves in the wrong direction. Deep ecologists argue in favour of small organizations following Schumacher's 'small is beautiful' approach. (1992: 14)

The roots of environmentalism in the biological sciences feed a profound respect for ecological diversity, which spills over into political thinking, and which is further fed by the more general left-libertarian creed of the new politics. The respect for diversity is also manifest in the principle of bioregionalism which, as Young notes:

> is the idea of people living in harmony with the land and the seasons. The natural world, the local environment, then determines the political, economic and social life of each community. (1992: 18)

Young goes on to suggest that, "for deep greens, an important part of the sustainable society is getting away from the centralized hierarchical nature of existing systems of government" (1992: 18), and that for deep ecologists:

> society would be organized on a smaller scale. There would be smaller organizations, smaller settlements, smaller units of production and so on. (1992: 17)

There is, then, general opposition to the centralized power of the contemporary state, opposition which coexists comfortably with the highly localized concerns that drive many, although by no means all, environmentalists.¹⁰ Thus, respect for biological and ecological diversity is com-

---

9. It is interesting to note that decentralization and egalitarianism are commonly collapsed into a single political characteristic in the environmental literature. It is by no means clear, however, that decentralized decision-making processes are necessarily egalitarian.
10. Rohrschneider's analysis of the 1982 Eurobarometer survey casts some doubt on the importance of local issues: "Experiences with ecological problems in one's immediate environment do not lead directly to favoring environmental regulations" (1988: 363).

patible with decentralization and, more generally, with the spirit of federalism. However, it is the environmentalists driven by global concerns who find themselves in a more complex and difficult political situation to which decentralization is a more problematic response.

Decentralization in a Global Context

Environmentalists have drawn attention to a set of transboundary and global environmental concerns for which decentralized political decision making provides little leverage, concerns which call for political action at the international level and point towards fundamental changes in the international political order.[11] However, it is by no means clear what direction such changes might follow, as Goodin points out:

> What makes the green message especially appealing is that it points to the need for concerted global action. What makes it especially unsatisfying is that it provides no account—apart from the apparently vacuous suggestions to 'think globally'—as to how that concerted global action is to be achieved. (1992b: 157-58)

Both deep and reformist environmentalists support decentralization, but the latter are more likely to acknowledge that there are pressing problems of large scope which cannot be addressed through a radical decentralization of political decision making. Young suggests that the resultant tension is resolved at times by arguing that a strong state is needed in the short term (1992: 22). Then, after a new environmental ethic is in place, and in a scenario reminiscent of early Marxist theory, the strong state could wither away to be replaced by new decentralized structures more coterminous with

---

While local experience led to an increase in concern with the national environment, Rohrschneider concludes that, "we did not find any evidence that personal experiences with pollution problems directly effect citizens' attitudes toward environmental protection" (1988: 364).

11. If, in the long run, a new environmental consciousness comes to prevail, then a decentralized system may produce decisions that will serve the global commons. In effect, this new consciousness could serve the role of Adam Smith's hidden hand; it could provide the orchestration that normally would not emerge from decentralized decision-making structures.

bioregions.[12] The fact remains, however, that in the short run decentralization provides little leverage on transborder problems, or on the spillover effects and externalities inherent in federal states.

There is a related tension between the decentralist impulses of environmentalism and its stress on what Plant refers to as a "planetary community" (1989: 253). The tension is minimal if one thinks of such a community as being based only on shared values. However, if we begin to articulate a political skeleton for such a community, it becomes increasingly difficult to reconcile planetary forms of government with decentralized decision making. While federalism on a global scale may provide the necessary reconciliation, this is not a case that has been made to date by environmentalists.

Goodin also points out a number of additional problems which reach beyond the transnational and global scope of many environmental concerns. First, the proponents of decentralization often fail to recognize that the price of decentralization may be a loss of community power despite greater local control:

> People are being given more and more power over less and less. Or, more precisely, more and more of what really matters will now ordinarily cut across communities and therefore lies in the hands of those who are to be responsible for negotiations with other communities. (1992b: 153)

The price of decentralization is jurisdictional fragmentation, and the price of fragmentation is a loss of political control to the specialists and elites of intergovernmental relations. Secondly, Goodin goes on to note that it is often assumed that a harmonious relationship among decentralized communities will emerge in a way analogous to the natural order:

> There is, after all, no central organization imposing order on nature. Rather, the plants and animals of each area simply adapt to their own locality, while at the same time incidentally feeding into the larger

---

12. Goodin makes essentially the same point with reference to how environmentalists see political parties: "In the ideal world to which greens aspire, a world of decentralized communities governed by direct democracy, the role of parties—green or otherwise—would largely fade away" (1992b: 146).

scheme of things. Ecologically, the global order emerges out of these local adaptations and interactions among them. (1992b: 153)

Yet to assume that a sound ecological order will emerge smoothly, if at all, from a multitude of decentralized political communities is to turn a blind eye to human history.

The Federal Solution?

Among those who recognize that decentralization must be orchestrated if planetary concerns are to be addressed, there is often reference to such ambiguous schemes as "federations of communities" and "self-sufficient collaboration" (Goodin 1992b: 151). Yet none of these take us very far in describing a stable relationship among decentralized communities, and it is here that federal principles can be brought into play. If one face of federalism is the decentralization of political authority, the other is the recentralization of authority, in at least some fields, through complex intergovernmental and representative institutions. Federalism may thus provide the solution to the problem of environmental policy coordination.

Federalism would appear to address the desire for both decentralized local control and strengthened global authority. Federal systems, after all, are designed to balance local control with the recognition of broader economic or security interests, which can only be pursued within political structures transcending local communities and interests. It could be, then, that federalism writ large is the system of governance towards which environmentalists are driving, even though this has rarely emerged as an explicit theme.[13]

The case for federalism extends beyond its potential capacity to bridge the competing interests of decentralization and global action. At the national level, and potentially beyond, federalism offers "multiple cracks" at political influence. For environmentalists who find national power elusive, federalism puts political success within easier reach; it allows progress to be made in areas of least resistance. When national power is not only elusive but hostile, federalism can offer a means of protection. During the Reagan and Bush ad-

---

13. A notable example is Chiras, who draws attention to the American federal experience and suggests that "a constitutional separation of powers and a system of checks and balances would be vital to the success of a world government" (1992: 174).

ministrations, for example, many states became virtual havens for environmental interests as the federal administration set out to roll back national environmental initiatives. Another advantage of federalism is that progress in one jurisdiction can be used as a model or prod for reform in other states or provinces. Federalism thus opens doors to policy innovation and policy diffusion.

Interdependence, which has been identified as a defining characteristic of federalism, is also a core principle of environmentalism. The Brundtland Report identifies the need for intergovernmental cooperation as the master solution for successful environmental management, and Walters takes this as an endorsation of both federalism and decentralization: "Given the all-pervasive nature of environmental management, it is difficult to conceive of one level of government as having exclusive power over it—indeed, to confer exclusive jurisdiction over sustainable development would be like conferring a legislative monopoly over common sense to one level of government" (1991: 424). Walters suggests that in a federal state, "there must be a decentralization of power over the environment such that each level of government can ensure that the resource and environmental issues related to each of its traditional spheres of constitutional jurisdiction are taken into account in the course of policy formation" (1991: 424). However, if federal models of environmental governance are to be developed, decisions will have to be made about which matters should best be left to "local authorities," no matter how these might be defined, and which should be entrusted to the larger national or transnational authority. Unfortunately, such decisions are notoriously difficult to make and, once made, to sustain. As Derthick explains, American federalism

> has not provided a stable set of understandings about how to distinguish the national from the local. Americans are forever searching for that distinction without finding it. It is no sooner declared to have been found than it is lost in a sea of social, economic, and ideological change. Interdependence among governments, always great, constantly grows. *The national relentlessly encroaches on the local.*
> (1992: 675, emphasis added)

There is little reason to expect that in the environmental field, where problems show a general disregard for jurisdictional boundaries, that this distinction will be any easier to find, or that the national will be any less likely to "encroach relentlessly" on the local.

The problem identified by Derthick is only one of many that will need to be addressed before federalism's potential can be assessed. To this point, however, models of governance in general, much less federal models in particular, have received relatively little discussion within the environmental movement. Even though political questions are front and centre to the movement, and even though there has been a wide-ranging condemnation of existing political structures, there are few concrete suggestions for institutional reform. As Goodin points out, "in any plausible model of policy coordination among decentralized green communities, there will be a role for centralized coordinating mechanisms" (1992b: 167). Yet, to date, the specification of such mechanisms has been avoided. In part this avoidance has been possible because considerable emphasis has been placed on two other strategies which enable writers to duck awkward questions of governance.

For those who are adverse to the creation of new political institutions, something that federal solutions imply, an appeal is often made to cooperation and implicitly to the hope that existing systems of governance might suffice if governments would cooperate on a common environmental agenda. Young suggests that faith in cooperation may have something to do with the scientific background of many in the environmental movement. In his discussion of the style of environmentalist publications in the early 1970s, Young notes "the characteristic academic belief that the main obstacle to intelligent action is ignorance rather than conflicts of interest: once the problem was explained with sufficient clarity and authority, then voters and governments alike would act on the advice which scientists were able to give them" (1990: 4). In any case, cooperation is seen as a means to overcome the problems inherent in divided jurisdiction and political sovereignty, as Chiras notes:

> Ultimately, efforts to align government policies with the tenets of sustainability require that all decisions pass through a sustainability filter. This, in turn, may help agencies transcend traditional boundaries and look beyond narrow, short-term solutions. It should help them develop strategies that compliment, rather than contradict, one another.
> (1992: 158)

Although a more realistic view would place conflicts of interest at the heart rather than at the periphery of environmental politics, faith in cooperation is not without foundation. It is clear that international cooperation and coordination, without any formal erosion of sovereignty, can make significant headway on environmental problems (Chiras 1992: 169ff). Boardman's work on international environmental regimes illustrates the cooperative international and transnational structures which are emerging in this very complex policy arena, although his work also shows that international regimes and agreements constrain the exercise of sovereignty even if there is no formal shift in the location of that sovereignty (1990; 1991).

Yet it should also be noted that the environmentalist's faith in cooperation often makes Pollyanna look like a hard-headed realist by comparison. Consider, for example, the following statement from a recent Liberal Party of Canada manifesto:

> The task of building a true environmental society is far too formidable to become the challenge of any one government or agency. It must become the challenge of all of us. Action must therefore be global in scope, and be interdependent. It must involve partnership and participation. It must include the federal and provincial governments acting in close cooperation and complementarity, but also local governments, native governments and authorities, environmental groups, academia, labour unions, industries as well as industrial and business associations, non-governmental organizations, and community organizations.
> (Lincoln 1991: 129)

While all of this may be true, it is also all but pointless to say. "We must cooperate" stops well short of being a coherent institutional or political strategy; indeed, it is a strategy that denies a role for politics in what is inherently a political problem. It is not surprising, then, that even those who recognize the positive role to be played by international cooperation also recognize that it may not be enough, and that we may require significant changes to international methods of governance. As Goodin points out, green supporters of decentralization "especially require but also singularly lack a theory of how the necessary coordination is to be achieved among all those autonomous small units" (1992a: 5). Without such a theory, green political thought remains seriously incomplete.

As a political strategy, cooperation assumes greater viability to the extent that communities share a common value system. It is not surprising, then, that environmental prescriptions for governance rely heavily on a second strategy, and that is the transformation of political and social values as a mechanism for intergovernmental coordination and cooperation. The belief in cooperation is thus be linked to the hope that a new set of environmental values, a new environmental consciousness, may come to infuse existing governments. It is unlikely, however, that value change itself will be sufficient to address the collective action problems confronting environmental policy. Rifkin, who is one of the most vocal proponents of a new environmental consciousness, admits that "an effective biospheric politics will necessitate a redrafting of political boundaries to make them compatible with the new ecological way of thinking about space" (1991: 286). Biospheric politics "will need to create a new, competing spatial map whose governing configuration more clearly follows the geographical lines of regional ecosystems on the local level, while encompassing the entire biosphere on an international level" (286). New lines, of course, will require new political institutions: "as biospheric consciousness is global and rooted in an organismic world-view, new international political institutions will need to be created to oversee and protect the entire biosphere of the planet" (286). Redrawing boundaries, moreover, is only part of the problem. The other part is putting into place an appropriate institutional relationship among the reconfigured political units, a task for which federalism may offer part of the solution.

Conclusion

Although environmentalism is one of the many new social movements seeking to transform the political landscape of western democratic states, it shares a number of important characteristics with other new social movements. For example, both environmentalism and feminism are highly politicized, transformative movements built around nonterritorial interests and/or communities, and both pursue an expanded political agenda which is entangled with federal values and institutions. The discussion of environmentalism can thus be used to shed some more general light on the challenge posed by the new politics to the future of federalism.

The environmental case study suggests that there are significant points of tension between the logic of the new politics and federalism, and that, as a consequence, the new politics may have a corrosive impact on federal values and institutions. At the same time, there are some important points of commonality between the new politics and federalism. In particular, the normative commitment of both to diversity and decentralization raises the possibility that federal models of governance may have a strong appeal to the proponents of a new political agenda. To this point, however, little has been done to develop explicit models of governance and to test such models against the logic of the new politics. Federalism's potential, its capacity to address the new political agenda, remains to be demonstrated.

It should also be stressed that even if federalism were to provide an appropriate new politics model of governance, existing federal arrangements would not be compatible with such new federal structures. Take, for example, the case of environmentalism. Contemporary federal states are too small to provide effective leverage on global and even continental environmental concerns.[14] At the same time, the constituent units of contemporary federal states—the provinces, lander and states—are not coterminous with ecological regions. Furthermore, it is not clear that political communities the size of Ontario, California, and New South Wales, or even Saskatchewan and Indiana, are what environmentalists have in mind when they call for greater decentralization.[15] To the contrary, it is quite likely that much smaller units would be preferred, units that would permit more direct forms of political participation and control, and which would correspond more closely to ecological boundaries.[16] Thus even a federalist response to environmentalism may be incompatible with, and potentially corrosive to, the existing institutional arrangements of contemporary federal states. Such states, like all nation-states, may be caught between the quest for greater decentralization and the institutionalization of a new global consciousness. There may be little room left in the middle for the nation state and nationalism, the latter being described in *A Blueprint for Survival* as that "dangerous and sterile compromise" (Goldsmith 1972). Indeed, the irony may be that existing federal institutions are particularly vulnerable to the pressure being exerted by the new politics.

---

14. Australia is an exception in the latter case, given that it alone among the federal states is also a continent.
15. For example, Goldsmith (1972) envisioned village-type communities of about 500, clustered together in larger communities of about 50,000, and in regional communities of 500,000.
16. There are, of course, existing federal units which might correspond quite closely to the environmentalist ideal. Possible candidates would include Tasmania and Prince Edward Island along with many of the smaller American states.

In summary, the potentially corrosive impact of the new politics on contemporary federal states suggests that, as we approach the twenty-first century, there may be significant limitations to the application of federal forms of political organization, that federalism may not be easily reconciled with the new social movements that are playing such an important role in shaping the emerging political agenda. This suggestion is particularly interesting because it runs counter to the oft-expressed view that federalism is the political option for the future, that it represents the badly needed institutional balance between economic globalization and the desire to maintain cultural pluralism, and local particularisms in the face of that globalization. The present analysis suggests that it may be an appropriate time to reexamine the future of federalism, and to do so within the context of those new social movements which promise to have such a significant impact on the unfolding of political life in western democratic states.

References

Note: This research is supported by the Social Sciences and Humanities Research Council of Canada.

Adamson, Nancy, Linda Briskin, and Margaret McPhail. 1988. *Feminist Organizing for Change: The Contemporary Women's Movement in Canada*. Toronto: Oxford University Press.
Boardman, Robert. 1990. *Global Regimes and Nation-States: Environmental Issues in Australian Politics*. Ottawa: Carleton University Press.
Boardman, Robert. 1991. "Approaching Regimes: Australia, Canada, and Environmental Policy," *Australian Journal of Political Science* 26, no. 3 (November): 446-71.
Bzdera, André. 1993. "Comparative Analysis of Federal High Courts: A Political Theory of Judicial Review," *Canadian Journal of Political Science* 26, no. 1 (March): 3-29.
Cairns, Alan C. 1977. "The Governments and Societies of Canadian Federalism," *Canadian Journal of Political Science* 10 (December): 695-726.
Chiras, Daniel D. 1992. *Lessons from Nature: Learning to Live Sustainably on the Earth*. Washington, D.C.: Island Press.
Commoner, Barry. 1990. *Making Peace With The Planet*. New York: Pantheon Books.
Crotty, Patricia M. 1987. "The New Federalism Game: Primacy Implementation of Environmental Policy," *Publius: The Journal of Federalism* 17 (Spring): 53-67.
Dalton, Russell J. 1988. *Citizen Politics in Western Democracies*. Chatham, NJ: Chatham House.
Derthick, Martha. 1992. "Up-to-Date in Kansas City: Reflections on American Federalism," *PS: Political Science & Politics* 25, no. 4 (December): 671-75.
Devall, Bill, and George Sessions. 1985. *Deep Ecology: Living As If Nature Mattered*. Salt Lake City: Peregrine Smith Books.
Fox, Warwick. 1989. "The Meaning of Deep Ecology," *Island Magazine* 38: 32-36.
Galligan, Brian, and Cliff Walsh. 1991. *Australian Federalism Yes or No*. Canberra: Federalism Research Centre, Australian National University.

Goldsmith, E. 1972. *A Blueprint for Survival*. London: The Ecologist.
Goodin, Robert E. 1992a. "The High Ground is Green," *Environmental Politics* 1, no. 1 (Spring): 1–8.
Goodin, Robert E. 1992b. *Green Political Theory*. Oxford: Polity Press.
Hardin, Garrett, and John Baden (eds.) 1977. *Managing the Commons*. New York: W.H. Freeman.
Inglehart, Ronald. 1977. *The Silent Revolution: Changing Values and Political Styles Among Western Publics*. Princeton, NJ: Princeton University Press.
Inglehart, Ronald. 1990. *Culture Shift in Advanced Industrial Society*. Princeton, NJ: Princeton University Press.
Kamieniecki, Sheldon, and Michael R. Ferral. 1991. "Intergovernmental Relations and Clean-Air Policy in Southern California," *Publius: The Journal of Federalism* 21 (Summer): 143–54.
Kara, Jan. 1992. "Geopolitics and the Environment: The Case of Central Europe," *Environmental Politics* 1, no. 2 (Summer): 186–95.
Kitschelt, Herbert. 1988. "Organization and Strategy of Belgian and West German Ecology Parties: A New Dynamic of Party Politics in Western Europe?" *Comparative Politics* 20 (January): 127–54.
Krasner, Stephen D. 1988. "Sovereignty: An Institutional Perspective," *Comparative Political Studies* 21, no. 1 (April): 66–94.
Lincoln, Clifford. 1991. "Our Planet Must Be Rescued." In *Towards a New Liberalism: Recreating Canada and the Liberal Party*, edited by Cleo Mowers. Victoria: Orca Publishers.
McKibben, Bill. 1989. *The End of Nature*. New York: Random House.
Millett, Kate. 1969. *Sexual Politics*. New York: Simon & Schuster.
Newsom, D. P. 1988–89. "The New Diplomatic Agenda: Are Governments Ready?" *International Affairs* 65: 29–42.
Offe, Claus. 1983. "'Reaching for the brake:' the Greens in Germany," *New Political Science* 11: 45–52.
Paehlke, Robert C. 1989. *Environmentalism and the Future of Progressive Politics*. New Haven: Yale University Press.
Pierce, John C., Taketsugu Tsurutani, and Nicholas P. Lovrich, Jr. 1986. "Vanguards and Rearguards in Environmental Politics: A Comparison of Activists in Japan and the United States," *Comparative Political Studies* 18, no. 4 (January): 419–47.
Plant, Judith. 1989. "The Circle is Gathering." In *Healing the Wounds: The Promise of Ecofeminism*, edited by J. Plant. London: Green Print.
Porritt, Jonathon. 1984. *Seeing Green: The Politics of Ecology Explained*. Oxford: Blackwell.
Rabe, Barry G. 1991. "Environmental Regulation in New Jersey: Innovations and Limitations," *Publius: The Journal of Federalism* 21 (Winter): 83–103.
Regens, James L. 1989. "Acid Rain Policymaking and Environmental Federalism: Recent Developments, Future Prospects," *Publius: The Journal of Federalism* 19 (Summer): 75–91.
Rifkin, Jeremy. 1991. *Biosphere Politics: A New Consciousness for a New Century*. New York: Crown Publishers.
Rohrschneider, Robert. 1988. "Citizens' Attitudes Toward Environmental Issues: Selfish or Selfless?" *Comparative Political Studies* 21, no. 3 (October): 347–67.
Roszak, Theodore. 1978. *Person/Planet*. Garden City, NY: Doubleday.
Simeon, Richard. 1983. "Criteria for Choice in Federal Systems," *Queen's Law Journal* 8.

Walters, Mark. 1991. "Ecological Unity and Political Fragmentation: The Implications of the Brundtland Report for the Canadian Constitutional Order," *Alberta Law Review* 29 (2): 420-49.
Welborn, David. 1988. "Conjoint Federalism and Environmental Regulation in the United States," *Publius: The Journal of Federalism* 18 (Winter): 27-43.
World Commission on Environment and Development (the Brundtland Report). 1987. *Our Common Future*. Oxford: Oxford University Press.
Young, John. 1990. *Sustaining the Earth*. Cambridge, MA: Harvard University Press.
Young, Stephen C. 1992. "The Different Dimensions of Green Politics." *Environmental Politics* 1, no. 1 (Spring): 9-44.

The Nation and the Future of Federalism

David G. Whitefield

The theme of these papers revolves around the issue of the future of federalism.* In what ways is its future in doubt? By which forms of political organization will federations be replaced? During a period when federal states such as the former Soviet Union, Yugoslavia, India, and even Canada are confronting upheaval, such systems seem self-evidently vulnerable and subject to replacement by presumably postfederal super states such as the European Community or the North American Free Trade Association. Alternatively, they may be subject to balkanization into smaller and more natural units, representative of constituents such as women or aboriginal peoples. Conspicuously, the so-called national question provides expression to one of the many sources of contemporary political instability and, as an alternative to federations, some political figures look to nations. Nations are often perceived as ancient and organic manifestations of popular culture and, unlike some federations, they are regarded as profoundly democratic. This paper will suggest that, as a state form, federations are much more deeply entrenched than nations which are "historical novelties" that were sometimes developed for purposes far removed from the popular interest.

For the European historian, there is no obvious reason to doubt that federations will continue to play a dominant role in political organization. Fed-

---

* This paper is based on a talk, as is apparent from its title, that was inspired by the writings of the distinguished historian Eric Hobsbawm, particularly by his recent book on the national question (1992). Modest exception is taken here to Hobsbawm's position on the questions of 'nation and autarchy' as well as to Gorbachev's arguments concerning Lenin on the federal and national questions. In addition to respect offered to Gorbachev and Hobsbawm, special gratitude is given to Dr E. J. Hundert of the University of British Columbia and to my colleague, Mr S. Hooper.

erations are as old as Europe itself.[1] Indeed, in one form or another, federations have been the general form of state system in many parts of the world, including North America where, long before the colonists revolution against the British Empire, federal relations had been formed among a number of aboriginal peoples.[2]

Over the millennia, specific federations have waxed and wained. They have been subjected to internal pressures generated by the power struggles among their constituents. They have been battered by difficulties arising from changes in the nature of the family and inheritance practices. They have been rended by conflict over the forms of property relationships that should prevail and by confrontations between adherents of various religious outlooks.[3] Federations have collapsed in the face of foreign conquerors or withered away as military elites became accustomed to the fruits of victory. There have been federations containing fixed territories and others laying claim to world domination. Some federations of historical importance—such as the medieval Roman Catholic Church—placed as much emphasis on ideological as on territorial sovereignty.

Certainly, the practice of federalism is ancient and, because of their utility, federations are likely both to survive and change. The central issue, therefore, concerns the form of that change, a form that may be determined by the nature of the popular forces of discontent.

Within many modern federations, the aspiration of peoples to resolve the national question appears to present a significant challenge to the stability of existing regimes. Indeed, as has recently been witnessed in relation to Yugoslavia, to the former Soviet Union, as well as to Québec, the legitimacy of the demand for national self-determination seems to be widely accepted as self-evident. In part, this may be explained by the common perception of nations as ancient formations, custodians of deeply entrenched organic culture, and as the tissue that binds past, present, and future generations.

---

1. For an interesting discussion of the formation of federations in "Dark Age" Europe, see Herrmann (1982). Unfortunately, this work is not available in English, but it is critically summarized in Whitefield (1987).
2. For studies of the Huron confederacy, see Trigger (1987). For the Iroquois, Wright (1992) and Richter and Merrell (1987). I am grateful to my colleague, Dr S. Carter, for introducing me to these works.
3. On these questions, as clear a discussion as any was provided by Engels (1884). Many of Engels's ideas are old-fashioned but, in their fuller development, they can be studied in Herrmann and Kohn (1988).

While for the European historian there is no doubt about the historic reality and viability of the federation, powerful reasons exist for suggesting that the nation subsists within the context of reification. Nations may best be viewed as imagined communities, the product not of time-honoured mass cultural forces but of relatively modern political economists and demagogues. Unlike the federation, the nation is an historical novelty, and all thinking persons who oppose demagoguery may be well advised to question the legitimacy of nationalist claims.

Obviously, this hypothesis flies directly into the wind of popular expressions concerning human nature. In the eighteenth century, a Scottish poet, Sir Walter Scott, faced the issue squarely by posing the following question.

Breathes there a man, with soul so dead,
Who never to himself hath said,
This is mine own, my native land? (1887: Canto 6, I)

But is the "native land" of Sir Walter Scott's poetry synonymous with the nation identified in the dull prose of the Charlottetown agreement which characterized the distinctiveness of Québec in terms of the civil code? Is Québec really distinguished by its advocates? What do we mean when we use the word nation?

The word has many meanings which reflect the historic and essentially European conditions within which it came into use and, in the remainder of this paper, an historical sketch will be presented of the main overlapping phases in the evolution of the word's meaning, which are: a collective; an autarchy; a liberal democracy; the nation as an invention; a popular democracy; an expression of religion or race; a sovereign state.

The Nation as a Collective. In this first phase, the word nation contains its original and somewhat condescending meaning in Latin to refer to Rome's allies in the Italian federation (Isidore of Seville, *Etymologiae*, IV, 2.1 & 4.4, cited in Wolfram 1988). Somewhat later, but without much more respect, it was used by the Romans to refer to the Goths, a federation of so-called barbarians who had conquered large parts of Italy. The Goths themselves were comprised of elements from several tribes (Wolfram, 1988: 5). In Latin's successor languages, the word nation retained a similar meaning. In the Scottish and French languages, it referred to groups of students; and it was in the same broad sense that nation was used—and only very rarely—in

German.[4] Both in French and Spanish, the word was most commonly used to refer to provincial peoples or areas. Alsace and Gascony—but not France!— were nations. In the eighteenth century, the word also applied to the peoples, from many origins, who lived in Québec. If, as some scholars argue, eighteenth-century culture survives and is contained in one of the modern official languages of Canada, then Canadian francophones must find quite incredible the inability of some Anglo-Canadians to acknowledge their country as a nation.[5]

The Nation as an Autarchic Economy. The next two meanings developed within the context of the struggle of the commercial and manufacturing strata against feudalism. Within late feudal society, the general state-form was the territorial principality—often organized into a number of federations such as the Holy Roman Empire, Sweden, or England. The names provided to these principalities included the county, the duchy or the realm—in German, *Reich*. The realm of England contained those territories which were peopled by persons who were subjects of the king's rule. In this environment, state policy was seldom directed to the service of manufacture or commerce, sectors whose condition was sometimes destabilized by changes in frontiers or embargoes resulting from dynastic wars.

Nevertheless, some territorial principalities became important centres of regional manufacture or trade and, in an effort to consolidate and expand these economic entities, pressure was extended to cease dealing with them as disposable 'subject' possessions but as permanent organic elements of the state. Within this context, the word nation was used as an alternative to realm and it was in this sense that it was used in petitions to Tudor monarchs.[6] It was also in this antifeudal meaning that it was used by Adam Smith in his famous *Wealth of Nations* (1776), by Alexander Hamilton and the Federalists in the debates concerning the constitution of the United States, and by Friedrich List in his work on the national economy.[7]

---

4. I am grateful to my friend Mr G. Tondino for sharing his knowledge and insight into Dark Age European history and, in particular, for sharing his knowledge concerning interethnic relations within various "tribal peoples."
5. I am grateful to my colleague Dr G. Donovan for drawing my attention to this point.
6. For an example, see Guy (1990: 43). For an additional example to the tendency to seek preference for "subjects" over other economic organizations, see Prothero (1913: 111–17).
7. Hobsbawm argues that classical political economy was directed toward strengthening world trade and was generally antagonistic to the national principle. "Non-classical" economists such as Hamilton and List, I suggest, were concerned with the formation of the United

The Nation as a Liberal Democracy. Conflict between the bourgeoisie and feudalism also invoked a political struggle against the independence of territorial sovereigns—the struggle against feudal absolutism. At the trial of Charles I, his prosecutors used the word nation as an alternative to the royal word "realm" when referring to the king's subjects living in England (Rushworth 1721). In this context, Englishmen were "citizens" who collectively possessed sovereign power. The concept of the nation as "sovereign citizens" was used in the U.S. Constitution debates and, as we all know, it was clearly enunciated by Abraham Lincoln after Gettysburg. The nation as sovereign citizens was also the meaning used by both Seyes and the Jacobins during the French Revolution.

In all these instances, of course, the question of qualifications for citizenship arose. In England and France, citizenship was reserved for males and there was a strong tendency to include only property-owning males. Birthplace and language had little or no part in determining citizenship. The American Tom Paine, although born in England, faced no special obstacle in becoming a member of the French national assembly. In America, however, only nonaboriginal, nonslave males born in the territories of the United States could achieve full citizenship—and full membership of the United States as a nation—through possession of the right to become chief magistrate.

The Nation as an Invention. The previous two meanings of nation developed during the struggle against feudalism. The next two emerged around 1848, as the aristocracy and capitalists found means to reach an accommodation. In that year, a force of extreme Jacobin-democrats and elements of the peasantry and the proletariat of the age of early industrialization rose up in rebellion across much of Europe. Terrified by this expression of the power of the masses, the bourgeoisie entered into an alliance with the remaining, often militaristic, vital forces of feudalism and formed new, quasi-democratic states. Within them, the recently mechanized press played a vital role, narrowly focussing politics on personalities and sensational incidents. Public participation in the process was organized through elections controlled by tight political parties with strong leaders such as Cavour, Bismarck, or

---

States and Germany into economic systems that would eventually allow them to compete with Britain in world markets. Given the level of development and weakness of the capitalist economic infrastructure of the American and German societies in the early nineteenth century, the federalists' discomfiture with *laissez-faire* seems quite reasonable.

Disraeli. Sometimes, plebiscites were used to obtain public support for the leaders' agenda. In Greece, Italy, Germany, and Britain, the formation of these new states was closely associated with the emergence of monarchy into a new age, within which kings identified themselves as custodians of usually invented tradition and of the "will of the people." The creation of a common language was among the more important of these inventions. In this regard, it is salutary to observe that, when Italy was 'unified' in 1861, only some 2.5 percent of the population spoke Italian.[8] In England, the formal language taught in the state schools, after the introduction of compulsory elementary education in 1875, was a product newly developed by pedagogues.

Several invented nations took the form of empires, with no fixed frontiers and populated by peoples of many languages and religions. In general, colonies were governed by migrants for whom nation acquired a special meaning. To the emigre, the nation existed, simultaneously, in two forms: first, as a nostalgic abstraction, the 'distant homeland' invented by the homesick; and, second, as a real community created and populated by expatriots living within an alien environment.

In post-Civil War America, as huge waves of immigrants were systematically placed in the melting pot, even the Hamiltonian United States was transformed. The masses were taught to swear allegiance to the flag, and, in the "sweet land of liberty," electoral control was seized by Tammany politicians who were supported and reported on by the so-called yellow press. Further north, Sir John A. Macdonald used the railroad and, in a period of less than six geological days, created Canada. The myth was developed that Canada contains two founding nations—England and France. In the Canada of 1867, Canadians of both Scottish and Irish origin could not have been outnumbered by the English—unless Sir John A. Macdonald was a Sassenach. And who knows how many Québécois were 'Basques'?

The Nation as Popular Democracy. The rebellions of 1848–50 transformed European politics. To avoid revolution from below and by including all classes in the ranks of the nation, ruling elites developed their own programs of revolution from above. The circumstances of 1848 also gave rise to the advance of the nation to another level of meaning. At the hands of Marxists and other non-Marxist socialists, the peoples' nation proceeded onto the stage.

---

8. Authority for this remarkable information is provided by de Mauro (1963).

Viewed macroscopically, socialism seems hostile to the nation. In the nineteenth century, socialist consciousness still embraced the entire world, peopled not by divided nations but by politically or objectively united classes. As the authors of *The Manifesto of the Communist Party* put it, "the proletariat has no fatherland" (see *Karl Marx and Frederick Engels Collected Works* 1976: v. 6, 477-519; v. 7, 3-7). Objectively true as this statement may have been, the authors also recognized a more immediate reality. The *Manifesto* was not quite the program of the workers of the world but of a small group of almost exclusively German-speaking exiles living in London, exiles who had recently formed the Communist League. In 1847, the Communist League held that the best prospect for revolution existed in the German confederation, a body of some thirty-nine sovereign states, and including two great powers. To advance their cause, Germany had to be transformed into a "nation, but a nation of a new kind." Precisely what this meant is unclear but it probably involved the formation of Germany as a Jacobin-democratic republic, economically liberal and with a very small state sector, reduced "to nothing more than a board of directors for managing the affairs of the bourgeoisie." Within that future greater German democratic republic, goods from the entire world would be imported at the speed of the oceanic steamboat and distributed at the speed of the railroad. Culture would be extended through compulsory education organized within the workplace. Under the future rule of the modern bourgeoisie, "all feudal, patriarchal, idyllic relations" would be swept away. Such would be the efficiency and popularity of this form of nation that it would be embraced by the entire world. Peacefully, even the walls of China would topple.

With the defeat of the revolutions of 1848-50 and the shattering, in the 1860's, of all obvious prospects of forming a united greater Germany, Marxist policy moved gradually in other directions. One took the route of denunciation of the nation as a *petit-bourgeois* objective and a means to divert and undermine the class struggle. Another acknowledged the need to come to terms with the nation but identified it, like religious denomination, as a private matter. Within that limited context, people could belong to any nation they liked.

In the long term, the most influential Marxist theory was developed by Lenin, for whom support for national aspirations was a matter of principle. The principle with which Lenin was concerned was to advance the revolutionary process within the czarist empire, a process that required the support of the nationalist *petit bourgeoisie*. In his writings, Lenin attempted, with some success, to liberate himself from utopian and universal political concepts, from principles. To him, questions concerning the superiority of federations over national-unitary forms of government were practical, to be decided according to specific political conditions. In practice, of course, the task of developing Lenin's ideas concerning the nation was adopted by Stalin, who was guided by another set of principles, under whose influence theoretical issues were confronted in terms of arbitrary dogma. As a result, many dogmatic revolutionaries in colonial countries turned to 'Marxist' slogans in their anti-imperialist rhetoric.

This process was further advanced by the inability of Marxists to liberate themselves from the popular belief that responsibility to provide for the needs of the people rested with the state. Especially, the state should guarantee the provision of economic and social benefits. Increasingly, this theory was adopted by the "inventive" national leaders whose programs to provide old-age pensions, workmen's compensation, employment protection, and free mass education were introduced by apparently antisocialist governments. In Britain, the socialistic process of providing services through the state was named "nationalization."

The Nation as an Expression of Religion or Race. Somehow, these historically novel meanings of the word nation are associated with modernizing policies. In western Europe, where these meanings originated, such policies were bound to be antifeudal. In many parts of eighteenth- or nineteenth-century Europe, of course, feudalism was still in its relative infancy, while in many parts of the world, feudalism had never existed at all. Even in these areas, however, ideas were strongly influenced by the power of westernizing forces and, within them, the word nation acquired an antirevolutionary connotation.

In Europe, conservative interpretations of the word emerged most explicitly in the territories subject to dispute between the Russian, Ottoman, and Austro-Hungarian empires. In the high days of the Holy Alliance, Russian power was decisive in the victory of the Greek independence movement. Religion was part of the polemic used in justifying czarist intervention: Greece, like Russia, was populated by adherents to the orthodox Christian religion.

Further north in the Balkans, religion was used to distinguish between two Slavic peoples speaking the same language. One group, the Croats, was identified as adherents to Roman Catholicism, and used the Latin alphabet. The other, allegedly orthodox, used the Cyrillic alphabet. Even further north, adherence to Roman Catholicism was seen, by both friends and foes of the

Irish national movement, as a necessary attribute of true Irishness. Under the influence of the Lodges of the Orange Order, protestantism became an ideological criterion of the true Scot.

With the great wave of migration from eastern to western Europe in the second half of the nineteenth century, religious criteria were also used to discriminate between peoples in Germany, where apparently Roman Catholic citizens of Polish origin were sometimes regarded in much the same way as the Irish in Britain. Politically, Bismarck's *kulturkampf* was partly directed against the influence of the Roman Catholic church-dominated Centrist party. For centuries, of course, some Jews had been treated as members of a distinct nation—distinguished by their religious practices and by belief in the theory that they were a "chosen people." The Dreyfus affair provides special insight into the relationship between religion and the nation and, in the light of subsequent events, it seems ironic that Germany was the country to which the "Jewish traitor" was accused of selling secrets. Irony apart, it is also important to recognize that adherents to the Jacobin theory of the "nation as citizens" came to Dreyfus's defence. For them, religion and the national principle were antipathetical.

In today's neoconservative world, by contrast, new impetus has been given to the identification of nation with religion. As we know, civil war is embracing Bosnia where, on the one side, stand socialist-atheistic anti-Bosnian Serbs and, on the other, independence-seeking Muslims. Whether this definition of nation is accepted by the actual peoples directly involved or is a convenient invention by western journalists is another matter. The same point might be made concerning the apparently ridiculous journalistic concept of the Islamic fundamentalist nation.

On the other hand, except in relation to Jews or Gypsies, the practical use of racist criteria for discrimination was relatively uncommon in nineteenth-century Europe. In most places, of course, visible minorities formed a very tiny proportion of the population. Outside of the harbour areas in the great port cities, members of other "racial" groups conducted themselves like the ruling elite; in the sport of cricket, the skills of Indian students at Oxford and Cambridge were deeply respected.

In the wider world where Europeans had settled, different ideas prevailed. In the post-Civil War United States, racist ideas were used in order to justify continued denial of citizen rights and full membership of the nation to emancipated slaves and their descendants. In South Africa, a tiny minority of Afrikaans- and English-speaking settlers developed a particularly vicious racist nation and similar ideas developed across most areas of European settlement.

Indeed, during the nineteenth century, the understanding of nation in terms of race may have been most common among migrants—and the development of the racist nation within twentieth-century Europe is also associated with a great waves of migration. The tragic events in Germany and eastern Europe were sparked, in part, by migration resulting from the victory of the 'national principle' at the Conference of Versailles; in Uganda, national independence resulted in migration by large numbers of 'Asians.' Although many of these migrants held British passports, they were denied entry into that country on the basis of no obvious grounds except race and political expediency.

The Nation as Sovereign State. Fortunately, the final meaning of the word nation is also the simplest. Regardless of any of our previous considerations, diplomats and bureaucrats will undoubtedly recognize their own special meaning of the word. Nations are states, with entitlement to membership of the United Nations.

In the reality of high places, nations may be comprised of an even smaller group. During his last days in office, President Bush announced that his final confrontation with Iraq was supported by the entire community of nations, a community presumably comprising, in addition to the Emir of Kuwait, the prime ministers of Britain and Canada, the president of France and, perhaps, Boris Yeltsin.

The Nation and Globalization

This sketch of the way whereby politicians and ideologues make use of a word has indicated that, contrary to common belief, political use of the word nation may not correspond to popular understanding and, by implication, that nations are myths. A quite different argument, of course, is presented by anthropologists and ethnographers, some of whom view the nation as part of a "species" of real communities which they identify with the word *ethnos*.[9]

A second implication may also be drawn, namely that the popular masses who comprise the human substance that is manipulated by the myth have

---

9. The concept has been developed most systematically by academician Yuri Bromley. For an example of his scholarship, see the work on Soviet and Western anthropology by Gellner (1980).

been entrapped by false ideology. The theory that vast numbers of common people are motivated by concern for the nation is quite widespread. The outbreak of the First World War, for example, is commonly associated with manifestations of mass enthusiasm for the nations' cause, enthusiasm which resulted in the mutual massacre of 'internationalist' workers and peasants. Similarly, leading figures of the Second International are accused of supporting the slaughter because they preferred exploitation by their own rather than foreign capitalists.

Such arguments have several weaknesses. For example, they fail to deal with the reality of widespread popular disapproval of the war. No statistics are provided for the numbers of people who danced in the streets of London, Paris, and Berlin as the guns roared in August 1914. They are not likely, however, to have been greater than the numbers who risked opprobrium and imprisonment by declaring conscientious objection or who supposedly sabotaged the war effort by striking for higher wages, rent controls, and improved social benefits. Nor is data available concerning the war-dancers' social status. Some social strata, including pedagogues and other employees of the state sector, may have a special vested interest in supporting nationalist ideas.

Empirical evidence concerning the impact of the politicians' perception of the nation is scarce while, of course, there is almost no direct historical evidence concerning the people's own view of what a nation means. Nevertheless, life itself may provide a few indicators.

Life suggests, for example, that nations are frequently regarded in terms of stereotypes. Germans are considered hard working and militaristic. The French are wine drinkers and lovers of fine cuisine. The English love only warm beer and everything associated with conservative royalty, including Brown Windsor soup. The Scots and Brazilians are especially skilled in Association Football while Americans are avid collectors of arsenals of weapons.

None of these stereotypes is completely devoid of truth, and it is possible that common people respond to the nation by either welcoming or rejecting such stereotypical practices. Throughout North America, for example, Italian, Chinese and other 'alien' foods are consumed ubiquitously and true Canadians consuming Neapolitan or Peking delicacies are aware that they are enjoying a touch of other nations. Indeed, with the intensification of the globalization process, the awareness and acceptance of other nations seems to be increasing.

Globalization, of course, is a complex phenomenon. Most obviously, it is an expression of the historic tendency toward the creation of a single capitalist world economic system. That process was interrupted, in the 1920's, by the Stalinist decision to engage in the experiment of building socialism in one country.

On the other hand, globalization may have created socioeconomic conditions that allow for the survival of distinctive cultural formations, such as nations in this final sense. To some degree, globalization may have given rise to a new and more informed awareness of other nations and to the recognition that at least some foreign customs are worthy of incorporation into our own. In Canada, this process is manifested in the increased popularity of international tourism, of language study, and of foreign works of art and literature. In a few countries, such as Canada, globalization has resulted in the emergence of a widely supported program to use the military as peacekeepers, as an instrument of defending peoples of other countries for whom we feel sympathy. Indeed, willingness to assist others may be a discerning stereotypical characteristic of the Canadian nation, as popularly understood.

Evidence from life, however, does not provide raw material for the European historian for whom literary archives and cemeteries remain more important sources. These suggest that federations will survive and, so long as there are political demagogues and idealists, so too will nations—as ideologues use the term. But the possibility exists that the process of economic integration and globalization will give rise to a new culture within which differences between peoples will be identified and celebrated in the world's emporiums and kitchens. Rather than inspiring fear and contempt, the essential material features of various nations will be purchased and cherished.

References

de Mauro, Tullio. 1963. *Storia Linguistica della Italia Unita*. Bari.
Engels, Frederick. [1884] 1942. *The Origin of the Family, Private Property and the State*. New York: International Publishers.
Gellner, Ernest, ed. 1980. Soviet and Western Anthropology. London: Duckworth.
Guy, John. 1990. *Tudor England*. Oxford: Oxford University Press.
Herrmann, Joachim. 1982. "Militarische Demokratie und die Ubergangsperiod zur Klassengesellschaft," *EAZ*, Volume 23. Berlin.
Herrmann, Joachim, and J. Kohn, eds. 1988. *Familie, Staat und Gesellichaftsformation*. Berlin: Akademie-Verlag.
Hobsbawm, E. J. 1992. *Nations and Nationalism Since 1780: Programme, Myth, Reality*. Cambridge: Cambridge University Press.

Marx, Karl, and Frederick Engels. 1976. *Karl Marx and Frederick Engels Collected Works.* New York: International Publishers.
Prothero, G. W., ed. 1913. *Select Statutes and Other Constitutional Documents Illustrative of the Reigns of Elizabeth and James I.* Oxford: Clarendon Press.
Richter, Daniel, and James H. Merrell. 1987. *Beyond the Covenant Chain: The Iroquois and Their Neighbours in Indian North America, 1600-1800.* Syracuse: Syracuse University Press.
Rushworth, John. 1721. *Historical Collections, Volume 7.* 2nd ed. London: Printed for J. Walthoe et al.
Trigger, Bruce C. 1987. *The Children of Aetaentsic: A History of the Huron People to 1660,* Kingston, ON: McGill-Queens University Press.
Scott, Sir Walter. 1887. *The Lay of the Minstrel,* edited by W. J. Rolfe. Boston, New York and Chicago: Houghton, Mifflin Company.
Wenskus, R. 1977. *Stammesbildung und Verfassung.* 2nd ed. Cologne.
Whitefield, David G. 1987. "Ethnography, History and Class Struggle." In *Ethnicity and Culture,* edited by R. Auger. Calgary, The Archaeological Association of the University of Calgary.
Wolfram, Herwig. 1988. *History of the Goths.* Berkeley: University of California at Los Angeles Press.
Wright, Ronald. 1992. *Stolen Continents: The New World Through Indian Eyes Since 1492.* Toronto: Viking.

Federalism: Russian Realities and Historical Experience

Yuri A. Krasin

Minsk. 8 December 1991. The presidents of three Soviet republics—Russia, the Ukraine, and Byelorussia—sign the document which officially dissolves the already weakened federative Union of Soviet Socialist Republics (USSR). Only the future will reveal if this was an act of great statesmanship or a rash act of personal and nationalist ambitions. There can be no doubt, regardless of motivations, that this date marks the end of the USSR's seventy-year history and, at the same time, the beginning of the quest for new forms of national statehood in the maelstrom of ethnic conflicts in the former Union.

The first step of this quest is to attempt to comprehend what has happened and the forces that are shaping the current situation. Among the problems that have beset the historical dynamic of the former Soviet Union and its components, few are more important than ethnic and nationality relations. Consequently, this paper focuses on those issues.

The Experience of the Soviet Federation

The establishment of the Soviet Union, in 1922, at first gave rise to considerable optimism, ill-founded as that optimism may have been, that a solution to the region's persistent nationality problems had been found. Nationality problems plagued the region for generations and had become especially acute by the end of the nineteenth century. The Soviet federation was created on the vast territories of the former Russian Empire, where over one hundred nations and nationalities had lived in a unitary state. Many of them had ancient historical roots and unique sociocultural identity, but were deprived of their own statehood and oppressed by the central authorities.

The federative structure of the Soviet state implied the implementation of other principles in nationality relations. The declaration of the establishment of the Union of Soviet Socialist Republics, adopted by the First Congress of the Soviets of the USSR, placed "mutual confidence and peace, national freedom and equality, peaceful coexistence and fraternal cooperation among the peoples" (First Congress of Soviets of the USSR 1923: Appendix 1, 8) in opposition to national hostility and inequality.

That agreement provided a glimmer of hope in a world of acute ethnic conflicts and colonial oppression. In the course of time, the hope turned to disappointment. The Soviet federal model collapsed. Now, it is time to carefully analyze the causes of that collapse in order to understand how present and future policies may avoid a repetition of past errors.

The very concept of the Soviet federation contained an inner contradiction. In principle, orthodox Marxism, oriented toward a strong state—the dictatorship of the proletariat—as an instrument of profound social transformation, rejected the idea of federative statehood. Even if Marx accepted it now and then, it tended to be an exception to the rule, a course to be followed only under special circumstances. Lenin had a similar attitude. "We are certainly in favour of democratic centralism. We are opposed to federation. We support the Jacobins as against the Girondists. . . . We are opposed to federation in principle, it loosens economic ties, and is unsuitable for a single state," he wrote in December 1913 (1970: v. 19, 500). Lenin did not formulate the concept of the Soviet federation until 1917, and only then as a response to pragmatic, not doctrinal, considerations. Having soberly analyzed the realities of the disintegrating Russian Empire, he realized that only federalism could preserve the integrity of a multinational state. The unitary line would be perceived as a continuation of the imperial policy of the subjugation of nations. That route would lead, in his judgement, to the country's breakup along nationality lines. Consequently, Lenin adopted a different approach: "Let Russia be a union of free republics" (v. 25, 37).

Lenin's interpretation presented federalism not as a permanent form of statehood equivalent to unitarism, but as something temporary and transitional. It was invested with a kind of inferiority complex. Federalism was regarded as a forced adaptation to specific Russian conditions and, in future, would have to be replaced by a mature unitary state. Lenin's interpretation was clearly spelled out in the documents of the Comintern's Second Congress (1920): "Federation is a transitional form to complete unity among the working people of different nations" (Second Congress of the Comintern 1934: 492 [translated by author]).

Lenin was far from considering federalism as a purely tactical stratagem, a verbal disguise for unitarism. Defending federalism as a real form of national self-determination, he resolutely opposed the supporters of "autonomization," including Stalin. Nevertheless, the kind of inferiority complex underlying the Soviet federation concealed the peril of its degeneration into an empty form deprived of real power. This particular circumstance later helped the "autonomists" take revenge for their defeat.

The future of the Soviet federation largely depended on the evolution of the Soviet state itself. Had democratic trends prevailed in that process, Soviet federalism could presumably have become a real form of a nation's self-expression at the state level. But, since totalitarian tendencies gained the upper hand, and Stalin's despotic regime became firmly established in the country, federalism turned into a fiction, a quasi-democratic disguise for the centralized bureaucratic power of the ruling elite, which was a parasite on the socialist idea and the masses' communal-egalitarian aspirations.

Federal power structures increasingly lost their political character, turning into a machine designed to impose the centre's will on the other regions. Unification took place both as an act of political will and also as part of the general modernization of Soviet society in the economic, sociocultural, and demographic spheres. This provided some material for ideological myths about "the nation's rapproachment," "people's inviolable friendship," a "new historical community—the Soviet people." Official ideology tended to ignore the potential dangers inherent in the retention and even revival of stagnant traditional structures and stereotypes of outlook and behaviour in national regions. Those processes were a kind of protective reaction to the limitation of national traditions, neglect of national specifics, and lack of attention to differences in national outlook. Disregarding historical traditions, central authorities reshaped republican borders at their own discretion, transferring national cultural centres and large population groups from one republic to another at will.

Even economic modernization, impressive as it may have been statistically, was not effectively correlated with the national sociocultural milieu, but mechanically superimposed on traditional structures. Thus, the new social and political relations and structures that were established tended to conceal more historically based values and relationships. The "man-commune," rather than "individual-society" relationship, was the axis around which social relations revolved. The family-clan group was the microcosm which determined individual behaviour. Nor was the population's ethnic variety and divisiveness reduced. Not having passed through market economy mechanisms that could mould nationalities into a single nation, central Asian republics, in particular, failed to achieve real national unity. That lack of effective integration and resolution of historical divisions has remained a major source of ethnic conflicts. As a whole, the Soviet system, federative in form and unitary in content, contained within it considerable potential for disintegration.

The democratic reform of Soviet society, which began in 1985 under Mr Gorbachev, had to expose and confront all those problems and contradictions of the nation-state. A rapid and well-conceived democratization of the centre and of the entire system of federal ties could have neutralized that destructive potential. This did not happen, however, because the democratization process at the centre of power lagged behind the rapidly growing centrifugal trends in the republics. The sovereignty explosion at the periphery undermined central power. Historically, the centre was based upon Russia. When Russia itself declared its sovereignty and the precedence of Russian laws over Union ones, the federation's breakup became inevitable.

In retrospect, it is useful to consider what the alternatives were and what was not done as a result of the lack of understanding of the issues involved, or for subjective reasons. What, in other words, was inevitable and what was unavoidable? The totalitarian system's collapse triggered the breakup of the Soviet federation, once the centre itself crumbled and its hegemony could be challenged. It is hard to imagine, given the degree of inertia that characterized imperial conservatism—which is still evident today—that it would have been possible during a period of crisis to undo centuries of accumulated ethnic tension, averting the unravelling of some important threads, and transforming the old federation into a new one. Painful consequences of acute ethnic conflicts would have to be experienced anyway. At the same time, the complete and rapid breakup of the Union was unpredictable, with the tragic aftermath and rough rupture of vital socioeconomic ties of the multinational society.

I believe the statesmen and sociopolitical forces had sufficient opportunity to maintain the minimum coherence which would have more evenly and less destructively enabled them to turn to the creation of new federative ties in the mainstream of a democratic reformation of post-totalitarian society. If, . . . but alas, history does not accept the subjunctive mood. The future of the independent states and their relations in the former USSR depends upon current realities.

The Commonwealth of Independent States (CIS)

The USSR was replaced by the CIS, which incorporated ten former Soviet republics, although only seven of them expressed their willingness to sign the Commonwealth charter. What is the CIS? Is it an embryo of future, principally new, federative relations of closely interconnected states of the former Soviet Union, or a powerless organizational structure which will complete, in a civilized manner, the former republic's divorce and divide the USSR's legacy and debts among them?

In January 1992, the Gorbachev Foundation hosted a meeting of specialists to analyze the political situation in the CIS and forecast its development. Various viewpoints were expressed, but pessimistic appraisals prevailed. There was little expectation that the CIS might be the embryo of a new Union. It was suggested that such a development could occur only if the major political groups within the CIS were prepared to provide the leadership in an effort to achieve real unity. The pessimism that such cooperation would be attained proved well-founded (Gorbachev Foundation 1992: 13).

The CIS emerged on the powerful wave of centrifugal forces which have not abated. Any movement toward unity is confronted by equally powerful factors that tend to encourage disintegration. There are several factors that press the political dynamic in that direction. The first factor has been the violent popular response throughout the former Soviet Union to the former totalitarian regime's imperial policy. For generations, that hostility, the national aspirations of non-Russians, has accumulated, pent up and contained by Moscow. With the collapse of the Soviet Union, those feelings are now overflowing. Local official elites, previously conformist and even servile toward Moscow, but discontented with their subordinate position, are resisting any return to their previous position. This sense of liberation also applies to national intellectuals, whose creative potential was limited by the cultural criteria that were defined in Moscow. Equally motivated are the masses of the local population, previously suffocated and repressed, their labour taken for granted and their culture disregarded. Inertia and continued "imperialist thinking" in Moscow have lent strength to the anti-Moscow sentiments in the former Soviet republics. Such anachronistic imperialist attitudes in Moscow have been apparent, for instance, in the Russian approach to the Crimea and in their assessment of political developments in the Dniester region.

A second factor is the effect which almost total political collapse has had on the mentality of the former republics. Formerly dependent on Moscow, the leaders of those republics have now been forced to rely more heavily on their own resources and, in the process, have become fiercely independent minded. Although such independence of thought is commendable, it has also occasioned a state of near anarchy in which there has been little coordination of economic, political, or military affairs among the former members of the Union. In the long term, such a condition cannot prevail, since all parties will ultimately suffer.

A third force at work against cooperation has been the ambition of the national elites. Freed from the domination of Moscow, local elites have seized their hour of opportunity and are reluctant to relinquish any of their newly won sense of autonomy. These national elites are not monolithic in their views. Some stress the capacity of their societies to achieve democratic reforms with Moscow's power reduced. Others are firmly anticommunist. Still others identify the possibility of religious freedom as the main achievement under the new order. Despite these differences, the local elites have a common denominator—the ambition to exercise power and secure the autonomy of those areas established on the ruins of the Soviet empire.

Conversely, one of the strongest arguments in favour of the CIS was the high level of integration that existed among the former Soviet republics, a point that Mr. Gorbachev stressed in his address to this conference. That earlier high degree of integration, resisted as it may be under present political conditions, has a long tradition and many favourable features. The legacy of such integration cannot be wiped away in a matter of months, but lingers in economic, social, cultural, and demographic conditions.

The highly negative views of the Soviet Union articulated by some leaders in the former republics need to be viewed in context. The Russian Empire and later the USSR were not simply a "prison of peoples" or a nation-wide *gulag*. Passing through very complex stages of its tragic history, Russia developed not as a classical colonial empire, in which the centre oppressed its colonies, but as a unique multinational state where dozens of different nationalities and ethnic communities connected by their common destiny coexisted and evolved together (*Narodny Deputat* 1992: 58–60). Russian culture presents an inimitable synthesis of diverse national cultures and traditions, influenced by both the West and the East. The Soviet state did not suppress these traditions, but assimilated their content. This particular synthetic function determined the very essence of Russian culture and provided the force of its attraction for the multinational population of a vast Eurasian region.

The centuries-old common historical and cultural experience of nations and ethnic communities living in the territory of the USSR was molded into common psychological and sociocultural stereotypes and ways of perceiving reality. That historical development and multinational synthesis created a profound basis for preserving cooperation and cultural ties, and will encourage new integrationist efforts in the future.

Thus far, however, destructive, "runaway," energy has prevailed. Those destructive, decentralizing forces inflict innumerable losses on all former Soviet republics. The consequences of the disintegration are especially evident in several areas of economic activity. For instance, engine-producing plants are concentrated in the Ukraine. Ninety percent of their products were previously supplied to Russia, and ninety percent of components necessary for their production came from Russia. With the separation of the Ukraine, that profitable and efficient two-way trade and integrated production has been disrupted. Workforce migration is another example. In 1992, over 60,000 Russians left Tajikistan; more than 50,000 of them were skilled specialists who had provided the republic with modern industrial production. It will be impossible to replace their skills in the near future. The same situation exists in other republics of the former USSR. Even the most fortunate Baltic states are having problems with their fuel and power resources and have lost their eastern markets. This rupture of economic ties is a major cause for the continuing recession in the former USSR.

The situation in nationality relations is even more severe. Ethnic tensions, which had been smoldering, have now become major conflagrations, some of them in the form of armed conflict. Nationalist fundamentalism has moved to the foreground. The fact that 55 million people of the former USSR live outside their nation-state formations has aggravated the problem, and, in some instances, created significant refugee movements. Ruptured Union ties have thus disrupted the lives of tens of millions of people, with incalculable damage not only to the personal lives of dislocated peoples but also to science, art, culture, and the spiritual values of those areas most seriously affected.

It would be in the best interest of all former Soviet citizens were it possible to retain ties between a majority of the former Soviet republics and to establish a new democratic federation. That course of action is the rational one, but, unfortunately, emotional considerations have been at the fore during the past two years of crisis, and reason has been overwhelmed by emotion, unbridled passion, private interests, and personal ambition. Hopefully, as the masses and the elites of the independent states experience the negative effects of the current crisis, they will come to appreciate the need for integration and unity. That learning process may require considerable time.

Certainly, as presently constituted, and given the present state of mind among CIS members, the organization has failed to become a durable structure for the establishment of even informal confederative ties among its member states. Unless the functioning of the CIS improves, it is unlikely to survive in its present form. Even if, in all likelihood, some zones of close cooperation will be preserved, along with some already existing ties, exceeding the framework of pure interstate relations. Those ties may not be very orderly and highly integrated; more likely is a patchwork arrangement, with each political unit varying in size and nature. At times, relations among the members may develop along bilateral lines, as has been the case between Russia and Kazakhastan. In the course of time, new interstate ties may prove to be stronger than Russia's traditional appeal to the other former Soviet states; a good deal thus depends on Russia itself and on its capacity to provide the necessary leadership. Even modest progress of this nature will confront major obstacles, but it is critical to avoid the confrontational level that has occurred in such areas as Yugoslavia.

Russian Federation

The crisis of Soviet federalism has directly affected the Russian Federation, whose structure, functions and difficulties mirrored the problems of the Soviet Union, and added a further difficulty—the absence of its own federal centre. Moscow sat at the heart of both the Soviet Union and Russia, providing the federation with a strong central core. Consequently, the weakening and ultimate collapse of the Soviet Union also undermined all structures of the central government in the Russian Federation and brought the latter dangerously close to the collapse that had already befallen the USSR.

The tide that carried nation-states to autonomy could not and did not stop at Russia's borders, which were often drawn at random under the totalitarian regime. Further, the status of national subjects within the Soviet federation tended to be arbitrary. In any case, many autonomous republics within the Russian Federation had certain reasons to claim the Union republic status. When the USSR's breakup began, they found themselves, together with Union republics, in the mainstream of nation-state independence efforts.

Despite the fact that the autonomous regions of Russia are not simply connected with Russia in the way in which most of the former union republics have been, but are, figuratively speaking, its flesh and blood, they also displayed separatist aspirations. Several zones of national tension have emerged on this basis: north Caucusus, the Volga, Baikal, and the north. These developments suggest that the future of the Russian Federation is an uncertain one.

The first step has already been taken: the federal agreement was signed on 31 March 1992, and was approved by the Sixth Congress of People's Deputies of the Russian Federation on 10 April. The importance of this step can be assessed by comparing it with the destiny of the new Union agreement, which has not been signed despite all the efforts. Nor has the signing of the federal agreement stopped centrifugal trends.

Two autonomous republics—Chechen and Tatarstan—have not agreed to sign the agreement. The Chechen Republic declared complete state independence. Tatarstan declared sovereignty and is ready to join the Russian Federation, but only as an associated member. Though the Republic of Bashkortostan has signed the federal agreement, it appended a supplement to the agreement, as a basis for relations with the federation. The supplement raises the issue of a general bilateral treaty that provides for Bashkortostan's selective approach to constitutional norms and laws of the Russian Federation. The constitution of the Republic of Sakha (Yakutia) establishes the principle of the priority of the republican constitution over the federal one and ensures the right to separate from the Russian Federation. The draft constitution of the Republic of Tuva contains ambiguous formulations about the priority of the republican constitution and the status of federal property in the republic's territory.

These collisions and constitutional quarrels underline the dangers that continue to confront any Russian Federation. The importance of these processes to Russia's future cannot be overemphasized. At the heart of these issues is the ethnic factor. Ethnic Russians constitute eighty-three percent of the population of Russian territory, yet any attempt to separate them from their multinational milieu is fraught with tragic consequences. Apart from northern Caucasian autonomies, the ethnic groups in the present federative states do not exceed the Russians either in their number or in their share in the socioeconomic and cultural spheres of their regions. Ethnic Tatars represent forty-nine percent, and ethnic Russians forty-three percent of the population of Tatarstan. In Bashkortostan, the indigenous population ranks third after the Russians and Tatars.

The USSR's breakup has already led to detrimental economic effects and contributed to national and human suffering. An experiment with the partition of Russia would be even more tragic. But even leaving aside this prospect, it is impossible to imagine that the breakup of the Russian Federation will ensure the Russian people ethnic homogeneity. Some researchers rightfully doubt the very possibility of identifying Russian ethnicity, which had emerged over a period of centuries through a process of migration, creating a melting pot of complex ethnic and nationality relations. An analogy to the American nation inevitably arises here. But in the United States, the national community was formed primarily as a result of a global migration to a new continent, whereas the Russian nation developed through a continuous fusion of various ethnic communities and cultures that already existed in the region. This ethnic assimilation has constituted a characteristic feature of Russian history.

Nonetheless, the effort to achieve isolation from the federation is characteristic not only of the national autonomies, but also of typical Russian regions. This effort is a consequence of the rejection of unitary totalitarianism. But, the transition to normal democratic federalism has also provided for a high degree of self-administration of the federation's subjects. This also reflects separatist aspirations and a desire to exploit, without cooperation with the other regions, existing advantages in economic and natural resources. It is rather indicative that in the course of economic reform, differences in economic potential have resulted in markedly different income levels in various regions of Russia. For example, while late in 1992 the average monthly per capita income in the northwest, Volga-Vyatka, and central black-soil regions was a little over 4,500 rubles, in the northern and western Siberian regions, it amounted to 8,000 rubles and, in the Far East, over 9,000 rubles. Fifty-six out of eighty-nine territories of Russia had a lower per capita income than the average in the federation.[1] Such differences tend to nurture separatist sentiments in the regions which are comparatively wealthier.

The policy which some national autonomies have pursued, of distancing themselves from the policies and programmes of the federation, has added fuel to the flames of regional separatism. Seeing some autonomies, for instance, paying almost no taxes to the federal budget, while getting subventions from it, and observing the growing prestige of ruling elites in independent autonomous republics, the population and the leaders of some Russian regions are tempted to emulate their example.

---

1. According to the data provided by the Center for Market Situation and Economic Prognostication, the Ministry of the Economy of Russia, *Izvestia*, 13 February 1993.

In the end, the growth of separatist trends in autonomies and regions of the Russian Federation is due to the weak centre and a distrust of the potential power of the federation. Small political entities also doubt their ability to resist the pressure of private interests as well as the capacity of any central government to act in the interest of all subjects of the federation. Thus, the separatism of autonomous republics is, in many ways, conditioned by both the appeal of national and local autonomy and by an antagonism toward any external authority. Such sentiments cross over ethnic boundaries; hence, many local ethnic Russians have lent considerable support to the separatist policies of the autonomies.

Even the idea that regional separatism will save Russia has recently been expressed. It has been suggested that, given the likelihood of a collapse of federal structures, it would be possible to preserve a sound social element only at the regional level, which could become the foundation for a renewal of Russia itself.

Whatever the positive motives may be in support of regionalization, such an approach undermines the foundation of Russian federalism—the very basis of Russian statehood. Its implementation would turn Russia into a conglomerate of peculiar independent principalities without any guarantees that they would again merge into a single federative organism rather than drifting even further apart, joining different geopolitical centres. Within the current confrontational political environment in Russia, without an agreement on a federal structure, Russian territory will become an arena of hostility and struggle, sterile soil for the development of modern democracy. Given Russia's nuclear military capability, this instability has serious implications for the global community.

The shaping of a stable Russian Federation is, thus, a cornerstone for the success of democratization in post-totalitarian Russian society and for Russia's transformation into a responsible and influential member of the world community. At the same time, the development of the Russian Federation is unthinkable outside the context of society's democratic reformation. Stability is only possible through improvements in the democratic process and institutions, including a reform of the federal system that provides for an effective distribution of powers between the centre and the rest of the federation.

In taking the first steps toward democratic federalism, one has to examine the lessons and principles tested by international experience, in particular the principle of equality between federation subjects. It is not easy to achieve this under the conditions that prevail in Russia. The present federal agreement consists of three independent documents regulating relations between federal power bodies and three different categories of the Russian Federation's subjects: (1) sovereign republics; (2) territories, regions, and the cities of Moscow and St. Petersburg; (3) autonomous regions and autonomous districts. In themselves, the categories and qualifications underline the extent to which the federation's subjects exist in a state of inequality.

At the outset, some experts proposed that the Russian Federation should be created as a purely territorial alliance, not one based on the ethnic composition of the regions. That approach would be the most feasible and, incidentally, had already been applied on a previous occasion in Russia, in 1918. At that time, the Russian Federation consisted of large commune-regions: the North, the central region, the Urals, the West, the Volga region, and western and eastern Siberia. Nevertheless, today, when national sentiments are so acute, and ethnic relations so tense, the notion of building the Russian Federation on a purely territorial basis, without close attention to ethnic differences and preferences, would be unrealistic. Such an abrupt transition would be perceived as an encroachment on national rights and would trigger a very strong reaction. At present, the three-stage federal agreement adequately reflects current Russian realities, combining the nationality and territorial principles of the federative structure.

Yet, I believe that the future of the Russian Federation will require gradually raising the status of territories and regions to the republican level and ensuring the equality of the federation's subjects. The federation's land structure itself should be supplemented with a programme that will ensure the establishment of conditions that foster cultural autonomy and the free development and self-expression of all ethnic communities living in Russia.

The future destiny of the Russian Federation will largely, if not decisively, determine the future of the entire Eurasian territory of the former USSR. For centuries, Russia has been acting as the linchpin for a multinational community of nationalities and ethnic groups in that vast land, and serving as a natural historical melting pot, constantly molding together achievements of the two civilizations—East and West.

Russia, with its poignant problems of overcoming the grave heritage of totalitarianism, is at the crossroads. Will it retain its historical ability to be an international integrator of the diverse sociocultural experience of the peoples in the vast Eurasian region, or lose forever that unique synthetic ability and stop being an influential force not only at the world but also regional level?

If Russia can become a democratic federation, providing for the rights of every ethnic community and every individual, it will create a powerful gravitational force for all states historically connected with it in the territory of the former USSR. Then the Russian Federation will have a chance to play an essential part in humanity's quest for the most progressive forms of future democratic federalism.

References

Gorbachev Foundation. 1992. *CIS: Current Situation and Destinies. An Analysis of the Political Situation and Forecast of its Development in the Commonwealth of Independent States.* International Foundation for Socio-Economic and Political Studies. Moscow, 1992 (translation provided by author).

First Congress of Soviets of the USSR. 1923. Shorthand report. Moscow (translation provided by the author).

Second Congress of the Comintern. 1934. Moscow. (translation provided by the author).

Lenin, V. I. 1977. *Collected Works*, Volumes 19 and 25.

Narodny Deputat. 1992. (6 November).

COMMENTARY

States and Nations

Alan C. Cairns

The three papers on this panel circle around overlapping themes, but they disagree on where we are and where we are heading. Rather than summarizing these papers, or contrasting them point by point, I will comment on several large themes that emerge when they are juxtaposed with each other.

All three papers view nations, states, and nation-states—the words are slippery—as evolving. For Roger Gibbins, the territorial bases of federalism—both country-wide and state/provincial—are challenged by the "new politics," in particular by environmentalism. He argues that the logic of the new politics threatens to erode, or corrode, existing federal systems. For David Whitefield, "nation" is an evolving concept, and he sympathizes with the Hobsbawm thesis that the late-twentieth-century nation is an endangered species, a product not of peoples but of politicians. For Yuri Krasin, surrounded by the disintegrating remnants of the USSR, and the "maelstrom of ethnic conflicts" that has followed its dissolution, the future is unpredictable.

Remarkably, none of the papers view ethnic nationalism positively as a liberating force. Gibbins sidesteps the issue. He sees a new politics, illustrated by environmentalism, as fostering new forms of transnational identities and as challenging the territorial basis of state authority, including federalism, with its overlapping territorial communities of the centre and the subunits. If the conflict is between federalism and nations, Whitefield awards victory to the former. Significantly, however, this is not the real issue, which he defines as finding "means to provide for the needs of real living peoples," a perspective that puts forms of government in a supporting role, and relegates nationalism to the sidelines. Krasin, fully cognizant of the historical context of the totalitarian suppression that lies behind the widespread ethnic strife in the former USSR, nevertheless sees much to deplore and little to applaud in the contemporary salience of ethnic nationalisms. None of the three presenters, accordingly, overtly sympathizes with the nationalist passions that mobilize tens of millions around the world.

The critique of nation by Whitefield, and of federalism and territorially based authority by Gibbins, are contemporary expressions of powerful political and intellectual fashions that form a subtext of social theorizing in the past century and a half. In one of its Marxist versions, that presupposed international working-class solidarity, the thesis, popularized prior to World War I, that the proletariat had no fatherland, was negated as the working class rallied behind national flags and engaged in the mutual slaughter of 1914–18. A more localized version of the thesis was the premise that state power in the service of fraternity could transcend the national question in multinational societies by fashioning, for example, Soviet or Yugoslav nationals, who would leave behind their anachronistic ethnic garments. We now know better.

Yet another version was the Laski thesis, presented by Brian Galligan and Georgina Lynch, that a capitalism which ignored political boundaries rendered federalism, with its divided jurisdictions, obsolete. To Laski, federalism paralyzed state action by both fragmenting power and locating it in political authorities that lacked the appropriate territorial and jurisdictional scope to manage an interdependent, disintegrating economic system. Laski's was an early version of the thesis that economic globalization renders the contemporary state system either irrelevant or dysfunctional for many of the tasks dictated by capitalist economic transformations. Somewhat illogically, Laski did not employ his thesis to challenge the state as such, but only the provincial dimension of federalist states.

In sum, the contemporary functional challenge to the state form that Gibbins attributes to environmentalism is not new. Further, the moral appropriateness of the state system is also recurrently challenged by those who see it as dividing a common humanity. This leads directly to the plea for a supranational authority when war, with its atrocities and inhumanities, is attributed to the state system. In a milder version of the preceding, state sovereignty is confronted by a new humanitarian internationalism—symbolized by Amnesty International—that no longer accepts the right of a state to do as it will with its own peoples.

The survival of the state system is related ambiguously to the linked question of the survival of ethnic nationalism. On the one hand, contemporary states that govern multiethnic or multinational societies are driven to generate pan-country-wide nationalisms, usefully described as umbrella nationalisms, or civic nationalisms, in order to contain the less comprehensive, but often more passionate subnationalisms that challenge their integrity. Thus, in the Canadian case, the fostering of pan-Canadian nationalism by the central government aims to moderate Québécois and aboriginal nationalisms by giving their adherents a Canadian identity that links them to the overall Canadian community, and dilutes the primacy of their aboriginal and Québécois senses of self. To its adherents, Québécois and aboriginal nationalisms are positive forces for liberation. From the perspective of the centre, however, unless moderated, they are destructive forces capable of undermining a historic constitutional order.

There is little evidence that ethnic nationalism is a voice from the past, a lingering survival destined for the graveyard. In the late fifties, under the spell of superficial modernization theories, many scholars, especially American, wrote epitaphs for ethnicity and its nationalist expressions. While now, in the nineties, ethnic nationalism is far from receiving universal acclaim, it is difficult to deny that it continues to be a powerful vehicle for ingroup human solidarity.

If ethnic nationalism is here for the foreseeable future, then the state system, in some form, is here to stay, for the nationalist elites who seek to break out of existing systems normally do so in pursuit of their own state. It also follows that state elites, both new and old, will continue to foster country-wide nationalism as a glue to hold multinational, multiethnic societies together. No matter how many new states are formed in response to nationalist assaults on old states, a state system resting on ethnically homogeneous peoples will forever elude us. Most new states, like the old states from which they have broken away, will be ethnically heterogeneous. The new majorities generated by independence soon encounter new or newly conscious minorities within their midst who keep alive the ethnic tensions that independence did not resolve. Hence the glue of ethnic nationalism, which is logically insufficient to hold heterogeneous modern nations together, requires supplementing by a civic nationalism that transcends particular ethnicities.

Further, the vast movement of peoples in the contemporary world will defy the efforts of governments, especially in the democratic capitalist world, to keep out newcomers who will add to the diversity of their populations. For these newcomers, of course, federalism will have little to offer, for they will typically be dispersed, and lack a territorial base. Federalism also has little to offer the 55 million people of the former Soviet Union, as noted by Krasin, who live outside of their "nation-state formations." Those who cannot achieve local majority status, accordingly, require protection from ethnic majorities wielding power over them.

Given the present and contemplated realities just noted, which seem to be in the nature of things, it is exceedingly unlikely that either the state system, or ethnic nationalism, or pan-country civic nationalism to support states governing ethnically heterogeneous societies will disappear. Inertia is on their side. Whatever their imperfections, they are known models. Inertia supplemented by imitation has resulted in both a world of states and a world of nations. The probability, therefore, is that the new politics, such as environmentalism, will neither erode nor corrode federalism and the state system, but will instead generate both national and transnational policy responses. In different language, perhaps the central political lesson of recent centuries is the adaptive capacity of the state system, its ability to regenerate itself, to drop old and add new functions, and to respond to threats to its own continuity by blunting and partly assimilating opposing forces.

If the requirements of effective policy will not render the state obsolete, perhaps the new transnational identities—such as feminism and environmentalism, for which state boundaries carry diminished meaning—will erode the citizen base of statehood. This too is unlikely. The choice is unlikely to be between environmentalism and Americanism, or feminism and Canadianism. The human capacity to sustain and compartmentalize multiple identities is a highly developed skill of contemporary citizens. Further, state identity is constantly bolstered by the state's control of the major instruments of socialization. The state's effort to domesticate challenging transnational identities is illustrated by the federal government's proposed Canada clause in its 1991 constitutional proposals which linked "the identity and aspirations" of Canadians to "a commitment to the objective of sustainable development in recognition of the importance of the land, the air and the water and our responsibility to preserve and protect the environment for future generations" (Canada 1991: 9-10).

Conclusion

Nations and states feed on each other. Territorially compact sociological nations lacking statehood spasmodically experience a sense of incompleteness, which they seek to overcome by obtaining a state of their own. In contrast, states with authority over heterogeneous peoples experience a different but dangerous sense of incompleteness—the absence of a supportive community base—which they seek to overcome by fostering a country-wide sense of national selfhood.

This dance between nations and states has its own momentum; it is never ending. It is a dialogue between the ubiquitous juristic state form that covers the planet and the underlying solidarities of ethnic communities. Where the two are discordant, federalism or assimilation fostered by a country-wide nationalism are the constitutional strategies of state actors, and enhanced autonomy, perhaps by federalism, or independence are the constitutional goals of ethnic elites. Barring ecological catastrophe, the likelihood of this nation-state game being displaced is close to zero. On the other hand, in the future as in the past, the game will evolve; thus, the kinds of questions that animated this panel at this conference will continue to be asked and ambiguously answered for the lifetimes of our children.

References

Canada. 1991. *Shaping Canada's Future Together: Proposals*. Ottawa: Ministry of Supply and Services.

III: *Ethnicity, Nationalism, and Federalism*

Federalism and the Siamese Twins: Diversity and Entropy in India's Domestic and Foreign Policy

Joyotpaul Chaudhuri

Introduction

This essay uses the classic distinctions in political theory and jurisprudence between unitary, confederate, and federal forms of political systems. Each of these forms have different versions, as is the case in the right-oriented federalism of Thomas Jefferson as opposed to the implied power federalism of Alexander Hamilton. India's union or federation is less of a classic federalism, and is a model which is more unitary then federal. The thesis of the essay is that the current state of the structure encourages the many religious, ethnic, and regional "rebellions" of domestic politics and weakens any notion of strategy in foreign policy. This, in turn, provides major barriers to both political and economic development. Alternatively, what is suggested is gradual decentralization as a prelude to a shift towards a more federal structure which, however, would enforce civil rights and procedural due process and provide safeguards against external aggression and domestic disorder.

The Siamese Twins of Foreign and Domestic Policy

Former U.S. President Richard M. Nixon has been a controversial figure both in issues of character and his understanding of the intrinsic moral issues involved in public policy in domestic or international politics. However, few would question Mr Nixon's grasp of the operational dimensions of foreign policy or his understanding of the interrelationships between domestic politics and foreign policy. In his speeches and writings in 1992 and 1993, he again returned to the theme that foreign and domestic policy are like Siamese twins: "Separate them and they die" (Schmemann 1993: A-4). Mr Nixon was speaking about the connection between "democracy" and foreign policy in Russia and the future relationship between U.S. domestic spending and foreign policy. In our global village, the link between domestic structure, process, and policy on the one hand, and a nation's role in international relations on the other, also holds for most other nations including India.

Currently, India has the second largest population in the world and given the comparative birth rates, will overtake China as the most populous country early in the next century. What happens to India's democracy, therefore, possibly has serious implications for regional as well as international stability, given the increasing interdependencies, nuclear proliferation, and the recent changes in the relationships between the world's most powerful nations.

Structure and process are inextricably linked in politics.[1] Yet, it is striking that the scholarly literature examining the linkage between India's semifederal structure and its foreign policy is somewhat sparse.[2] The descriptive literature on India's federalism is extensive and there is a somewhat smaller analytical literature on central-state relations (see Arora and Mukarji 1992). However, the literature is spotty with respect to analysis of the federal structure and the possible adaptations in the context of what Nixon has called the Siamese twins of domestic and foreign policy.[3] Possibly, this is due, in part, to the fact that while there are federations, federalism, as political theory, is a New World and American phenomenon and was not part of the mainstream of western political thought.

The Comparative Foundations of Federalism: Jefferson and the Native Americans

With reference to the first state constitution in the United States—the Virginia Constitution of 1776—Jefferson commented on the dangers of a mechanical federalism which allowed for an elective despotism to emerge in the states. The Virginia Constitution concentrated powers in an elected legislative assembly, and Jefferson warned that:

---

1. Analysis of structure complements analysis of other "behavioral" elements of contemporary conflicts in India. For an example of the latter analysis see "Modern Hate" by Rudolph and Rudolph (1993).
2. For a discussion of some of the relationships see Verney and Frankel (1986). See also, Ghosh (1980), and Sharma (1984).
3. See the essays by Balveer Arora, Baladas Ghoshal, and Joyotpaul Chaudhuri in Chaudhuri (1992a).

the concentrating of these in the same hands is precisely the definition of despotic government. It will be no alleviation that these powers will be exercised by a plurality of hands, and not by a single one. Let those who doubt it turn their eyes on the Republic of Venice.

([1854] 1985: 152-57)

The Jeffersonian vision of federalism, in contrast to the main strands of European thought, involved the clear demarcation and decentralization of power not only at the federal-state level but within the constituent state as well. This involved not only Jefferson's well known theory of wards in local government, but also included separation of powers.

An *elective* despotism is not the government we fought for, but one which should not only be founded on free principles, but in which the powers of government should be so divided and balanced among several bodies of magistracy, as that no one could transcend their legal limits, without being effectively checked and restrained by the others.

([1854] 1985: 152-57)

Jefferson's advocacy of a decentralized federalism did not ignore the link between the structure of domestic politics and foreign policy. The Jefferson who sent the first U.S. force into the Middle East, the negotiator of the Louisiana Purchase as well as the first secretary of state, was not unsophisticated in the handling of foreign policy and international relations. Jefferson opposed a large centralized standing army, preferring to depend on a coordinated system of national security, where the member states were active partners. Large standing armies were seen as threats to federalism as well as to the development of a stable system of international relations and law.[4] Jefferson broke with classical democratic theory, which argued that participatory government was most appropriate only in small and homogeneous concentrations of people, rather than large expanses of territory with a heterogeneous diversity of interests.

Jefferson's views were echoed by Ben Franklin, who also pointed out that American Indians, including the Iroquois, were able to govern large expanses of territory with a coordinated but decentralized system of governance.

---

4. See Tucker and Hendrickson (1990). See also my book review in *American Political Science Review* (Chaudhuri 1991).

While the superior technology and weaponry of the Europeans eventually eroded Indian sovereignty, both the Iroquois in the northeast and the Creeks in the southeastern United States had already demonstrated—in the isolated laboratory of the New World—the viability of decentralized federal systems in connecting very diverse cultural groups, which balanced local power with coordinated foreign policy and defense. The Iroquois regional alliance included a quite diverse groups of Mohawks, Oneidas, Onondagas, Cayugas, Senecas, and, later on, Tuscaroras. Spatially, their territory covered westward from New York to Illinois, and southward to the Cherokee country of the Carolinas.

The Creeks in the southeast also fashioned an elaborate but coordinated division of powers, which politically interrelated large, diverse groups of people with vastly diverse languages and cultures over spatially extensive territories. More than just a federation of tribes, the Creeks were also committed to checks and balances and to human freedom. It is the latter value which is also at the root of some of their conflicts with the settlers over slavery. The regular linkages included the Muscogee Creeks, the Alabamas, Seminoles, Miccosukees, and Euchees together with other links with Sawnees and Natchez. The Creeks, despite their diversity and decentralization, coordinated their external relations with the Cherokees and other groups, attempted diplomatic overtures to England, and were able to take the field (unsuccessfully) against Andrew Jackson at the Battle of Horseshow Bend (see chapter 2 in Chaudhuri 1992b).

The principles of the Jeffersonian and American Indian approaches to federalism, apart from their differences, had several key points in common: (1) Both were different from the Athenian "democratic" city-state and the English unitary nation-state models; (2) Both models involved a balancing of decentralization and cooperation; (3) Both assumed the existence of considerable diversity at the local level; (4) Both allowed for political participation; (5) Both had separation of power as well as checks and balances in order to minimize large concentrations of power; And, (6) both allowed for considerable freedom from government. The contributions of the New World to federalism are unique and much larger in scale and importance than European examples, including the league of the Greek city-states.

The eclipse of American Indian power and the rise of the Hamiltonian implied powers doctrine and centralization in the development of an American commercial republic, in part, has turned our attention somewhat from the unique foundations of both models of federalism. Yet, the rise of diverse religious, ethnic, and regional forces, combined with new economic aspirations, suggests that the American and New World experiences still contain far more instructive power than the more dominant, unitary nation-state centralized models of power.

India's federalism greatly reflects its British heritage, with a single legal framework, a great degree of centralization, and a parliamentary model of governance. The combination of ethnic, economic, and religious crises points towards a reexamination of structural issues, in addition to the more commonly examined issues of electoral politics and process. These issues are particularly salient in federations resting on Hobbesian and Marxist foundations.

Hobbes and Marx

In contrast to Jeffersonian and Native American perspectives, Hobbes's English positivism of John Austin's utilitarian followers, and Marxist materialistic jurisprudence led the way in Europe to centralized monist conceptions of the state under varying labels. Despite other great differences, both English- and Soviet-trained lawyers and legal architects instinctively return to the undivided sovereignty of the centralized state.

The great merit of Jefferson's approach to federalism, as well as the Iroquois and Creek approaches, is that they are essentially and uniquely pluralists in their approaches to sovereignty and the law. Sovereignty and power were distributive, shared, and applicable in specific, limited contexts. A comparative lack of contextual limitations are characteristic of unitary states. Pluralist conceptions of sovereignty not only existed historically in many societies, but they were also briefly held by the English guild socialists. In relatively recent American jurisprudence, the late Myres McDougal and Harold Lasswell of the Yale Law School, also argued for a contextual approach to sovereignty and international law (see, among other works, McDougal 1947). There are many other contemporary critics of centrist conceptions of state power.[5]

The limitations of the dominant Austinian, Marxist, and other centrist conceptions of the state domestically and internationally are, in part, contributing factors in the rise of explosive dissatisfactions of ethnic and fun-

---

5. See the reprint of Northrop's *The Taming of the Nations* ([1989] 1952), with a new introduction by Joyotpaul Chaudhuri.

damentalist politics since the end of World War II. India is no exception—South Asia, including India, is probably the most culturally and religiously diverse region in the international system.[6] The entire region cries out for loose-knit regional political systems and federalist arrangements. Yet the combination of great power politics and the heritage of English law has essentially led to the creation of monistic states which are having great difficulty, despite the use of considerable force, in containing the ethnic, religious, and linguistic forces at work. In turn, throughout South Asia, the Siamese twins of domestic and foreign policy have ethnic, religious, and linguistic forces at the nexus of their interactions.

India alone in South Asia has a semblance of a federal system, in addition to its electoral democracy, but its federalism is not of the Jeffersonian variety with its combination of a bill of rights and a decentralized distribution of power.

A Profile of Indian Federalist Structure

India's federalist structure, in spite of its considerable achievements in the face of monumental challenges, is different from Jeffersonian federalism in several crucial areas. Historically, the American states helped create the central government. In India, power was transferred to a central government by the British, and the central government plays the decisive role in the formation and the empowerment of the states. The states do not have constitutions as is the case for American states. The Indian constitution is over 170 pages long and contains over 390 articles.

Elements of federalism exist in that there is a division of power between the centre and the states. State jurisdiction includes public order, police, welfare, health, education, local government, industry, agriculture, and land revenue. The existence of these state powers has resulted in a wide diversity of politics and policies in the states, and the states have assumed real political personalities.

However, state powers are counterbalanced by a long list of concurrent central powers, which can preempt the states. In addition, there is a long list of exclusive central powers including foreign affairs, defense, citizenship, railroads, postal/telegraph services, customs, currency, banking, and income

---

6. For a further development of this theme, see the author's essay, "State Structure and Sovereignty in India," (Chaudhuri 1992a).

taxes. As well, there is a multitude of special powers and "duties" in articles 352, 355, 356, 360, 256, 257, 249, and 365, which speak to central authority in state emergencies, national emergencies, and financial exigencies.

In matters of rights, the Indian system differs from the Jeffersonian approach to religion, speech, and press. Liberties exist in India more extensively than in second- and third-world countries and the concept of equal protection is embedded in the constitutional framework. However, diluting the notion of rights are the cases of preventive detention, the lack of an independent system for the enforcement of justice, and the predominance of the parliamentary system which Jefferson warned can lead to elective despotism. As in the Hamiltonian and positive law departures from Jeffersonianism, the equivalents of the doctrine of "clear and present" and clear and probable danger has diluted the commitment to rights in the Indian system. However, these erosions do not diminish India's comparative and considerable achievements in providing civil liberties, given the history of civil liberties and civilian-military relations in most of the third world. Nevertheless, erosions in India are real.

Entropy and Indian Federalism

A British model of an unitary state, with minor adaptations from the American system, provides the skeletal semifederal legal framework of the Indian political system. Yet, the culture of India—including the church/state experiments of Akbar, the governance of Asoka, the economic ideas of Gandhi, and the *de facto* political systems of the past—is more federal and plural than what is captured in the legal framework, limiting the usefulness of copying the English model. Indian society has a substantial common core held together by a synthesis of many common trends of architecture, music, literature, dance, art, philosophy, history, symbols, and group memory. It is in the area of religion, particularly in the gulf between ritualistic Hinduism and fundamentalist Islam—magnified by modern mass communications—that the strands are the weakest.

Complementing the unifying symbolism is the existence of deeply entrenched regional loyalties. It is profoundly unrealistic to assume that a slightly modified unitary state can dilute the realities of those elements of Indian culture that are truly regional. For this reason, the Jeffersonian approach to federalism is even more appropriate for twentieth-century India than the diversities of Jefferson's eighteenth-century America.

Continuing confusion on the nature of Indian federalism may continue to compel centralized statist solutions. The problem with central statist solutions in an essentially parliamentary system is that prudent but decisive leadership is made extremely difficult by the rise of interest groups and increasingly undisciplined utilitarian party "democracy." This was quite evident in the handling of the dynamic leading up to the destruction of the sixteenth-century Babri Masjid (mosque) in December, 1992 by an avalanche of right-wing Hindus, led by an alliance which included the Bharatiya Janata Party (BJP). The latter party has successfully appealed to some groups by fusing anti-Muslim, anti-affirmative action, and anti-welfare state symbols. The prime minister was deeply mired in the search for an utilitarian consensus in the midst of the competing utilities of party, party coalitions, state, and religious factions. As long as the prime minister is a captive of his heterogeneous party, fragile coalitions, and parliament, it would take an extraordinary leader to simulate the kind of presidential leadership that is possible in a presidential federalism. The contrasting images of Eisenhower at Little Rock or Kennedy at the University of Alabama during the great regional difficulties of *de jure* desegregation come to mind. In contrast, while constitutionally specific emergency powers were available to the Indian prime minister, they were not used in the Babri Masjid case until after the destruction of the mosque. Accommodation to interest groups showed the weakness of parliamentary quasifederal systems. On the other hand, emergency powers have been frequently used in the past in the north and south, for far less serious national emergencies. This is largely due to the inherent weakness of interest group politics in a parliamentary system wherein the monopoly of the Congress party has long disappeared.

The changes in India's international role, the interrelationship between domestic and foreign policy, the rise of subnational forces and interest groups, and the eclipse of any serious balancing of executive/legislative powers are all pointing towards a drifting semifederalism. The drift often leads to the emergency use of force. The economic realities, together with the breakup of the Union of Soviet Socialist Republics, has already stimulated new initiatives in scrapping a planned socialist economy and a movement towards liberalization of the economy. Major changes with respect to foreign investments, allowing the rupee to float, and privatization of some public-sector corporations have both occurred and/or are under way. However, the unitary features still stand in the way of further liberalizations and effective development in several ways. First, the attention of the central government is focused on parliamentary survival since India has had a series of minority government coalitions. Secondly, the central government is still dictating the pace of liberalization, thereby preventing the state governments from rapidly buying into the liberalization and engaging in initiatives of their own—within national guidelines. Thirdly, the attention of the central government is considerably diverted by centralized decisions in the wake of subnational crises and events. Finally, the parliamentary system's inability to provide communal and regional stability affects the quality and quantity of foreign investments, as well as the coordination of domestic and foreign policy.

Domestic Entropy

The increasing shift of activism from the centre to localities and regions can be seen in a variety of contexts, including Kashmir, Punjab, and the northern Hindu belt. In the case of the Babri Masjid issue, despite clear authority in the current federal structure, the centre, mired in interest group politics within the Congress party and in parliament, was helpless in the wake of forces gathered from a variety of regions. Yet, some public opinion polls showed that the majority of people opposed the destruction of the Babri mosque. A *Statesman Daily* editorial summarized the polling results on the issue of the Muslim Babri mosque, which supposedly sat atop the birthplace of heroic god-like Ram of orthodox Hinduism. This issue has provided the cutting edge of right-wing Hindu groups in several key states. The groups include the Bharatiya Janata Party (BJP), the Vishwa Hindu Parishad Party (VHP), the Rastriya Sevak Sangh (RSS), the Bajrang Dal, a paramilitary group, and the Shiv Sena, a militant group in Poona and Bombay. The membership of these groups, particularly the core elite, belong to the upper castes for the most part.

The Hindu fundamentalist groups have been strongest in Uttar Pradesh, Himachal Pradesh, Madhya Pradesh, and the urban centres of Bombay, Poona, and Ahmedabad. The groups are much weaker in the south, in Punjab, Kashmir, and eastern India. Up to now, Bihar, which has had caste-based conflicts, has been able to put together a political coalition of lower caste Hindus and minorities, including Muslims. Consequently, Bihar was relatively quiet after the destruction of the mosque.

Brahminic northern Hinduism is only one segment of Hinduism and represents far less than a majority. However, in interest group politics, intensities are part of the countervailing calculations, as opposed to mere numbers. Parliamentary democracy with decaying party cohesion exaggerates interest groups intensities rather than leading the so-called silent majority.

The use of emergency powers has added to the deep fissions in Kashmir and Punjab. There is no question of the existence of terrorism in both states, but the central government's use of emergency powers has resulted in greater alienation rather than developing popular support against terrorism and subversion.

In the case of the Babri Masjid, the centre was unable to mobilize the latent integrationist tendencies and goodwill that is broadly present, as the *Statesman Daily* noted:

> The respected research organization, MODE, reports that at the end of November, 1992, 77% of the respondents in an opinion poll were in favor of leaving the Babri Masjid where it was; 67% were against the VHP's plans to start Kar seva on December 6; 84% thought that it was a shameful thing for a secular country like India to tolerate such a controversy; and if the structure were to be demolished, 93% thought it would lead to communal strife and violence.
>
> Another opinion poll after the event found 68% unhappy, while 70% were surprised that it had happened. (Irani 1992: 1, 12–27)

What we know of public opinion illustrates that the current quasifederal arrangements are more attuned to factional interest groups, and yet, there is a reservoir of tolerance that does not have a vehicle for expression.

The disciplined national political party that was Congress has disappeared. It is now a collection of regional, class, and personal factions. The core group of nationalist leaders have all died and the current leadership groups have essentially regional followings. The vibrant political parties are regional parties like the CPI(M), the Janata Dal, the BJP, and the regional congress organizations.

The achievements of Indians have been largely regional achievements. Agriculture in the Punjab, rural community development in Bengal, science education in the Tamil Nadu and Karnataka, and literacy in Kerala are examples of diverse regional energies. India's centrist federalism has shown its weaknesses in handling both diversity and the economy, which, in turn, has affected foreign policy as well as domestic policy.

Entropy in Foreign Policy

The decline of India's role in international relations cannot be exclusively attributed to the absence of the old Nehru leadership in the days of the Bandung conference. Increasingly, prime ministers have had less and less experience in handling foreign policy. The quasifederal structure has not handled interethnic relations very well, and the centre has had to pay more attention to mere domestic survival, given the string of coalition governments. Thus, one would be hard pressed to point out what Prime Minister Chandrasekhar's foreign policy was during the Iraq/Kuwait crises, busy as he was trying to keep his minority government alive.

Rather than global strategy, India's foreign policy after Nehru and possibly Indira Gandhi, has been more and more linked with domestic crises and events. India's relations with the Middle East is linked with its efforts to counter Pakistan and Islamic fundamentalism at home. India's relationship with Pakistan and, therefore, indirectly with other countries, is also partly linked with the crises in Kashmir. In May 1990, Pakistan and India came very close to a nuclear confrontation wherein domestic and international factors were closely interlinked (see Hersh 1993).

India's relationship with Sri Lanka is also interlinked with its relationship with Tamil militants in India. India's relationship with Pakistan is also now interlinked with Sikh politics in the Punjab. In turn, India's embassies in London and the United States have had to turn their attention considerably to countering Punjabi and Kashmiri dissidents abroad. India's relationship with Iran and Bangladesh are also directly linked with interethnic and interreligious relationships at home. The line between internal and external affairs has eroded if not vanished. The centrist semifederal governmental structure is a barrier to problem solving. Every local rebellion is easily turned into a national issue rather than being resolved locally. India, even more so than many traditional societies, has had buffer institutions between the centre and its parts. With the increasing rise of the English parliamentary and centrist semifederal model, a vortex reaction of pushing problems to the centre, as has often been the case in South Korea, rather than a decentralized diffusion and problem solving is the result. De Tocqueville clearly warned that the lack of buffer institutions leads to centralist tendencies and despotism—elective or otherwise—in order to meet interest group demand in a democratic system.

The parliamentary system in the Indian states adds to the difficulty. The state chief ministers, like the country's prime minister, are primarily instruments of their party. Jeffersonian federalism at the state and federal level, with directly elected executives, would provide both coherence and balance in replacing the juggling of interest groups and party factions which has become one of the main tasks of chief ministers. A new federalism in India will have to harness the centrifugal forces at work without abandoning the broader commitments to a just community and to human dignity.

Handling the Centrifugal Forces

Baladas Ghoshal rightly argues against giving outright independence to ethnic, linguistic, or religious groups in India:

> Given the past history of the subcontinent a further division of or granting independence to any of the constituent units of today's India will not solve any religious, linguistic, or other ethnic disputes. The same is true for Pakistan. The case of Bangladesh was very different because the two former wings of Pakistan were not only physically separated by another country, they had hardly anything in common except religion. (1992: 45–46)

The whole continent is rife with what V. S. Naipaul (1990) has called a "million little mutinies." Even giving each of these mutinies their space will not resolve the cleavages of the subcontinent. The existing culture areas have overlapping population centres and there are many Kashmiris, Sikhs, Muslims, and Christians outside of central cluster areas in Kashmir and Punjab. "Ethnic cleansing," apart from its hideous immorality, would be an impossibility given the mixed ethnic and religious residential patterns in India. Thus, even in Kashmir, the cleavages are complex. The majority of the population is Muslim, but many of the big property holders are Hindu Brahmins. Further, the Muslim population dominates the valley whereas the Jammu area has a substantial Dogra/Hindu population. The Ladakh area is primarily Buddhist. Neither a centrist state nor a series of ethnic enclaves (there would have to be over a thousand in India) can provide an appropriate political structure. Moving gradually towards federalism is a better alternative. The move can begin with administrative decentralization and delegation prior to making constitutional changes. Changing the Indian constitution is a far easier matter than is the case in the United States. Parliament plays a large role in Indian constitutional changes and is not as dependent on ratification as is the case in the United States.

Decentralization

Moving towards a true federalism is fraught with dangers. The United States moved from confederacy to federalism, yet it faced the dangers of a return to confederacy prior to the civil war. Moving from quasifederalism to federalism also has to be done cautiously in order not to overbalance the centrifugal forces already at work.

Administrative and then legislative decentralization can be a prelude to gradual constitutional changes; however, while giving more power to the states, any right of outright secession must not be acknowledged given the possible domino effect of any such move. For a start, much greater administrative decentralization is possible than is currently present in a variety of areas including the Punjabi, Kashmiri, and economic matters. Even though the country is moving away from socialism toward welcoming competition and foreign investments, the states are, unfortunately, still playing a junior subsidiary role. Within broad export and import guidelines, the states can be allowed greater leeway in licensing, contracting, initiating, and negotiating international trade agreements. In the case of the European Common Market, its architect, Monet, clearly foresaw that increased free economic trade and American-style interstate commerce could diminish even centuries-old Franco-German antagonism.

The increased state-initiated trade can, among other things, eventually lessen the political tensions in the border states and neighbouring countries. In the long run, the superordinate goal of a loose-knit regional federalism could become one of the soundest ways to approach the political and economic development of South Asia.

In the process of decentralization, the central state could and should still maintain the primary responsibilities for foreign policy, national security and defense in a nuclear age, civil rights, and major tax collection. The clear national enforcement of civil rights, when combined with decentralized trading, can help lessen interethnic tensions. The Indian political system has gradually moved to an utilitarian rather than Jeffersonian democratic model.

Rajiv Gandhi encouraged Muslim separatism when he placated Muslim fundamentalists and led the legislation exempting Muslims from uniform divorce laws for the protection of women. Later he wooed fundamentalist Hindus in securing their right to temporarily worship Ram in the Ayuddha Masjid area. Similarly, the Sikh militants and the Tamil militants were, at one time or another, encouraged by the congress leaders as a means to counter and embarrass the opposition to the Congress party in several regions.

One is reminded of Bush's earlier support of Saddam Hussein as a counterbalance to Iran. The logic of Jefferson federalism is different from balance-of-power theories—domestically or internationally. Jeffersonian federalism has a structure of rights and decentralization jurisdictions rather than reacting only to the shifts in group power.

Procedural Due Process and Civil Rights

Justice William O. Douglas has pointed out some of the key similarities and differences between the American and Indian conceptions of federalism. The broad commitments to federalism, accommodation of diversity, equal protection and rights are noted by the late Justice Douglas. These are not insignificant similarities as compared to the majority of other political systems. However, Douglas noted the existence of an Indian provision for preventive detention and the lack of a due-process clause as far as procedural requirements are concerned (1956: 27).

The lack of procedural due process prevents the even-handed pursuit of justice in dealing with Hindu-Muslim conflicts as in the Babri Masjid case or in handling unrest in Kashmir and the Punjab. The real threat to the civil rights of Muslims could have justified a decisive military presence in Ayuddha. Instead, the central troops were immovably sequestered several miles away. After the destruction of the mosque, the union government then dismissed the BJP state governments in three states. Inaction was followed by overreaction in contrast to the standards of federalism of Eisenhower, in Little Rock and Kennedy, in Alabama.

The adoption of procedural due process can go a long way in distinguishing between actual terrorism and the safety and security of the average citizen. Procedural due process would give the justice administration and the judiciary a series of rights by which to check the excesses of administrators and parliaments when civil rights of minorities are violated. Douglas noted the lack of state constitutions in India, and early in the 1950s, he also warned us of the inherent possibilities of centralization.

> The blue prints for the new India emanate from Delhi; and they embrace comprehensive programs of reconstruction, rehabilitations, and industrialization. This central planning may produce in India problems of centralization that parallel America's. If it does, it will affect the measure of federalism actually existing. (1956: 43)

Douglas also noted the lack of real separation of powers in the Indian constitutions and the predominance of the parliamentary system (33). The prime minister's executive work is really an extension of parliamentary democracy and now, in the 1980s and 1990s, is really the extension of the ruling party or coalition. In the wake of the recent ethnic crises, primarily out of the Masjid issue as well as from Punjab and Kashmir, it is clear that the coherence of the Congress parliamentary coalition and party elite is the key to administrative power in India. Even though India has an independent judiciary, its power is restricted in dealing with many interethnic and interreligious issues because of at least three major factors.

First, the absence of procedural due process largely limits the judiciary to statutory interpretation and a fairly strict adherence to constitutional hermeneutics. Secondly, constitutional and judicial interpretation can be easily amended by the legislature except for limited provisions. Article 44 of the Constitution calls for a uniform civil code. In keeping with this principle, the Code of Criminal Procedure, in 1973, called for uniform maintenance for divorced Muslim and Hindu women. Thus, under Rajiv Gandhi's leadership, parliamentary modification of the code and constitutional principles negated a judicial decision which upheld uniform rights in a divorce case involving a Muslim divorcee. The new legislation allowed Muslims to follow Muslim family law rather than a uniform code. Thirdly, in the same vein, parliamentary interest group politics has played religious, ethnic, and caste groups off against each other.[7] Thus, Rajiv Gandhi reopened Hindu access to the Babri mosque pending "judicial decisions." Because of the structure of federalism and these intensely short-run interest calculations in politics, the judiciary has a very limited role in solving the major issues brought to a head by Kashmir, Punjab, and the Bharatiya Janata party. Nothing short of decentralization, the strengthening of procedural due process, and revisiting the federal structure can address the issues involved.

---

7. For a similar observation, see the editorial entitled, "India at the Edge" (1993), which appeared twenty-four hours prior to the testing of a ban against a proposed march and demonstration in Delhi planned by the Bharatiya Janata Party.

Caste Equity and Civil Rights

Finally, it should be noted that another major difference between the American and Indian constitutions is due to the persistent efforts of the untouchable so-called father of the Indian constitution, B. R. Ambedkar. The Indian constitution, unlike the American constitution, accepts the legitimacy of remedial action—affirmative action—in striving for equality for India's untouchables. These provisions have been unevenly enforced by the centre. The South has done a better job than the North on affirmative action. As evidence, one can point out that it is in the strongholds of the BJP and Hindu fundamentalism that there has been the greatest outcry against further remedial action. The affirmative action issues are civil rights issues where the centre should remain active despite decentralization on other substantive state matters. Lack of sustained attention to civil rights can result in additional troubles in the northern tier of states as untouchables and tribals become more politically conscious. Central attention to civil rights, accompanied by decentralization of other powers, can counter the communal parochialism of local governments without bureaucratizing everything else as is now particularly the case.[8] Delayed attention to structural reforms can continue to weaken India's role in the larger world order.

The Internal/External Nexus

With the passage of time, India's foreign relations are increasingly related to domestic politics. Both the structure (quasi-federalism) and process have utilitarian impacts on this relationship between these Siamese twins. In the times of Nehru, India had an architecture of foreign policy relatively independent of domestic realities. Nonalignment, third-world leadership, development of the United Nations and international law were objectives which were pursued independent of domestic politics.

However, the Chinese invasion in 1962 was a watershed in the change of architecture as India rapidly paid attention to modernization of its armed forces. The continued difficulties in Kashmir further began to define India's relationship to the United States. India's relationship to Pakistan has also been shaped by domestic factors. Thus, the pressure for India's intervention

---

8. For a criticism of Panchayhat Raj, see Tummala (1992).

in East Pakistan—now Bangladesh—came from domestic pressure groups in eastern India as well as from other considerations.

The presence of a large Muslim population in India has also insured that India cannot afford to appear anti-Islamic and must have strong relationships in the Muslim world. The relations with Iraq, Egypt, Afghanistan, the Arab Emirates, and Indonesia are partly shaped by domestic factors of both religion and economics. The increasing role of domestic forces is accelerated by the decline of the Soviet Union, which has affected India deeply. International calculations are seldom major determinants in current foreign policy. The rise of the CJP has heightened India's interests in demonstrating their secularism, given the impact of the mosque controversy in Pakistan and Bangladesh—both in their domestic and their foreign policies. India's politics in the Punjab has repercussions in its relations with the United States.

The very centralization of Indian "federalism" adds to India's difficulties in the articulation of foreign policy. Centralization insures that problems in the Punjab and in Ayuddha will directly impact on foreign policy. A more decentralized and more truly federalized structure is more likely to create appropriate buffers with respect to resolving regional problems regionally. The creation of a more federal arrangement involves flexibility and accommodation, but it does not necessarily mean the creation of new states. Indian leadership has occasionally overstated the demands of independence by the Sikhs and the Kashmiris, at least, in the past. Indian centrist governance is as responsible as anything else for the rise of Kashmiri and Punjab subnationalism.

The other subnationalist movements, like Jharkand, Gorkhaland, and Bodoland, could be approached with relative decentralization and autonomy at local and district levels.

Conclusion

The development of this essay shows the central importance of structure and its relationship to the crises in Indian politics. While modernization, economic insecurities, and changes in mass communications are important variables, the current governmental structure is the major barrier in addressing both domestic and foreign policy issues. Ex-President Nixon is absolutely correct that in our interdependent world, foreign policy and domestic policy are Siamese twins. Wendell Wilkie, in the 1930s, pointed out that we have one world but do not appear to know it. However, a loose-knit federalism balanced with central administration of foreign policy, national security, and justice issues is likely to keep the linkage between the Siamese twins accommodating and enriching—insuring the survival of both twins—in the Indian milieu. As A. M. Rosenthal of the *New York Times*, speaking of India's "great adventure" noted, "In 1947, India became the only large newly freed nation to reach for economic decency by building a democratic, secular, pluralistic state" (1993: A-15).

As a result of the cataclysmic attacks on secularism of December, 1992 and early 1993, Rosenthal wonders about the great adventure but hopes that it is not over. The cataclysms brought out the weaknesses of a parliamentary system which is dependent on the internal leadership of the ruling party in a fairly centralized "federal" state. The politics of Kashmir, Punjab, and the rise of the BJP show that interest-group democracy has shaken the structure and that the structure deserves reexamination. For the great adventure to continue, the real alternatives are those of the dangerous road of greater statism or gradual movement towards a true federalism. In different ways and to different degrees, the latter alternative involves the common strands of decentralization and tolerance in the ideas of Jefferson, Asoka, Akbar, and Gandhi.

References

Arora, Balveer, and Nirmal Mukarji. 1992. *Federalism in India: Origins and Development*. New Delhi: Vikas.

Chaudhuri, Joyotpaul. 1991. Book Review in *American Political Science Review* 85, no. 3 (September): 1009–1010.

Chaudhuri, Joyotpaul, ed. 1992a. *India's Beleaguered Federalism: The Pluralist Challenge*. Center for Asian Studies Monograph Series. Tempe: Arizona State University.

Chaudhuri, Joyotpaul. 1992b. "Indian Governance: Diversity and the Social Structure." In *Founding America, The Political Legacy of Rights, Religion, Commerce, and Diversity*, edited by J. Chaudhuri. Dubuque: Kendall/Hunt Publishing.

Douglas, William O. 1956. *We the Judges: Studies in American and Indian Constitutional Law From Marshall to Mukherjea*. Garden City, NJ: Doubleday and Company.

Ghosh, Partha S. 1980. "Domestic Sources of India's Policy of Non-Alignment," *India Quarterly* 36: 348–62.

Ghoshal, Baladas. 1992. "State and Nation in India: Will It Survive?" In *India's Beleaguered Federalism: The Pluralist Challenge*, edited by J. Chaudhuri. Center for Asian Studies Monograph Series. Tempe: Arizona State University.

Hersh, Seymour M. 1993. "On the Nuclear Edge," *The New Yorker* (March 29).

"India at the Edge." 1993. *New York Times* (24 February): A-14.

Irani, C. R. 1992. Editorial in the *Statesman Daily* (Calcutta): 1, 12–27.

Jefferson, Thomas. [1854] 1985. *The Writings of Thomas Jefferson, Volume 8*, edited by H. A. Washington. New York: Riker Thorne and Co. Selection on elective despotism republished

in *Free Government in the Making*, edited by Alpheus Mason and Gordon Baker. New York: Oxford University Press.
McDougal, Myres S. 1947. "The Law School of the Future: From Legal Realism to Policy Science in the World Community," *Yale Law Journal* 56 (8): 1345.
Naipaul, V. S. 1990. *India: A Million Mutinies Now*. London: Heinemann.
Northrop, F. S. C. [1989] 1952. *The Taming of the Nations*. Introduction by Joyotpaul Chaudhuri. Woodbridge, CT: Oxbow Press.
Rosenthal, A. M. 1993. "On My Mind: The Struggle for India," *New York Times* (26 February): A-15.
Rudolph, Susanne Hoeber, and Lloyd I. Rudolph. 1993. "Modern Hate," *The New Republic* (22 March).
Schmemann, Serge. 1993. "Moscow Journal," *New York Times International* (19 February): A-4.
Sharma, M. M. 1984. "Domestic Determinants and India's Foreign Policy," *Indian Journal of Political Science* 43/3-45/4: 172-84.
Tucker, Robert W., and David C. Hendrickson. 1990. *Empire of Liberty*. New York: Oxford University Press.
Tummala, Krishna K. 1992. "India's Federalism Under Stress," *Asian Survey* 32: 538-53.
Verney, Douglas V., and Francine R. Frankel. 1986. "India: Has the Trend Toward Federalism: Implications for the Management of Foreign Policy? A Comparative Perspective," *International Journal* 41 (Summer): 572-99.

The Failure of Federalism: Yugoslavia

W. Harriet Critchley

Under various names and constitutions, Yugoslavia has existed as an independent state for nearly three-quarters of a century.[1] For the last forty-eight years, the state has had some form of federal structure.[2] In spite of this history, federalism has failed as a constitutional framework for a polity that embraces a multiethnic society.

To be sure, federalism did function for the thirty years between 1945 and 1974, but only to the degree that it was imposed by an authoritarian regime. After the death of Marshal Tito in 1980, the authority of the federal regime was progressively weakened to the point where, in the latter half of 1991, it simply disintegrated. What had been a federation of six republics and two autonomous regions dissolved within less than a year (June 1991 to May 1992) into the four independent states of Slovenia, Croatia, Bosnia-Hercegovina, and Macedonia and one, much smaller, "new" federal Yugoslavia consisting of Serbia, which had already reabsorbed Montenegro and the formerly autonomous regions of Vojvodina and Kosovo. What caused this massive disintegration of a federal system? Why did it happen so rapidly and with such violence?

---

1. Starting in 1918, the names of the state, in English translation, were: the Kingdom of the Serbs, Croats and Slovenes, the Kingdom of Yugoslavia, the Socialist Federal Republic of Yugoslavia, the Federal Republic of Yugoslavia. The current (1993) Yugoslavia is a rump state which has not received international recognition. (Note: This article has been written for those who are not specialists in Yugoslav history, economics, and politics. As such, it contains very few footnotes or sources and those few are confined to English language publications. Readers interested in pursuing the details in non-English works, should contact the author.)
2. The constitutions of 1946, 1953, 1963, 1974, and 1992 established the varying federal structures.

The answers to these two questions can be found in the chronological coincidence of three factors: ethnic history, the struggle between two different visions of federalism, and growing economic disparities within the federation. Any one of these factors would present a serious challenge to a federal constitutional order; when combined, each factor exacerbated the effects of the other two and, in the process, produced a truly deadly mixture. Each factor will be examined in turn before their combination is discussed.

Ethnic History

Yugoslav means "South Slav," a term which identifies a distinct group of people, or series of tribes, that migrated into the Balkan region from the northeast beginning in the seventh century. By the end of the Middle Ages several mediaeval kingdoms had existed. Historically, three of the most important of these kingdoms were the Serb, the Croat, and the Bulgarian. Each existed at a different time, but their boundaries overlapped substantially. The existence of these mediaeval kingdoms is the earliest historical source for the territorial claims made by contemporary Yugoslav ethnic groups.

At a later date, all of these areas were absorbed into either the Austro-Hungarian empire or the Ottoman empire. For some five hundred years as the Ottoman empire first expanded into the Balkan region, then contracted in a territorial sense and stabilized, then declined, and finally disintegrated in the early twentieth century, the borders between the Austro-Hungarian and Ottoman empires underwent a series of changes.

Generally speaking, the religion adopted by the local population in any subregion was influenced by that subregion's location within one of the two empires. South Slavs living within the Austro-Hungarian empire (that is, most Slovenes and Croats) tended to adopt Roman Catholicism, while South Slavs living within the Ottoman empire (that is, most Serbs) tended to adopt the Eastern Orthodox religion, or Islam.[3] However, as the boundaries between the two empires changed—especially to the west, north, and south—and as some subregions moved from one empire to the other, there were influxes of "other" South Slavs and non-Slavs.[4] Many areas of mixed Serb and Croat population were border areas at one time, as figure 1 shows.

---

3. The South Slavs who adopted Islam did so voluntarily for the most part. They are the contemporary Bosnian Muslims.
4. For example, in the nineteenth century much of Bosnia-Hercegovina changed from being a part of the Ottoman empire to being a part of the Austro-Hungarian empire.

Figure 1. The Austro-Hungarian military frontier. Reproduced with the permission of the International Boundaries Research Unit, University of Durham, from G. Englefield (1992: 3).

Again, over time, some South Slavs who had adopted Islam left their peasant holdings and gravitated to the towns and cities to take up trading and merchant occupations. As a result, the Muslim component of mixed population urban areas increased, while the Roman Catholic or Eastern Orthodox component of the surrounding rural areas increased.

With the collapse of the Austro-Hungarian and Ottoman empires in the course of World War I, the allies at Versailles decided on the creation of an independent South Slav state. This new state was named the Kingdom of the Serbs, Croats and Slovenes. Its component parts included a small independent Serbia, a small independent Montenegro, some remnants of the Austro-Hungarian empire (contemporary Croatia, Slovenia, Vojvodina, parts of Bosnia-Hercegovina), and some remnants of the Ottoman empire (contemporary parts of Serbia, parts of Bosnia-Hercegovina, Macedonia). Thus, the new state contained South Slavs who followed one of three religions at a time when religion had a major role in ethnic identity: Serbs were Eastern Orthodox; Croats and Slovenes were Roman Catholic; Slavic Muslims were beginning to think of themselves as Bosnians.[5]

The Kingdom of the Serbs, Croats and Slovenes was a unitary state with a constitutional monarch (a Serb), a multiparty parliamentary democracy, and more than a score of ethnically based political parties. This constitutional order collapsed in 1928 after three national elections and seventeen cabinets—all within ten years. Until 1991, this was the only attempt to establish a democracy in this territory.

In 1929, the Kingdom of Yugoslavia was established. It lasted until 1941 and was essentially a royal dictatorship. The king (a Serb) ruled a unitary state in which the administrative subunits were given geographic, rather than ethnic, names. In this and other ways, the regime attempted to foster a "Yugoslav nationality" in place of the ethnic identities that had so undermined the previous constitutional order.

The years from 1941 to 1945 were an extremely complex period in the ethnic history of the South Slavs in Yugoslavia. First, it was a period of international war and invasion for the Kingdom of Yugoslavia. Germany, Italy, Bulgaria, Albania, and Hungary invaded and occupied large chunks of the territory, while two Axis puppet-states were created in a part of Serbia and a part of Croatia. Secondly, this was a period of ideological civil war within the kingdom: the old regime and its supporters versus the fascists and their supporters versus the communists and their supporters. It was not uncommon for one of the three sides in this ideological civil war to collaborate periodically with some of the foreign occupiers, to the detriment of its civil war enemies. Finally, this was a period of interethnic war: that is, of local wars in areas of mixed population between Serbs and Croats, between Serbs and Slavic Muslims, between Croats and Slavic Muslims, and between Serbs and Albanians. One characteristic of this complex three-wars-in-one period was the commission of unimaginable atrocities on all sides. Forty-five years

---

5. The new state also contained substantial non-Slav minorities: Albanians, Hungarians, Romanians, Germans, and Gypsies, to name only the largest.

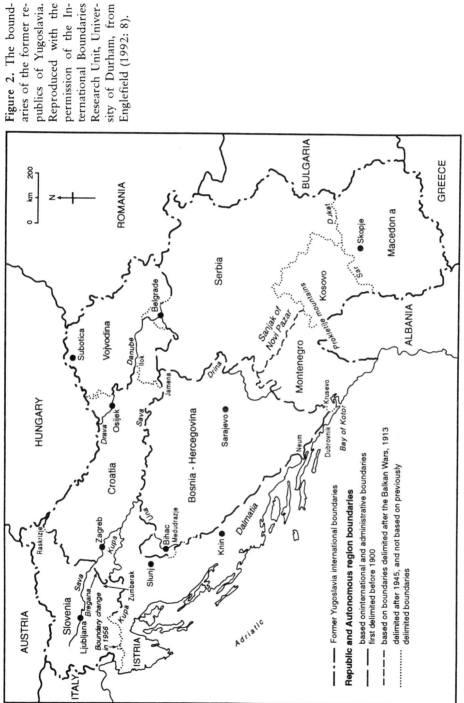

Figure 2. The boundaries of the former republics of Yugoslavia. Reproduced with the permission of the International Boundaries Research Unit, University of Durham, from Englefield (1992: 8).

Table 1. Overall ethnic population, Socialist Federal Republic of Yugoslavia

Serbs	36%	Macedonians	6%
Croats	20%	Montenegrins	3%
Muslim Slavs	9%	Hungarians	2%
Slovenes	8%	Others	9%
Albanians	8%		

Source: Compiled in part from Englefield (1992: 16). Percentages do not add to 100 due to rounding.

later, in 1991, individual, family, and ethnic group memories of those horrible events were still extremely fresh, and those memories engendered extreme fear and hatred as well as a strong desire for revenge.

In 1945-46, Yugoslavia was re-created, this time as a socialist federal republic. The republic was led by Marshal Tito, the victorious communist resistance leader of the early 1940s. Although it was a one-party state, that party—the League of Communists of Yugoslavia—had a federal structure which mirrored the constitutional/administrative structure. One of the regime's central policies was to foster a Yugoslav national identity and to suppress the expression of ethnic identity. Nevertheless, the units of the federation—the six republics—had ethnic titles: Serbia, Croatia, Slovenia, Bosnia-Hercegovina, Montenegro, and Macedonia (figure 2).[6] In addition, this constitutional order, and the central federal policies stemming from it, resulted in the official creation of two "new" ethnic groups: the Bosnian Muslims (that is, Slavic Muslims in Bosnia) and the Macedonians were declared "peoples" or "nations."

Allocating ethnic titles to the federation's constituent republics had one important weakness. The titles masked the degree of ethnic mixing in most of the six republics. The clearest way to show the problem is by examining the two sets of population statistics in tables 1 and 2.

---

6. Two parts of prewar Serbia were declared autonomous regions: Vojvodina in the north and Kosovo in the south. The degree of autonomy in these two regions gradually increased, but in 1989 they were reabsorbed into Serbia.

Table 2. Ethnic population by federal subunit, Socialist Federal Republic of Yugoslavia.

Republic	Population	Ethnic Composition
Slovenia	2.0 million	90.0% Slovene 2.9% Croat 2.2% Serb
Croatia	4.6 million	70.0% Croat 11.0% Serb
Bosnia-Hercegovina	4.4 million	43.0% Muslim Slav 32.0% Serb 18.0% Croat
Montenegro	0.6 million	62.0% Montenegrin 13.5% Muslim Slav 9.2% Serbs
Macedonia	2.0 million	68.0% Macedonian 20.0% Albanian
Serbia	5.8 million	66.0% Serb 14.0% Albanian 2.3% Muslim Slav
Kosovo	1.7 million	85.0% Albanian 13.0% Serb
Vojvodina	1.8 million	54.0% Serb 19.0% Hungarian

Source: Compiled in part from Englefield (1992: 16). Percentages do not add to 100 because of the existence of other minorities in each subunit which have not been included in these figures.

The data show clearly that the former Yugoslavia was a multiethnic state of impressive proportions and that all the units of the federation—with the exception of Slovenia—had mixed populations and substantial minorities. Indeed, even the percentages presented in table 2 mask the degree of ethnically mixed populations in some subregions, such as parts of Croatia and Bosnia-Hercegovina.

These figures were accurate until mid-1991. Since then, voluntary and forced migrations, ethnic cleansing, and casualties of the fighting in parts of Croatia and Bosnia-Hercegovina make them quite inaccurate for nearly all former republics and autonomous regions.

Although the post-1945 regime in Yugoslavia suppressed expressions of ethnic identity, the underlying reality and "ethnic memories" stretching from mediaeval times to the atrocities of 1941–45 remained. That reality began to reappear with the changes embodied in the 1974 constitution and the death of Tito in 1980. It resurfaced in two ways. First, in the population at large, there was increasing expression of ethnic identity (as opposed to "Yugoslav" nationality) and a growing perception of social and economic problems in an ethnic context; secondly, among local and regional politicians, there was an intensified use of "ethnicity" to revisit current grievances and past hatreds.

Federalism

The struggle between two different visions of federalism is the second of the three factors which help to explain the failure of federalism in Yugoslavia. Many South Slavs who were not Serbs—especially the Croats—were unhappy with the constitutional arrangements of the various Yugoslav states from 1918 to 1941. They regarded these unitary states as Serb-dominated, to the detriment of other ethnic groups. At the same time, some Serbs were also unhappy with the constitutional arrangements for, while they did provide an answer to their desire for all Serbs to be in one state, their degree of political control was not, in their view, commensurate with the sacrifices and casualties that Serbs had sustained throughout history in support of their own political independence and that of other South Slavs.

The inauguration of a federal state in 1945–46 was met with some relief and optimism as people attempted to recover from their horrible experiences during 1941–45 and to rebuild their communities and the economy. Their optimism was increased by the official state promotion of "the myth of Partisan solidarity": that Tito (a Croat) had led the multiethnic partisans as their numbers and units eventually spread throughout Yugoslavia and as they achieved liberation from the occupying forces, thus proving that the South

Slavs could collaborate successfully as Yugoslavs. In spite of that early optimism, dissatisfaction with the new constitutional arrangements, albeit suppressed, soon emerged and would grow over the years—especially among the Serbs, the Croats, and the Slovenes. The Croats and the Slovenes noted that Belgrade was both the federal capital and the capital of Serbia, and that a large proportion of senior civilian and military leadership positions were held by Serbs. The Serbs, for their part, began to see themselves as essentially losers in an anti-Serb conspiracy, especially when Vojvodina and Kosovo were carved out of Serbia to become autonomous regions.

This general dissatisfaction came to be expressed in the only politically acceptable fashion that was possible in those days—in two different visions of federalism. On the one hand, some people wished to see a more centralized federal structure which would give more power to the federal level and less to the republics. This vision was supported by many Serbs. On the other hand, some people wished to see a more *de*centralized federal structure with more power in the hands of the units (the republics and the autonomous regions) and less power at the federal level. They wanted a structure which was closer to a confederation. This vision was supported by many Croats and Slovenes.

The constitution of 1974 attempted to resolve the growing tension between these two visions of federalism by creating a more decentralized structure. At the federal level, the position of president was replaced by an eight-person "collective presidency" (with each of the eight representing one of the eight units) wherein one of the eight was elected chairman on an annual rotation basis.[7] The federal assembly was composed of delegates from each of the eight units (six republics and two autonomous regions). The jurisdiction of the federal level of government was confined to foreign affairs, defence, and some joint economic concerns. At the same time, more powers and authority were given to the legislative assemblies of the units.

Rather than resolving the tensions, this new constitutional order increased dissatisfaction on all sides, particularly after Tito's death. At the unit level, politics in the governments of the republics and autonomous regions was increasingly identified with the majority or dominant ethnic group in that unit. Throughout the 1980s, politicians at the unit level increasingly used ethnicity as a component of their policies and debates. Serbs in the Serbian republic worked for a more centralized federation, while Serbs elsewhere in

---

7. This constitutional provision did not come into practice until 1980, after Tito died.

Yugoslavia grew more and more unhappy with the governments and polices of the non-Serb republics in which they resided. Croats and Slovenes, for their part, wanted further decentralization to convert the federation into a confederation. Albanians in Kosovo and Macedonia wanted more autonomy and political power. Among some Croats, Bosnian Muslims, and Albanians there was a growing fear of becoming minorities in a "Greater Serbia" and losing their own autonomy and political power: that is, a fear that the Serbs, by annexing territory to Serbia or reincorporating the autonomous regions or centralizing the federation, would use their overall dominance to the detriment of locally dominant non-Serb ethnic groups.

As the constitutional situation deteriorated, elections at the republic level which took place in the late 1980s and 1990 brought noncommunist governments to power in four of the six republics. Therefore, communist/noncommunist/anticommunist political divisions were added to ethnic and republic divisions. The struggle between the two different visions of federation continued and even sharpened right up to mid-1991, when Slovenia and Croatia declared their independence.

Economic Disparities

Economic disparities provided the third challenge to the continuance of federalism in Yugoslavia. When the Kingdom of the Serbs, Croats and Slovenes was created in 1918, the new state had to combine territories which all supported peasant agricultural economies, but which had a variety of currencies, land-holding systems, and transportation networks which were both rudimentary and rather incompatible with each other. Little progress was made towards the creation of a common economic infrastructure in the ensuing twenty-odd years. During 1941-45, the three wars in one wreaked havoc on the population through disease and casualties, and on their rudimentary economy. Efforts at economic recovery after 1945 were impressive by prewar standards, but they resulted in uneven economic development across the new federal state. Some republics—particularly Croatia and Slovenia—used industrialization and tourism programmes to foster their economic development and garner hard currency for further development. Compared with other parts of the postwar federation, they became rich. Other republics—Serbia, Montenegro, and Macedonia—remained heavily agricultural on what was a poor agricultural land base, experienced little industrialization, and so remained the least economically developed and poorest regions of the state.

Within the post-1945 federal state, attempts to even out the levels and pace of economic development across the federation, by transferring federal revenues from the richest republics to the poorest and by making greater federal investments in the poorer areas, were not very successful. Instead, these efforts at balancing economic development exacerbated political differences and jealousies among the units of the federation. The richer, more developed republics and autonomous regions resented paying for the economic development of the poorer units. They wanted the monies from contributions to federal revenue and additional federal investment for the economic development of their own republics and autonomous regions. The poorer units resented receiving so-called federal charity and the attitudes the richer units displayed towards them.

In 1965, federal economic reforms were introduced which favoured more decentralization in the form of decreasing the revenues paid to the federation and allowing for more economic planning and policy control at the republic/autonomous region level. These reforms created dissatisfaction on all sides, however. Economic disparities increased, as did mutual resentment among the various units of the federation.

Conclusion

I have suggested that the failure of federalism in the former Yugoslavia was caused by the chronological coincidence of three factors: ethnic history, the struggle between two different visions of federalism, and economic disparities within the federation. Now that each of these factors has been examined, the fact that their coincidence in recent years exacerbated the overall constitutional problems in the federation should be obvious.

The disintegration of the federation is mirrored in the fighting that began in the summer of 1991, and continues as this analysis is being written. Before June 1991, the armed land forces in Yugoslavia consisted of the multi-ethnic federal army and militia-like territorial defence forces in each republic. The latter were locally organized units which were semitrained and whose weapons were in local armouries. The first months of fighting involved federal army units, but some of these units were under a chain of command that was neither disciplined nor effective. These army units were fighting with various types of irregular forces: army deserters who were fighting for their own ethnic group; units of the territorial defence forces in various localities (only some of which were under the control of republic authorities); and, following a centuries-long guerrilla warfare tradition, *ad hoc* units raised in many localities which took orders from no one. As the fighting continued, it became increasingly a guerrilla war between *ad hoc* local units in areas of mixed population, with each unit defending its own small local territory against units in adjacent localities. Neither republic-level nor regional political authorities control many of the units fighting within their territory. Hence, the repeated violation of a whole string of ceasefire agreements over the past two years; the multiple roadblocks that humanitarian aid convoys must negotiate over even relatively short distances; the voluntary and forced migrations; and ethnic cleansing.

The chaos, anarchy, and horrors that exist in parts of the former Yugoslavia are best described in the following quotation by Ugrešić (1992: 12):

> Under the slogan of democratization the governments of all the republics have made their lands unmistakably poorer and their people unhappier. Instead of genuine democracy, they have created small, obedient national [ethnic] statistics; instead of free media, media under control; instead of overthrowing the old state apparatus, they have strengthened small state replicas; instead of a free judiciary, a controlled one; instead of demilitarization, a new militarization.

The extreme interethnic violence, severe social disruption, and economic disaster that has ensued from the failure of federalism in the former Yugoslavia suggest very strongly that in the aftermath there will not be hospitable soil for the re-creation of a federation, or the establishment of democratic states in the various independent pieces of the former Yugoslavia for the foreseeable future. At least one generation has been poisoned psychologically.

As the elements of exactly the same situation exist in areas of mixed ethnic population in the former Soviet Union—for example, Moldova, Georgia, Azerbaijan—and in the Czech and Slovak states, what can be learned from the failure of federalism in Yugoslavia in the hope of avoiding such tragedy elsewhere? There seem to be at least five key lessons. First, the suppression of ethnic identities—particularly where there are interethnic tensions—provides no long-term solution to those tensions. Eventually and in various political, economic, and social ways, the tensions resurface with, perhaps, more intensity because of the previous suppression. Secondly, decentralization (and even centralization) of a federal constitutional order is not a substitute for genuine political pluralism. Thirdly, self-determination as a principle for founding territorially and demographically small and fragile "nations" or independent states is a formula for political and economic disaster.[8] Fourthly, the political leaders in multi-ethnic states who play on ethnically defined identities, problems, and resentments for short-term political gains should be widely and immediately recognized as the criminals they are. Finally, human rights—and especially minority rights—must receive prominent and meaningful acknowledgment in any federalist constitution, because this recognition is the central exercise in establishing a positive environment of trust and confidence-building among the citizens of a multiethnic federal state.

References

Englefield, G. 1992. *Territory Briefing—Yugoslavia, Croatia, Slovenia: Re-emerging Boundaries.* Territory Briefing Series 3, International Boundaries Research Unit. Durham: University of Durham.

Ugresic, Dubravka. 1992. "Parrots and priests: 'before' and 'after' in Yugoslavia," *Times Literary Supplement* (15 May).

Zametica, John. 1992. *The Yugoslav Conflict.* Adelphi Paper 270. London: International Institute for Strategic Studies/Brassey's.

---

8. On this point and a number of other matters raised in this analysis, see Zametica (1992).

The Future of Federalism:
Lessons from Canada and Québec

Alain-G. Gagnon and Guy Laforest

In the past few years, the world has witnessed the dissolution of three important federations—Czechoslovakia, the Soviet Union, and Yugoslavia—and the current Russian federation is also under threat from various centrifugal forces. Does federalism have a future beyond bipolarity in the globalized world of late modernity? The tensions created by globalization and the resurgence of nationalism do not necessarily push in the direction of fragmentation. In federal regimes of the past and even of today, numerous leaders, as if their eyes had suddenly been opened by the ghosts of Plato and Hobbes, have been obsessed with unity and have attempted to create—whatever the cost—a sense of national allegiance to the federation as a whole. Their goal was to transform federations and complex societies into nations, to create, for instance, a Yugoslav identity to rival and ultimately to supersede the Bosnian, Croatian, and Slovenian identities. The failure of many such endeavours should encourage the abandonment of such a strategy. To shed some light on this dilemma and to provide some suggestions for a more prudent path for federal undertakings, this paper examines the case of Canada and Québec.[1]

The current situation in Canada is one that denies federal qualities while it cultivates similarities. This shift is viewed by some as a way to provide the ingredients necessary to reunite the country following the unfortunate patriation of the British North America Act without Québec's consent in 1982, the undisputed failure of the Meech Lake process (1987-90), and, in 1992, the defeat of the poorly conceived Charlottetown accord. It seems that while Québec was busy discussing its constitutional future and assessing its aspirations as a national community, a process best represented by the Bé-

---

1. For a comparative account of such federal endeavours, see Burgess and Gagnon (1993).

langer-Campeau Commission, and while its most outspoken and liberal-minded intellectuals were debating ways to re-establish federal practices, the federal government and the anglophone provinces were developing a political strategy that would short-circuit Québec's ambition to express itself as a national community. The most effective measure to achieve this was found in the proposal for a third order of government (aboriginal government) which would further undermine Québec's search for nationhood.

In light of so many missed opportunities to find a pan-Canadian solution that Québec would find acceptable, the future of Canadian federalism is undoubtedly in jeopardy. It is thus appropriate to examine if, and how, Canadian federalism can be transformed to find a way out of this impasse. At the centre of the constitutional problem, we believe, is the continued failure of political élites to recognize competing visions. To assess the future of Canadian federalism, we will examine three main issues which constitute, in our view, the crux of the present predicament. First, an examination and assessment of the legacy of Pierre Elliott Trudeau will provide many of the reasons why Canadian federalism has failed to accommodate asymmetry. Secondly, it is essential to look at the rich history of Canada and Québec and draw lessons from prevailing constitutional practice. Thirdly, we believe that Canadian federalism will not be able to survive the next quarter-century unless a way is found to reconcile the country's diversities with a modicum of "constitutional morality," as J. A. Corry so aptly put it some fifteen years ago. We believe that the conclusions we have reached with respect to the future of Canada are equally valid for the future of federalism in general.[2]

The Trudeau Legacy

A little over twenty-five years ago, in 1967, Pierre Elliott Trudeau published what we regard as the most important book in the political and intellectual history of both Canada and Québec: *Le fédéralisme et la société canadienne-française* (1967).[3] The work, a collection of pieces written in the 1950s and early 1960s, was released into a fascinating political climate in which Trudeau had only recently been appointed the federal minister of justice. President Charles de Gaulle of France had just taken Canada and the world

---

2. See Corry (1978: 1-15), in which he introduces the concept of "constitutional morality."
3. The text was subsequently published in English as *Federalism and the French Canadians* (1968). Quotations in this article are drawn from the English edition.

by storm with his now-legendary words, "*Vive le Québec libre,*" proclaimed from the balcony of Montreal's Hôtel-de-Ville during his visit to Expo '67. In the autumn of the same year, René Lévesque broke with the Québec Liberal party, published *Option Québec*, and founded the Mouvement Souveraineté-Association. In November, the Estates-General of French Canada met in Montreal. In early December, the Royal Commission on Bilingualism and Biculturalism published the first volume of its report, which dealt with bilingualism. That volume contained a general introduction, written by André Laurendeau, which remains to this day the most eloquent defence of a reconciliation between the claims of Québec nationalism and those of a broader patriotism in support of the Canadian federal political community. Six months after the publication of his ideological statement, Trudeau caught the attention of the whole country when he brilliantly argued the federal case in a lively exchange with the premier of Québec, Daniel Johnson, at the constitutional conference of February 1968. Two months later Trudeau became prime minister of Canada. In a sense, the rest is history. In another sense, the rest is also the subject of this article as we explore the destiny of federalism.

The historical importance and contemporary relevance of Trudeau's views can be aptly demonstrated by focusing on one selection from his 1967 book. This piece, entitled "Federalism, Nationalism, and Reason," had first been given as a paper at a joint meeting of the Canadian Political Science Association and the Canadian Association of Law Professors, in 1964. Ironically, it was translated into French by Pierre Vadeboncoeur, one of Trudeau's high-school comrades at Collège Brébeuf and, briefly, a colleague sharing similar views during the *Cité libre* years, before he became, with Marcel Rioux, one of Trudeau's most forceful ideological adversaries.

There are three reasons why this particular piece is relevant to our topic. First, as the title indicates, Trudeau suggests that one can rationally adjudicate the claims of federalism and nationalism. Secondly, he offers his own narrative of the history of federalism and nationalism in Canada and Québec. Thirdly, and most crucially, it is possible to compare Trudeau's theoretical insights of 1967 with the political goals of his virtually uninterrupted reign as prime minister between 1968 and 1984.

Trudeau, not unlike such thinkers as Elie Kedourie and E. J. Hobsbawm, believes that nationalism fades with the passage of time. At the end of his article, Trudeau concludes that nationalism will never provide a solution to federalist issues in Canada. More generally, he predicts that nationalism will come to be seen in developed societies as an outdated and unsophisticated tool. Nationalism is ultimately bound to be rejected as a principle of good government, to be replaced by political instruments which will have to meet the criteria of functional rationality (1968: 215). Federalism, ideally, should be based on reason and not be warped by relying on the kind of primitive emotions generally linked to nationalism. What should a state do, however, when circumstances are less than ideal, when one or a plurality of sociological nations threaten to pull a federation apart, when a state risks dismemberment? The first response, for Trudeau as political theorist, remains the use of reason. But suppose it fails? In 1967, Trudeau did not hesitate to contemplate the alternatives, and his suggestions are quite instructive for our study.

As Michael Oliver recently argued in a brilliant comparative study of Laurendeau and Trudeau, the latter made a fundamental distinction between two kinds of nations, even though he granted that both employ nationalism as a kind of cement to unify the community (1991: 35). In the one case, however, "nation" is synonymous with a "state"; in the other case, it corresponds to a "people." The two entities—the juridical nation and the sociological one—should be considered separately. The modern state, Trudeau argued, uses nationalism as a cement to maintain its integrity, to preserve the popular consensus on which its legitimacy rests. Because it is difficult to persuade by reason alone, the state is tempted to use the nationalist idea because it is a convenient and efficient instrument: "Hence, from the emotional appeal called nationalism is derived a psychological inclination to obey the constitution of the state" (1968: 189). This temptation exists in all states, but Trudeau believes that its use is almost irresistible for the governments of federations. Federations are said to be fragile because they are built on the pillars of compromise and compact. According to Trudeau, a solidifying nationalist cement will be required to maintain their viability. However, in a paradoxical fashion, this reliance on an ideological construct at the federal level is likely to render nationalism legitimate at the regional level. Indeed, Trudeau envisages this development as virtually inevitable. How, then, is the federal state to avoid the rise of nationalist demands at the regional level, to ensure that what is logically acceptable does not become logically desirable? Trudeau's answer to this question is one of the most remarkable passages in this whole article:

> One way of offsetting the appeal of separatism is by investing tremendous amounts of time, energy, and money in nationalism, *at the*

federal level. A national image must be created that will have such an appeal as to make any image of a separatist group unattractive. Resources must be diverted into such things as national flags, anthems, education, arts councils, broadcasting corporations, film boards; the territory must be bound together by a network of railways, highways, airlines. . . . In short, the whole of the citizenry must be made to feel that it is only within the framework of the federal state that their language, culture, institutions, sacred traditions, and standard of living can be protected from external attack and internal strife.

(1968: 193)

Trudeau's argument could be summarized as follows: nationalism is a potent political phenomenon which is likely doomed by history, but it is inferior to theoretical reason represented by the federalist principle; however, to ensure the triumph of federalism in pluri-ethnic and multinational states, practical reason suggests that it may be appropriate to resort to the use of an alternative nationalism to create a more compelling allegiance to the centre. In 1993, practical reason tells us that we have to find some other means to achieve this goal.

Interestingly, in his 1967 composition, Trudeau openly admitted the multinational nature of Canada. He recognized that Québec was a nation, at least in the sociological sense: "In Quebec today the same forces are at work: a new and modern society is being glued together by nationalism, it is discovering its potentialities as a nation, and is demanding equality with all other nations" (1968: 202). In the juridical sense, however, there had to be only one nation at the federal level. We believe that the resources of political imagination will have to produce more refined conceptual tools if federations are to survive the winds of the late twentieth century. In his article, Oliver notes that Trudeau does not condemn with equal vigour the sociological nationalism of Québec and the juridical nationalism of Canada. Trudeau studied in detail the political options of a state facing the sovereignist demands of sociological nationalism, but he provided no such analysis of the policy choices available to those defending themselves against the imposition of the language and symbols of juridical nationalism designed to foster a greater loyalty towards the federal community (1991: 351).

This differential treatment, according to Oliver, can be attributed to three factors. First, Trudeau argues that sociological nationalism hinders political stability. Secondly, he believes that sociological nationalism will inevitably seek to duplicate itself at the juridical level, to create a correspondence between nation and state. We believe that this postulate is wrong and that more often than not it is the nation-building attempts at the federal level which push sociological nations towards secession. Thirdly, Trudeau has always viscerally hated the sociological nationalism of French Canada. This hatred is characteristic of his writings, from the days of *Cité libre* to his introduction to *La grève de l'amiante*, the book he edited on the famous asbestos strike of 1949, to *Le fédéralisme et la société canadienne-française* and, most recently, his various attacks on the Meech Lake and Charlottetown accords.

There is deep tension in the pages of "Federalism, Nationalism, and Reason." For practical motives, Trudeau argues that nationalism can come to the rescue of a federal state, can in a sense help federalism triumph as a more rational principle of government. In Trudeau's own words, this view resembles practical irrationality. In the same pages, however, he takes pains to criticize previous forms of nationalism not only in Québec but also in Canada. The historical account of federalism and nationalism in Canada that Trudeau offers in this article demonstrates clearly that, in 1967, Trudeau, in ideal circumstances, would have preferred the complete dismantling of nationalism to maintain the country's integrity. In the real world of politics, this was not achievable, however, and Trudeau had to work out another plan of attack.

In the real world of Canadian politics, particularly after his re-election in February 1980 and after the referendum on sovereignty-association in Québec in May of the same year, Trudeau came to realize that reason alone could not create the cement for the Canadian state. Something else would be required: a national patriotism, coupled with a sentiment of national belonging, had to be invented—a new myth for the Canadian nation. These goals were achieved through the patriation effort of 1982, and particularly through the entrenchment of the *Canadian Charter of Rights and Freedoms* in the *Constitution Act*. In his frequent interventions during the constitutional crisis of 1987–90, known as the Meech Lake saga, Canada's former prime minister revealed the nature of his vision:

> And once again, it means an even greater tendency, a greater weight on the side of provincialism, at the expense of a federal institution or legislation which, up until now, has given Canadians a feeling of belonging to one Canada. In the same way the Canadian Charter of Rights and Freedoms was important to Canadian unity, as were the patriation of the Constitution and the new Canadian flag. All of those

things are important in the sense that they help Canadians to realize that they share with *all* other Canadians, *throughout* the country, the same set of fundamental values. (1990: 31)

After 1980, Trudeau resolved to use the means at his disposal to invent a new national tradition for Canada. Through the Charter, he attempted in his own words, to "constitutionalize Canadians" beyond their provincial/ territorial identities. In this perspective, the people or the nation in Québec is denied, perhaps even in the sociological sense. The citizens of Québec are members of the Canadian nation, subjected to the same Charter rights as those in other provinces. Scholars such as Alan Cairns, Peter Russell, Rainer Knopff, and F. L. Morton have all insisted on the nation-building characteristics of the Charter.[4] The interpretation of the Charter by the judiciary, the branch of government in Canada that least reflects the federal principle, has contributed to this standardization of norms and public policies throughout the country, reinforcing such values as the equality of provinces and the equality of individual rights and citizenship. By strengthening the value of equality, the Charter renders considerably more difficult the implementation of such notions as 'distinct society' and 'special status' for Québec in the spirit of asymmetrical federalism, which is also the Aristotelian principle recognizing Québec's peculiar circumstances in North America. Concomitantly, the Charter promotes a political culture of constitutional minoritarianism, enabling a variety of groups and of individuals as members of groups to see themselves as important players in the definition of the political community and in the functioning of the political system. Multicultural groups and feminist organizations, native peoples and language minorities, and many others belong to the vast assembly of Charter patriots likely to give unconditional allegiance to Canada as a nation and to the institutions protecting and promoting their rights.

As a country-building device, the Charter has not had the same impact in Québec as it has elsewhere in Canada. We cannot affirm categorically that the nationalist spirit of the Charter will not overtake Québec at some point in the future, but for the time being, the debate about the legitimacy of the Charter and of the whole 1982 constitutional reform continues unabated in Québec. Although Premier Robert Bourassa finally came 'on side' during the

---

4. Russel et al. (1990: 11). See also Knopff and Morton (1992: 43–44). In addition, one may consult Cairns (1990: 86–88).

macroconstitutional effort that led to the 1992 Charlottetown Accord, known as the "Canada Round," the provincial Liberal government, through the voice of its constitutional affairs minister, Gil Rémillard, has continued to express the consistent view that the reforms of 1982, made without the consent of Québec, remain illegitimate in that province.

As Québec society sinks into yet another episode of its language debate, the nation-building dimension of the Charter becomes harder to hide. The conflict between Canada and Québec does not, in essence, turn on the philosophy of liberalism. As the federal constitutional proposals of September 1991 made very clear, the Canadian political culture and the Charter encompass a complex equilibrium between individual and collective rights: "The fact that community rights exist alongside individual rights in our Constitution goes to the very heart of what Canada is all about" (Canada 1991: 3). The same remark can be made with regard to Québec. The fundamental rights of Canadians, such as freedom of expression and freedom of association, can be overridden by the notwithstanding clause—the derogatory clause—of the 1982 constitution, whereas language rights are completely shielded from such an assault. Because language is at the centre of politics and identity in Canada, Trudeau, when forced to choose in 1981-82, preferred to safeguard the language provisions of the Charter from the bite of the notwithstanding clause. The desire to create a nation and promote a pan-Canadian code of fundamental values was his primary motive, rather than the expression of any particular liberal philosophy.

But shared values, as the Canadian political philosopher Will Kymlicka recently concluded, do not necessarily lead to a shared identity (1992: 37). And we would add that, in the end, members of the different sociological nations in a federal regime will resent the government and leaders who try to create a national identity through such a standardization of values and norms. This specific aspect of constitutionalism in Canada brings us back to the tension at play in Trudeau's article, "Federalism, Nationalism, and Reason":

> Thus, a critical point can be reached in either direction beyond which separatism takes place, or a civil war is fought.
>
> When such a critical point has been reached or is in sight, no amount, however great, of nationalism can save the federation. Any expenditure of emotional appeal (flags, professions of faith, calls to dignity, expressions of brotherly love) at the national level will only

serve to justify similar appeals at the regional level, where they are just as likely to be effective. Thus the great moment of truth arrives when it is realized that *in the last resort* the mainspring of federalism cannot be emotion but must be reason. (1968: 194)

Two points must be made at this crucial juncture in our reflections concerning federalism and the Canada-Québec experience. First, though lacking the foresight to predict the future, one must juxtapose Trudeau's prediction with his earlier words on ways to counter separatism. The reader will recall that Trudeau had argued that immense resources could be directed towards inventing a nation at the federal level. Still, the passage we have just quoted demonstrates that he believed such an enterprise to be ultimately doomed. According to Trudeau's 1967 argument, the 1982 nation-building project cannot survive the passage of time. The differential application of the notwithstanding clause among various forms of equality—applied, for example, to gender but not to language, one of the fundamental cleavages of Canadian politics—is testimony to the fact that the Charter was not a product of liberal reason.

We shall be more concise about our second point because we will come back to it in our conclusion. In 1967, Trudeau argued that in a federation exposed to a multiplicity of nationalist demands, the pressures thus created may reach a point beyond which separation must take place or civil war will emerge. There is no place in his thinking for the kind of multi-national federalism to be found in James Tully's major theoretical contribution to constitutional politics in Canada. It will become more and more obvious that Trudeau falls prey here to a Manichaean logic. It would be sheer folly for contemporary federations and their leaders to do the same.

Lessons From Past Experiences

Political practices and the recognition of conventions are fundamental to the understanding and exercise of power. The comprehension of these practices and conventions lays the groundwork for the type of justice to be achieved.[5]

James Tully, a highly regarded Canadian political philosopher, argues that "what lies at the bottom of the Canadian federation is neither a unifying con-

---

5. On the multiple conceptions of justice, one should refer to Noël (forthcoming). Citations in this article are from the manuscript.

stitution nor shared vision, but the multiplicity of activities of multilateral negotiations" (n.d.: 12).[6] Obviously, there is no official admission of the multiplicity of nations in Canada. Nevertheless, we feel that this reality is the key to understanding the relationships between Québec and other Canadian national communities competing in "the bosom of a single state." Tully identifies three recognized conventions that ought to characterize just constitutional negotiations in all federal states. (1) The members of the federation should be recognized in their own terms through the negotiations and in the constitution (the convention of mutual recognition and continuity, or "self-identification"). (2) Constitutional agreements should be based on negotiations that are fair by the customs of each member involved (the convention of multilateral negotiations). (3) Negotiated constitutional agreements should require the consent of those affected and/or their representatives (the convention of consent or *Quod omnes tangit* 'what touches all must be approved by all'). If any federal relation among any number of members satisfies all three conventions it is a just relation (n.d.: 18–19).

The three conventions identified by Tully are not mutually negotiable. They need to be adopted concurrently. There is no room for trade-offs of the sort imagined by Trudeau: for example, in return for the acceptance of the *Canadian Charter of Rights and Freedoms*, a province will be permitted to use a notwithstanding clause. Federal conventions require the approval of all parties involved to guarantee continuity. We believe that Tully has identified the foremost constitutive elements that give a country its federal quality. At a time when many federal regimes have dissolved or are in trouble, his insights should be pondered with the utmost attention.[7]

Two of Tully's conventions were disregarded in the constitutional discussions of 1981–82 in Canada. The government of Québec has still not consented to a reform which diminished its power (third convention). Moreover, Québec's desire to be seen as a nation or a distinct society rather than as a province was ignored (first convention). In the hearts and minds of many

---

6. Compare this with Alan C. Cairns's assertion: "At first glance the Canadian government acts straightforwardly as the senior government of a federal system that contains ten provinces and two territories, and thus as the government of the coast-to-coast community of all Canadians" (n.d.: 14–15).
7. Acceptance of these conventions has not fared well in recent constitutional negotiations in Canada. See Gagnon and Latouche (1991), especially *"Comment organiser le Canada: le point de vue des commissions royales et des partis politiques"* (21–90).

Quebecers, the constitutional negotiations of 1982 represented a "breach of trust" (Laforest 1991: 147-63). It is notable that, even in times of adversity, Québec has continued to respect established federal practices, all the while requesting corresponding behaviour on the part of others. At stake is the urgent need to disentangle the notions of legitimacy and legality.[8]

The danger that 1982 presents for Québec is that the constitutional changes adopted and the way in which they were imposed may become acceptable constitutional practice, thereby fundamentally modifying constitutionalism in Canada. The passage of time is not without political implications for Québec's place in the federation. The *Constitution Act* of 1982 is a dangerous precedent for Québec because it challenges the previous belief that fundamental changes to the constitution could not be made without its consent. The decision on the part of the Supreme Court of Canada to view Québec's opposition as insufficient to stop reforms that are intended for the whole country was an explosive rebuke of legitimacy in favour of legality. As long as the rule of 'substantial provincial consent' is met, such changes are legal. This decision was a sharp break with former practice, and its significance was not lost on Quebecers and their representatives in that province's National Assembly. A profound sense of betrayal has swept the Québec people, as this breach of former federal practice remains unrectified. Indeed, the three principles identified by Tully for a just relation to exist in a federal state have been suspended in Canada.

A recognition of all national communities is a prerequisite to the continuity of Canada and many other similarly complex federations. Alan Cairns's identification of three competing nationalisms in Canada is a clear reminder that Canadian nationalism and aboriginal nationalism are not coterminous. In addition, it should be stressed that, of late, aboriginal nationalism has been encouraged by the central government as a means to undermine Qué-

---

8. In "Conscience and the constitution," (*Columbia Law Review* 1993), Dennis Patterson brings up the complementary notion of the "practice of persuasion" on which the entire federal government strategy during the referendum campaign of October 1992 was based. The intent was to avoid discussing normative and substantive issues by appealing to the most visceral components of the Canadian identity, as Patterson points out: "The modalities of justification are the ways in which propositions of law are shown to be true or false. . . . The decision may require resort to conscience, but conscience does not do any normative work. . . . The reasoning is either persuasive or it is not. Conscience does not persuade, nor is it persuaded: only argument can do that" (327, n. 118).

bec nationalism by challenging Québec's territorial integrity (Hall 1991).[9] A recognition of the aboriginal community in the province by the central government would make it more difficult for Québec to realize its own national aspirations. This is currently the most serious threat to Québec's sovereignty and is the most risky option ever considered by Ottawa and the anglophone provinces to extinguish the Québec question. In a recent essay, two English-Canadian academics, David Bercuson and Barry Cooper, recommend that if Québec were to secede, its borders should be redrawn along ethnic lines (1991: 157). The new state would only occupy the territories traditionally inhabited by the French in Québec. This is not the road to multinational federalism but the path towards Yugoslavia and Bosnia. We consider this to be the path of imprudence.

The argument of this paper is that, for federalism to be legitimate, the imposition of instrumentalities that conflict with the interests of the federating nations must be avoided. The original compact (real or understood) made between the nations of Canada was based on the understanding that the agreement would allow for diverse means of continued development, and the establishment of the necessary instruments to strengthen their respective national aspirations within the newly formed political entity. This remains the goal and the hope of most nations in the federations of the late twentieth century. Many of them will secede only as a last resort.

Federal societies are expected to reflect "deep diversity" (Taylor 1993: 181–84),[10] which leads them, in turn, to construct federal institutions characterized by accommodation. Social and political engineering to rebuild Canada according to a more flexible model (read, asymmetrical federalism) is, therefore, an appropriate and necessary solution at this juncture of our com-

---

9. For a counterargument, see Brun (1992: 69–85).
10. For Taylor, there are two levels of diversity: We face a challenge to our very conception of diversity. Many of the people who rallied around the Charter and multiculturalism to reject the distinct society are proud of their acceptance of diversity. . . . What is enshrined here is what one might call first-level diversity. There are great differences in culture and outlook and background in a population that nevertheless shares the same idea of what it is to belong to Canada. . . . To build a country for everyone, Canada would have to allow for second-level or "deep" diversity, in which a plurality of ways of belonging would also be acknowledged and accepted. Someone of, say, Italian extraction in Toronto or Ukrainian extraction in Edmonton might indeed feel Canadian as a bearer of individual rights in a multicultural mosaic. . . . But this person might nevertheless accept that a Québécois or a Cree or a Déné might belong in a different way, that these persons were Canadian through being members of their national communities. (1993: 182–83)

mon existence. Far from denying the past, the goal should be to recognize ways in which the construction of a country can become a positive endeavour, respectful of contributions made by all partners of the compact. The patriation of the *British North America Act* by the government of Canada in 1982, without the support of the Québec's National Assembly, is a clear reminder that Ottawa did not respect established political conventions, and this action was an unsettling development for most Quebecers who had come to see Canada as a compact.

The work of Baron de Montesquieu, for whom decentralized federalism was an acceptable and fortunate device to accommodate people, institutions, and mores, is of interest here. For Montesquieu, it would be inappropriate for a government (read Ottawa) to introduce edicts or laws that are incompatible with the mores of a people (read Québec). It would be inadmissible to see a government that decides to "establish things shocking to the existing ideas [*la manière de pensée*] of a nation." This, for Montesquieu, would simply be tyranny. Not surprisingly, such tyranny is more likely to be found in centralized states (1989: 293).[11]

This reflection takes us back to Tully, who believes that it is more important to examine the "character of Canada" in terms of the diversity of its myriad cultures and mores that largely account for variegated political conflicts than to ponder lack of experience, oversight of bureaucrats, politicians' entanglements, and the multiple angles of the issues at stake.

Constitutional Morality

The failures of the Canadian federal system can be associated with the decision of Ottawa to invade fields of exclusive provincial jurisdiction, making any serious expressions of cooperative federalism impossible.[12] Incrementally,

---

11. The work of Alexis de Tocqueville is also instructive: see *Democracy in America* (1945, vol. 1.1.8: 169), where the author says: "In great centralized nations the legislator is obliged to give a character of uniformity to the laws, which does not always suit the diversity of customs and of districts; as he takes no cognizance of special cases, he can only proceed upon general principles; and the population is obliged to conform to the requirements of the laws, since legislation cannot adapt itself to the exigencies and the customs of the population, which is a great cause of trouble and misery."
12. See a series of contributions to *Le Devoir*, written by a former speech writer, André Burelle, for Prime Minister Trudeau, 30 April, 1–6 May 1993. *"Pour une remise en question du fédéralisme unitaire"* (1-2 May) and *"Fédéralisme dominateur et fédéralisme*

the federal government has imposed its views on Québec and asked that it surrender some of its sovereignty for the so-called good of the country. This process, while denying recognition to Québec's national aspirations, left little place for asymmetrical federalism to take hold.

According to one of the most respected students of Canadian federalism, the late J. A. Corry, the main criticism Québec could formulate against Ottawa and the anglophone provinces is their insensitivity to the conditions of existence for Québec in North America. The dominant interpretation of federalism in the rest of Canada builds on a twentieth-century vision, a vision that largely ignores the need to respect deep diversity, as noted by Corry:

> Quebec's objections about them [federal priorities and patterns built into shared programmes] have not been primarily the distribution of powers under sections 91 and 92 but rather the stamp of English-Canadian preferences and outlook on most of what the federal government does. That is why English Canadians have to think more sympathetically about what it would be like to stand in Quebeckers' shoes, and try to modify their preferences and outlook to take account of the preferences and outlook of Quebeckers in a wide range of matters. Here indeed we do need a new and more scrupulous constitutional morality. (1978: 9-10)

This argument remains pertinent in view of the contemporary constitutional deliberations that occupied Canadians during the Meech Lake *débâcle* (1987-90), the constitutional 'conferences' that traversed the country in 1990-92, and the referendum campaign of October 1992 on the Charlottetown Accord (see Bariteau et al. 1992). The challenge for all federations that want to survive into the next century is to accommodate diversity and to enrich it while building a stronger entity.

At the basis of these repeated constitutional failures in Canada, there is a common denominator which could be summarized as a substantial insensitivity on the part of too many Canadians to the presence of multiple national communities aspiring to share and continue building a country together. Aboriginal nationalism and Québec nationalism, in particular, demand to be accommodated in a revamped federal system that will be capable

---

(4 May) are the best examples of this tendency.

of facing the difficult and rewarding challenges that diversity, and its entrenchment, present to all Canadians.

It is significant that the Charlottetown Accord proposed different means for dealing with Québec nationalism and aboriginal nationalism respectively. This incongruous treatment emerges when examining the application of the *Canadian Charter of Rights and Freedoms* to Québec and to aboriginal peoples. The differences are also highlighted in an analysis of the Charlottetown Accord by Alan Cairns, in which he argues:

> For Quebec, the Charter, and indeed the whole constitution, was to be filtered through the interpretive lens of the distinct society, which "includes a French-speaking majority, a unique culture and a civil law tradition" . . . [whereas] the original s. 25 Aboriginal non-derogation clause in the 1982 Charter, by contrast, is not simply an interpretive clause but is a categorical protection—in its pre-Charlottetown Accord form, Charter rights and freedoms "shall not be construed so as to abrogate or derogate from any aboriginal, treaty or other rights or freedoms . . .," a protection that the Charlottetown Accord would have strengthened. (n.d.: 50–51)

The intention of the federal government was, first, to recognize territorial claims on Québec's territory and to erect a third order of government to fulfil aboriginal demands and, secondly, to challenge Québec's right to self-determination by recognizing another order of government whose powers were to be superimposed over the existing 'provincial' order of government.[13]

In failing to live up to the constitutional morality identified by Corry— a crucial explanation for the continued failure to accommodate Québec's national aspirations in a federal setting—power holders in Ottawa have attempted to make the *Canadian Charter of Rights and Freedoms* the cement that binds together all Canadian citizens, with little, if any, respect paid to their national aspirations. They have claimed for themselves Trudeau's legacy. We have seen earlier that this does not bode well for their purportedly federal dreams. As we enter the next millennium, we believe that if fed-

---

13. Guy Laforest's *"L'accord d'Ottawa-Charlottetown et la réconciliation des aspirations nationales du Québec"* (1992) and Daniel Latouche's *"Le partage des pouvoirs"* (1992) are very sensitive to this very point.

erations are to survive it is essential that they be built on the notion of 'constitutional morality.' Should they fail to build on such a morality, federations, we submit, are fated to enter a period of political instability and distrust.

Conclusion

Québec's desire to express its specificity should not be interpreted as a mutiny, but rather as a profound attachment to the federal spirit. For, as Tully pointed out, the conventions of mutual recognition, multilateral negotiations, and consent are required to maintain the federal spirit. It is clear, however, that the emerging Canadian nationalism has not been able to tolerate such expressions of federalism and, indeed, views them as challenges to the construction of a Canadian state that is based on the one-nation concept, which—at the cost of a civil war—has long inspired Americans.

As the process of European integration continues, tensions could arise in many settings. It is also possible that countries such as Russia may have little choice but to take the road of deep diversity if they are to make it into the next century. In unitary and federal countries characterized by deep diversity, such as Canada (Québec), the United Kingdom (Scotland, Wales), South Africa, Spain (Catalonia, Basque country), France (Brittany, Corsica), and, to a lesser extent, Switzerland (Jura), a great deal of political imagination will be required in the future.[14] This does not mean that there has not been progress in some of these regions; merely that more needs to be achieved if those countries want to meet the emerging challenges posed by political and economic integration, as well as by the important movements of population that the so-called end of communism has unleashed throughout Europe.

Recently Charles Taylor has suggested that for modern countries to survive, accommodation both to "first-level diversity" (cultural differences) and "second-level or deep diversity" (different models of citizenship) would need to be recognized as legitimate; and argues that "the world needs other models to be legitimated in order to allow for more humane and less constraining modes of political cohabitation. Instead of pushing ourselves to the point of

---

14. In the case of Québec, Hobsbawm (1992) suggests that it had something to do with a major societal transformation, that is, the displacement of values and mores aligned with Catholic teachings by nontraditional ones associated with a desire to redefine the national community.

breakup in the name of a uniform model, we would do our own and some other peoples a favour by exploring the space of deep diversity" (1993: 183).

Hobsbawm's (1992: 180–83) thesis predicting the diminution of nationalism, when measured against the Canadian example, appears to be deficient. In Canada, Québec nationalism has inspired Canadian nationalism which, in turn, has propelled aboriginal nationalism, and so on. However, for federalism to survive present-day challenges, and for the owl of Minerva not to leave its perch,[15] it is essential that federal states dispose of any expressions of elementary nationalism and move towards acceptance of the deep diversity suggested by Taylor. It should also be pointed out that Canadians outside Québec often equate federalism with a strong central state. This has led to deep frustration among Quebecers because they tend to believe that federalism is designed to allow for the expression of diversity in a country while maintaining unity.

For Canada to survive, it will have to adhere to the three conventions of federal practice identified by Tully. A failure to subscribe to these conventions would make Canada's future less than promising. To extricate themselves from the current political quagmire, Canadians will have to find the energy to pursue negotiations until continuity is reestablished, until mutual recognition is adhered to, and until consent is finally granted by the three national communities which constitute the country. Now more than ever, there is an urgent need for some constitutional morality: a morality that would allow for sensitivity to the Québec question and that would refrain from imposing identical requirements on all communities for association with the Canadian state. Canada, after all, has been built on many competing, but reinforcing, identities. To require that Quebecers put the principles of provincial equality, pan-Canadian uniformity, and individual rights above everything else is, by definition, to relinquish the premises of federalism among complex societies.

In closing, we suggest that Corry's notion of "constitutional morality," the need to respect "political conventions" put forward by Tully, and the recog-

---

15. Indeed, as Hobsbawm reminds us: "After all, the very fact that historians are at least beginning to make some progress in the study and analysis of nations and nationalism suggests that, as so often, the phenomenon is past its peak. The owl of Minerva which brings wisdom, said Hegel, flies out at dusk. It is a good sign that it is now circling round nations and nationalism" (1992: 183).

nition of "deep diversity" suggested by Taylor are pertinent to the survival of many countries. Many avenues are being suggested by analysts, but central to all of them is a deep-seated commitment to pluralism and tolerance. Such is the path of political prudence in the late twentieth century.

References

Bariteau, Claude, et al. 1992. *Référendum, 26 octobre 1992: les objections de 20 spécialistes aux offres fédérales*. Montreal: Les Editions Saint-Martin.
Baron de Montesquieu, Charles Louis de Secondat. 1989. *The Spirit of Laws, Volume 19*, translated and edited by Anne M. Cohler, Basia Carolyn Miller, and Harold Samuel Stone. Cambridge: Cambridge University Press.
Bercuson, David, and Barry Cooper. 1991. *Deconfederation: Canada without Quebec*. Toronto: Key Porter.
Brun, Henri, 1992. "*L'intégrité territoriale d'un Québec souverain*." In *Répliques aux détracteurs de la souveraineté du Québec*, edited by Alain-G. Gagnon and François Rocher. Montreal: VLB Editeur.
Burgess, Michael and Alain-G. Gagnon, (eds.) 1993. *Comparative Federalism and Federation: Competing Traditions and Future Directions*. London: Harvester Wheatsheaf.
Cairns, Alan C. 1990. "Constitutional Minoritarianism in Canada." In *Canada: The State of the Federation*, edited by Ronald Watts and Douglas Brown. Kingston: Institute of Intergovernmental Relations, Queen's University.
Cairns, Alan C. n.d. "The Charlottetown Accord: Multinational Canada vs. Federalism." In *Canada's Constitutional Predicament after 1992*, edited and introduced by Curtis Cook with an afterword by Charles Taylor. Montreal & Kingston: McGill-Queen's University Press. (forthcoming).
Canada. 1991. *Shaping Canada's Future Together: Proposals*. Ottawa: Supply and Services Canada.
Corry, J. A. 1978. "The Uses of a Constitution." In *The Constitution and the Future of Canada*, Special Lectures of the Law Society of Upper Canada. Toronto: Richard De Boo.
de Tocqueville, Alexis. 1945. *Democracy in America*, translated and edited by Henry Reeve, rev. Francis Bowen. New York: Vintage Books.
Gagnon, Alain-G., and Daniel Latouche. 1991. *Allaire, Bélanger, Campeau et les autres: les Québécois s'interrogent sur leur avenir*. Montreal: Québec/Amérique.
Hall, Tony. 1991. "Aboriginal Issues and the New Political Map of Canada." In *"English Canada" Speaks Out*, edited by Jack Granatstein and Kenneth McNaught. Toronto: Doubleday Canada.
Hobsbawm, E. J. 1992. *Nations and Nationalism since 1780: Programme, Myth, Reality*. 2d ed. Cambridge: Cambridge University Press.
Kymlicka, Will. 1992. *Recent Work in Citizenship Theory: A Report Prepared for Multiculturalism and Citizenship Canada*. Ottawa: Supply and Services Canada.
Knopff, Rainer, and F. L. Morton. 1992. *Charter Politics*. Scarborough: Nelson Canada.
Laforest, Guy. 1991. "*L'esprit de 1982*." In *Le Québec et la restructuration du Canada 1980-1992: enjeux et perspectives*, edited by Louis Balthazar, Guy Laforest, and Vincent Lemieux. Sillery, PQ: Septentrion.

Laforest, Guy. 1992. "*L'accord d'Ottawa-Charlottetown et la réconciliation des aspirations nationales du Québec.*" In *Référendum, 26 octobre 1992: Les objections de 20 spécialistes aux offres fédérales*, edited by Bariteau, Claude, et al. Montreal: Les Editions Saint-Martin.

Latouche, Daniel. 1992. "*Le partage des pouvoirs: ceux des autochtones, ceux du Québec et ceux qu'on a peut-être oubliés.*" In *Référendum, 26 octobre 1992: Les objections de 20 spécialistes aux offres fédérales*, edited by Bariteau, Claude, et al. Montreal: Les Editions Saint-Martin.

Noël, Alain. n.d. "Deliberating a Constitution: The Meaning of the Canadian Referendum of 1992." In *Canada's Constitutional Predicament after 1992*, edited by Curtis Cook. Montreal & Kingston: McGill-Queen's University Press. (forthcoming).

Oliver, Michael. 1991. "*Laurendeau et Trudeau: leurs opinions sur le Canada.*" In *L'engagement de l'intellectuel: mélanges en l'honneur de Léon Dion*, edited by Raymond Hudon and Réjean Pelletier. Québec: Les Presses de l'Université Laval.

Patterson, Dennis. 1993. "Conscience and the constitution," *Columbia Law Review* 93 (January): 293–307.

Russell, Peter, Rainer Knopff, and F. L. Morton. 1990. *Federalism and the Charter*. Ottawa: Carleton University Press.

Taylor, Charles. 1993. *Reconciling the Solitudes: Essays on Canadian Federalism and Nationalism*, edited by Guy Laforest. Montreal & Kingston: McGill-Queen's University Press.

Trudeau, Pierre Elliott. 1967. *Le fédéralisme et la société canadienne-française*. Montreal: Editions HMH.

Trudeau, Pierre Elliott. 1968. *Federalism and the French Canadians*. Toronto: Macmillan.

Trudeau, Pierre Elliott. 1990. "There Must Be a Sense of Belonging." In *Pierre Trudeau Speaks Out on Meech Lake*, edited by Donald Johnson. Rev. ed. Toronto: General Paperbacks.

Tully, James. n.d. "Diversity's Gambit Declined." In *Canada's Constitutional Predicament After 1992*, edited by Curtis Cook. Montreal and Kingston: McGill-Queen's University Press. (forthcoming).

COMMENTARY

Ethnicity, Language and Nationalism

Mathew Zachariah

Professor Harriet Critchley's paper on the failure of federalism in Yugoslavia is as tragically timely as today's newspaper headlines. She discusses, in detail, the manner in which that the experiences of ethnic groups within the former Yugoslavia during the 1941-45 period placed an indelible black mark on ethnic relations, and that hostile reactions to these experiences were actively suppressed from 1945 by Marshal Tito's government. Negative actions—such as suppression of distasteful views—are unlikely to keep ethnic groups within a federal state together unless a positive normative structure is put in place that enables people to forgive, forget, and unite in building a new national vision. The case of the former Yugoslavia gives social scientists with opportunities to identify the limits and possibilities of promoting interethnic harmony. One of the lessons Professor Critchley mentions is that the use of coercion to suppress ethnic nationalism is bound to fail.

Professor Critchley also mentions that economic disparities between the different republics became more apparent thereby exacerbating ethnic and political conflicts. This, I submit, is close to the heart of whether any federalist structures will survive in the long run. No ideological propaganda to promote a transethnic identity is likely to be effective unless it is supported by a perception of just and fair treatment of all citizens. Such a perception, of course, must be grounded in objectively observable fair treatment of people of different classes and cultural groups.

Professor Joyotpaul Chaudhuri's paper addresses the extreme strains that India's federalism has been undergoing, especially in the past decade. We are all familiar with the secessionist movement in the Punjab, and the serious ethnic and religious problems in other parts of India. What I found most interesting in Professor Chaudhuri's paper is his thesis that participatory government is possible in federal structures if a decentralized system of governance is gradually and carefully put in place. His point that India's highly centrist federalism is unworkable in the wake of regional ethnic, caste, linguistic, and religious assertiveness makes eminent sense. Professor Chaudhuri notes that India can be proud of its considerable achievements in providing civil liberties as compared to a number of other southern hemisphere countries. Yet, its record in protecting human rights can also be subjected to considerable criticism. India is a country, says Professor Chaudhuri, that "cries out for looseknit regional political systems and [genuinely] federalist arrangements." His plea for gradual decentralization is combined with a simultaneous plea for greater attention to procedural due process and civil rights.

During the Constituent Assembly debates leading to the proclamation of India's republican constitution in the late 1940s and in the first year of the 1950s, a deliberate decision was made by the fathers—yes, they were almost all men—of India's constitution to use the expression "the Indian Union" instead of expressions like "the Indian Federation." The reasoning went something like this. Foreign powers were able to conquer India, plunder its riches, destroy its culture, and stunt its growth only when Indians were divided among themselves. Therefore, an ideology of Indian nationalism that would bind all Indians irrespective of caste, creed, and language must be promoted; phrases like "the Indian Union" were meant to help promote such an ideology. A corollary argument was that a strong central government was necessary to ensure India's survival as a national entity. This view has been, and continues to be, dominant in the minds of many persons who shape India's domestic and foreign policies. Any argument, however persuasive on other grounds, to change India's highly centralized structure must take due account of this historical memory of conquest and colonialism.

The data that Professor Chaudhuri mentions in his paper suggest that ordinary people—or the masses, to use an oft-used Indian term—have a pan-Indian vision most of the time. That vision, characterized by a remarkable generosity of spirit, is partly the precious legacy of the great men and women who fought for Indian independence; it was insistently promoted in a number of ways beginning in 1950, when India became a sovereign republic. In national radio and television programmes, documentary films which are required to be shown before every movie feature presentation, in much of the print media, and in postindependence school curricula, the message that, for over 5,000 years, India has developed a unique civilization that is the heritage of all Indians was consistently promoted. It is very unfortunate that the deadly combination of economic and population pressures, exploited by narrow factional interests, appears to be dissipating this pan-Indian vision.

Professor Chaudhuri mentions that the original Jeffersonian formulation recommended a decentralized federalism for the United States. I particularly appreciated his highlighting the fact that American First Nations peoples practised forms of decentralized federalism before the arrival of Europeans, and that Benjamin Franklin, for instance, was aware of it. Some Indian historians have been rediscovering that decentralized governance has always been part of Indian political thought. We can recall that Gandhi's views on relatively self-sufficient Indian village governance structures were, in part, built on this historical insight.

From a comparative international perspective, the stresses and strains of the Canadian confederation are instructive for a number of reasons. Professor Alain-G. Gagnon of McGill University and Professor Guy Laforest of Laval University in their paper brought to us a Québec perspective on the future of federalism. This perspective is very evident, for instance, in their use of the phrases "Québec" and "Canada" as though Québec is already outside Canada.

Gagnon and Laforest, using the distinction between juridical and sociological nations, notes Pierre Elliott Trudeau's recommendation in his 1968 book, *Federalism and the French Canadians*, that the appeal of separatism can be offset by building up federal nationalism with new symbols such as the national flag to create emotional attachments, and the creation or revitalization of federal institutions such as the Canadian Broadcasting Corporation and the National Film Board. This recommendation was put into effect during Trudeau's prime ministership in the 1970s and early 1980s. The Canadian Charter of Rights and Freedoms was the constitutional capstone of this relentless effort to create a Canadian nation. Québec's opposition to the charter created a crack in that capstone even as it was being put in place. The failures of the Meech Lake and Charlottetown accords bode ill for the creation of a renewed, resurgent federalism that can "accommodate asymmetry," to use the authors' phrase. Gagnon and Laforest interpret recent attempts to recognize aboriginal claims to self-government as an attempt "to superimpose a third order of government" in Canada, which would have the effect of further undermining Québec's search for nationhood. This view also further complicates the possibility for the development of a pan-Canadian consensus necessary for a renewed federalism.

The authors give pride of place to the three principles enunciated by James Tully for the creation and maintenance of just relations between ethnic communities in a federal state. They are: (1) the members of a federation should be recognized in terms of their own self-identification in constitutional negotiations; (2) multilateral negotiations leading to constitutional agreements should be fair in terms of the customs of each negotiating party; (3) what touches all must be approved by all. The authors refer to three national communities using, to good effect, a distinction between juridical nationalism and sociological nationalism. They refer to three competing nationalisms in Canada: Québec, aboriginal and Canadian. If Canadian is negatively defined as non-Québec and non-aboriginal, one is left with the question of how one would apply Tully's principles to, say, people of Ukrainian origin who form sizable communities in western Canada. Similarly, we know that the category "aboriginal" includes within it a number of different nations and tribes. How a federal Canada will placate all these distinct societies is a great challenge.

One of the remarkable things about tensions within Canadian federalism—viewed in a comparative international perspective—is the relative absence of violence and the continuance of civil dialogue. How may we account for this? My hypothesis is that, unlike in the former Yugoslavia and in India, economic hardships and disparities have not been permitted to reach the point of poisoning the possibility for continued conversations about cultural survival. Federal equalization programs and payments have probably played a very important role in not exacerbating ethnic and linguistic disagreements in our country.

The future of federalism can be viewed from many angles, but I wish to focus on two perspectives and sketch them rather simplistically here. In one, the preoccupation is one of order and control, which is the concern of those who own or control the commanding heights of the economy and polity. The other is the perspective of those who are owned and controlled, but who are constantly testing the limits of the system to enlarge possibilities to become more human. Oppressor and oppressed, the rulers and the ruled, the bourgeoisie and the proletariat, subjects and objects; these are bipolar distinctions that express the differences of these perspectives. These two perspectives are potentially or actually in conflict at every level. Tensions in federal structures arising from differences in ethnicity, language, religion etc., that express themselves as nationalistic yearnings are, at base and in part, expressions of people who wish not to be objects but subjects in human history. We may tie this idea to the world system perspective which sees the world in terms of centres, semiperipheries, and peripheries, which I cannot discuss in detail. It is worth noting that the problems of federalism are being managed much better in a core country like Canada than in the semiperipheral and peripheral countries of Russia, Yugoslavia, and India. Policies that promote respect for people in the areas of human rights and multiculturalism, policies that encourage participation by broad sections of people in issues of governance are an implicit acknowledgement of the humanity of the governed.

In the world today, there are over 170 sovereign states, within which there are over 5,000 ethnic groups, each with its own linguistic and cultural traditions. Whether federal or unitary states, they have to contend with and satisfy some of the aspirations that professors Gagnon and Laforest have expressed in the final paragraph of their essay. States have to respect and encourage diversity and allow for asymmetry instead of uniformity, if people are to learn to live and let live. It is in this context that current discussions about the creation and maintenance of civil society, of acknowledging democratic yearnings, of developing respectful bargaining cultures take on increasing importance. The concept of federalism continues to hold great potential for accommodating diversity and promoting the very abstract, yet noble, ideal of human community that rises above ethnic, religious, and national divisions.

IV: CONTEMPORARY CHALLENGES TO FEDERALISM

Federalism and the Environment: With Australia as a Case Study

Brian Galligan and Georgina Lynch

Federalism versus New Environmental Politics?

Federalism is a venerable system of government with a long prehistory dating from medieval and ancient times (Davis 1978; Elazar 1987). With a modern history of more than two hundred years, from the drafting and ratification of the United States constitution in 1787, the American model has come to dominate discussions of federalism because of the dominance of the United States in world politics, especially since the Second World War, and the coherency of the American federalist argument which gave federalism a coherent democratic pluralist rationale (Diamond 1961; Wheare [1946] 1963). A somewhat different tradition of European federalism was manifest in Switzerland. When the Australian constitution was drafted in the last decade of the nineteenth century, it incorporated elements from both the American and Swiss models, as well as being influenced by the Canadian hybrid of federalism and parliamentary responsible government. While the modern German constitution was heavily influenced by the American model, it also drew on the long German federal tradition (Von Beyne 1988).

Federalism was overused by European powers in cobbling together incongruous ethnic and tribal amalgamations to cover their belated withdrawals from colonialism in Africa and Asia. Despite its failure in such instances (Franck 1961), however, federalism in one form or another remains the institutional basis of numerous systems of government around the world (Elazar 1987: 43-44). In fact, with the increasing political integration of Western Europe and the breakup of the Soviet Union into independent republics, including the Russian federation and a looser Commonwealth of Independent States, federalism is at the heart of the emerging constitutional order in much of the modern world—so much so that federalism and transnational associations will likely be for the twenty-first century what nation states were for the twentieth century and empire and colonialism for the nineteenth. Variations of this old political institution are being revived in the new constitutional order.

For its part, the environment has emerged as one of the core elements of the new political agenda along with feminism, sustainable economic development, human rights, and peace. The "new politics" is an amalgam of causes and interests not derived from the old left-right ideological divide of industrial society or the regionally based ethnic or national groupings of people. Rather it tends to be postmaterialist and universalist, galvanizing individuals and groups behind international concerns, such as the world's environmental problems. There is heightened awareness that the environmental issues, ranging from species extinction to the degradation of land, seas, and atmosphere which beset our planet, transcend national boundaries.

Because of this internationalist focus of the new politics, it is said by many of its exponents to be at odds with the "old politics" of established parties and institutional arrangements based on geographical entities such as nation states or federal systems, as Roger Gibbins points out:

> Environmentalism has become the social and political issue of the 1990s, one that challenges many of the economic shibboleths of western industrial states. . . . It also potentially challenges many of our political shibboleths, including federalism and national sovereignty. Simply put, environmentalism challenges the territorial organization of political life. (1991: 55)

Gibbins argues that environmentalism tends to corrode political lines on maps, both national and federal, and thereby enhances the national integration of Canada (Québec excepted for special reasons), and its continental integration with the United States. According to this argument, federalism is an institutional arrangement of the old politics and incompatible with the new, of which environmentalism is a notable part.

There is a somewhat different argument about the obsolescence of federalism, which has salience among more traditional opponents of federalism in federal countries like Australia. Federalism, it is said, following Dicey ([1959] 1985), provides weak government, whereas the magnitude and urgency of environmental issues and problems in modern times require strong action by national government. This is reinforced by derivatives of Laski's old argument that federalism was obsolete because it fragmented political power when government needed to be concentrated in order to deal with the nationalization of economic forces (Laski 1939; Greenwood 1976). The increasing internationalization of economic and environmental issues has reinvigorated and extended this critique, with greater national power and centralization of government considered necessary in order to respond to international forces, as well as to impose national standards. In the absence of viable international government, strong sovereign nations are seen as the best hope for dealing with international issues.

Beyond the Sovereign Nation State

Our argument has more resonances with the new politics critique of authors like Gibbins, than the old nationalist view of the modern-day Laskiites. We agree that there is a "growing disjuncture," as Stephen Krasner says, "between the nature of sovereignty in the contemporary world and functional objectives," but these are broader than security and economic ones with which he is concerned (1988: 86). Krasner is right to emphasize the historical persistence of the institutions of the nation state and their shaping of society and individuals for more than a century, but he goes too far in asserting the continuing primacy of the nation state in the face of increasing internationalization, when he claims that

> the sovereign state is the only universally recognized way of organizing political life in the contemporary international system. It is now difficult to even conceive of alternatives. The historical legacy of the development of the state system has left a powerful institutional structure, one that will not be dislodged easily, regardless of changed circumstances in the material environment. (1988: 90)

On the contrary, it is no longer difficult to conceive of alternatives, especially in Europe where Community membership and laws are eroding national sovereignty. But, as well, in smaller countries like Australia, national policy is being increasingly internationalized with the deregulation of financial and currency markets, the dismantlement of tariff protection, and the adoption of international law standards concerning human rights and indigenous peoples (Capling and Galligan 1992; Kelly 1992). A notable example was the high court's 1991 Mabo decision which reversed two hundred years of common-law doctrine in ruling that Australia was not *terra nullius*, but that the land had been legitimately owned by aboriginal people. According to Justice Brennan's leading opinion in that case, international law is a legitimate and important influence on the development of the common law, especially when international law declares the existence of universal human rights. A common law doctrine founded on unjust discrimination in the enjoyment of civil and political rights demands reconsideration.

(Mabo v. Queensland 1992: 30)

Internationalization is eroding the sovereignty of the nation-state to such an extent that appealing to its consolidation and strengthening, as the neo-Laskiites do, as a way of coping is obsolete. Erosion of the sovereign nation-state does not necessarily entail a similar threat to federalism, but can be seen as congenial with it. That is, providing federalism is understood not in terms of an association of discrete geographical entities defined by regional lines on a map, as referred to by Gibbins, but as a system of diffuse power centres, divided sovereignty, multiple citizenship, and overlapping jurisdictions. In all of these aspects, federalism is highly compatible with the emerging new order of transnational associations and international centres of policy making and rule setting which overlap, intrude upon, and constrain the sovereign nation-state.

The point can be made by reference to the Europe of the future, which will more closely resemble a quasifederation of member states with limited sovereignty. In a recent exposition of Britain's actual move "Beyond the Sovereign State," through closer political and legal ties with the European Community, Neil MacCormick poses the challenges to be faced in adapting to the new order:

Can we think of a world in which our normative existence and our practical life are anchored in, or related to, a variety of institutional systems, each of which has validity or operation in relation to some range of concerns, none of which is absolute over all the others, and all of which, for most purposes, can operate without serious mutual conflict in areas of overlap? If this is as possible practically as it clearly is conceptually, it would involve a diffusion of political power centres as well as of legal authorities. It would depend on a high degree of relatively willing co-operation and a relatively low degree of coercion in its direct and naked forms. (1993: 17)

These might be daring propositions for the British who, MacCormick points out, are still locked into obsolete ideas and prejudices of national and parliamentary sovereignty, which no longer reflect Britain's growing entanglement in Europe, but they are highly compatible with the political culture of federalism. A diffusion of power centres and a variety of institutional systems—each of which has jurisdiction over some range of concerns, but none of which is absolute over all the others—are characteristics of federalism. Moreover, cooperation and accommodation rather than coercion are also operational requirements for an effective federal system.

To sum up, our argument is that a system of diffuse power centres is broadly compatible with the new politics of the environment. The sovereign state and national sovereignty are being eroded through international forces and transnational associations of a political kind, as with the European Community, or standard-setting kind, as for Australia. Erosion of the nation-state and its associated monosovereign jurisprudence is not necessarily incompatible with federalism and may even enhance it by reducing some of the pressures towards the dominance of national government at the expense of the states, which has been a definite trend in postwar decades in countries like the United States and Australia. In other words, federal nations may be more compatible with increasing internationalization, including with respect to environmentalism, than are unitary states with overblown traditions of national sovereignty such as the United Kingdom. But this requires a theory of federalism as more than the lines on maps or associations of distinct geographic territories.

Federalism as Diffusion of Sovereignty and Jurisdictional Concurrency

The theory of federalism which we draw upon is not the juridical one which sees federalism as essentially a system of separate governments with distinct domains. This can be either in the form of the geographic metaphor with the emphasis on precise boundaries, or lines on maps, as invoked by Gibbins above. More significantly, it can be in the form of the coordinate model of federalism, which views national and subnational governments as having separate and discrete spheres of jurisdiction. This has been the dominant model of federalism in the Anglo tradition from Bryce to Wheare. Rather, we see federalism as primarily a system of derived, divided, and diffuse sovereignty: derived from the constituent people who retain sovereignty in the prime republican sense, divided vertically between national and subnational governments as specified in a controlling constitution, and diffuse among a multiplicity of subnational governments as well as between the national and subnational governments. In addition to diffused sovereignty, policy roles and responsibilities are not separate and distinct spheres as the coordinate model would have it, but intermingled and concurrent.

Two key misconceptions about the way federalism works, or ought to work, are associated with the notion of federalism as separate and distinct spheres of government. One is that the division of powers between governments is coordinate rather than concurrent. The other is that the structure is hierarchical with the national government at the top of the pyramid and subnational governments at the base, or that the national government is at the centre and the subnational governments on the periphery. Both these misconceptions have major implications for the way we think about federalism that are relevant to considerations about its suitability for dealing with the new politics of the environment.

Coordinate means that powers are allocated between the Commonwealth and states so that each has separate and distinct policy responsibilities. Concurrent, in contrast, means that policy jurisdictions are shared by both governments. The two basic paradigms have quite different diagnostic and prescriptive consequences. If coordinacy is the standard, then it follows that there should be a crisp divide, with particular policy responsibilities being allocated to one or the other level of government. Accordingly, where, in practice, there is much shared responsibility, the proffered solution is to sort out and reallocate roles and responsibilities. The coordinate paradigm is highly congruent with judicial adjudication of jurisdictional disputes, because courts make either/or decisions.

The coordinate view has strong support from classic writers on federalism such as Bryce and Wheare, who have been dominant influences in the Anglo tradition. In explaining American federalism to his English, Australian, and Canadian readers, Bryce likens it to a great factory where two sets of machinery were at work with their moving parts crisscrossing but never touching or hampering one another. In one telling passage, he combines presumptions of coordinacy with those of central hierarchy: the aim of those who drafted the American constitution, Bryce claims, "was to keep the two mechanisms as distinct and independent of each other as was compatible with the still higher need of subordinating, for national purposes, the State to the Central government" (vol. 1, 1888: 425). Wheare, on the other hand, links coordinacy with independency:

> The federal principle requires that the general and regional governments of a country shall be independent each of the other within its

sphere, shall be not subordinate one to another but co-ordinate with each other. ([1946] 1963: 93)

Wheare was sufficiently realistic to acknowledge concurrency as a practical feature of all modern federal governments, but did so by coupling it with the principle of paramountcy: in the case of conflict, there had to one level of government, typically the central one, with authority to decide the case ([1946] 1963: 75).

A second pervasive, but incorrect assumption about federalism is that it sets up a hierarchical structure in which the central government is at the apex and provincial or state governments make up an inferior base. The hierarchical model of federalism provided a congenial structure for those who preferred or presumed an inevitable centralization of power: the one reinforced the other and there was enough evidence from the pattern of intergovernmental relations in the postwar decades to support a half-plausible case.

The hierarchical model of federalism has been criticized on both theoretical and practical grounds by American scholars such as Grodzins (1966) and Elazar (1984, 1987). In his famous 'marble cake' analogy, Grodzins emphasized that government functions became confused and activities of participating agencies so complex that there tended to be a mixing and blending rather than a discrete interaction between separate jurisdictional entities. Intergovernmental relations were essentially messy, with governments and parts of governments often competing for a share of the action.

The theoretical construct for such a nonhierarchical policy process was further articulated by Elazar with his notion of a policy-matrix in which no government has a monopoly or complete authority (1987: 33–34). As Christine Fletcher points out, Elazar's matrix highlights two main points concerning public policy making and intergovernmental relations: the first is that authority is "non-centralized," as is appropriate to a system with no dominant central authority or apex, and the second point is the "mercurial quality" of public policy making in a federal system (1991:85). This is supported by Elazar's conceptual paradigm, that, "in a matrix, there are no higher or lower power centres, only larger or smaller arenas of political decision-making and action" (1984: 15). Nor can federalism be understood as a centre-periphery model with the national government somehow at the centre of things, as Elazar points out:

> The matrix model of federalism is policentric by design. The essence of the federal matrix is conveyed both in the original meaning of the term—a womb that frames and embraces in contrast with a single focal point, or centre, that concentrates—and in its contemporary meaning—a communications network that establishes the linkages that create the whole. (1987: 13)

In this view, federalism is a system of complex and diffuse power centres with an intermingling and overlapping of jurisdictional responsibilities and policy activity.

The Suitability of Federalism

So far we have argued that federalism, being a matrix of diffuse power centres, or multiple governments, with concurrent responsibilities and powers, is broadly compatible with the emerging international order in which transnational relations and associations are becoming more significant and sovereign nationhood less so. But more precise assessment of the institutional suitability of federalism for dealing with the environment is required. In fact, because the environment is so significant it can serve as a test case for thinking through the suitability of federalism for modern governance in new politics areas.

At the same time, we need to keep in mind some general considerations about the character and functioning of institutions. One is that institutions are designed for political and policy processes rather than for particular outcomes. Hence, criteria for assessing institutional suitability need to be in terms of capacities rather than outcomes. Another is that an institutional system has to handle a diverse range of policy issues and respond to a variety of interests, as well as to changing agendas. Flexibility is thus essential. Furthermore, institutions depend on human agents to staff and operate them, and, more broadly, on the political culture of the polity in which they are immersed. As well, historically rooted, established systems tend to perpetuate themselves over time, shaping, at least in part, the actors who operate them and the larger political community in which they are embedded, as emphasized by institutionalists like Krasner cited earlier. This means that established institutions cannot be easily changed. Finally, institutions have to be workable and practically robust, which is a further reason why there is a certain prudence in sticking as far as possible with what has worked in the past, provided it can handle new issues.

Keeping such considerations about institutional design in mind, it is appropriate to test the suitability of federalism on three grounds: one, its congruence with increased internationalization of which the environment is a prime policy instance; two, its fit with democratic aspirations; and three, its ability to address the dimensions of the particular policy area in an appropriate way.

On the first issue, we have already argued that federalism is not incompatible with internationalization. While it is true that internationalization is eroding the sovereignty of the nation-state, federalism is already premised on the denial of national sovereignty in favour of divided sovereignty and diffuse power arrangements. This does not establish that federalism is appropriate for dealing with internationalized environmental issues: only that federalism is broadly compatible with the postsovereign nation era, because it entails a diffuse system of multiple governments none of which are sovereign.

The second issue has to do with the political aspirations and preferences of citizens to which the institutional system must be responsive. The strong preference of green ideology is for enhanced local participation, as encapsulated in the slogan "Think globally and act locally." Decentralization is the "truly distinctive feature" of green politics, with a preference for loose networks of small local activist groups (Goodin 1992: 147). In fact, the institutional preference of green purists borders on the anarchic extreme of decentralization with an unrealistic lack of plausible coordinating institutions (151). A federal system is far removed from what these green purists might prefer, but at least it goes part of the way towards the decentralization of decision making. The enhancement of democratic participation through multiplying governments and decentralizing large parts of policy making is a key legitimating feature of federalism, especially in countries like Australia where there are no regionally based ethnic divisions (Galligan 1989; Gerritsen 1990).

The third issue is concerned with institutional capacity to address the complexity of environmental management. If a policy area were unidimensional and geographically defined, then it might be properly dealt with by a single government with appropriate powers over the relevant areas. But, if it is multidimensional—like the environment—with international, national, and regional aspects then clearly a multilevel system of government is more appropriate. Our contention is that federalism within a country plus international arrangements with other countries to address global issues can provide an institutional basis for dealing with environmental issues. In the rest of the paper, we show how increased internationalization is affecting Australian environmental policy and how Australia's federal system is being made to cope with the new environmentalism.

Internationalization of Australia's Environmental Agenda

The Australian constitution, under the Commonwealth or national government, has responsibility for negotiating and concluding international treaties, agreements, and conventions which are binding under international law by virtue of the section 51(29) external affairs power. As the number of international agreements dealing with the preservation of the world cultural and natural heritage sites increases, the utilization of section 51(29) has widened the Commonwealth's base of authority in addressing issues regarding the environment and its management. Increasingly, Australia's environmental protection agenda is influenced by international forums.

For instance, the United Nations General Assembly Resolutions 44/228, authorizing the United Nation Conference on Environment and Development, held in Brazil in July 1992, was embraced in full by Australia through the acceptance of Agenda 21, which deals extensively with actions that governments and international organizations, and industry, and the community can take to ensure lasting changes in human economic developments. While something of a wish list of good intentions, adoption of this United Nations agenda indicates the source and intention of Australia's environmental policy thinking. Furthermore, implementation of these objectives independently of the global community would be ineffectual in many instances so that the realization of such environmental conservation goals requires collective action by nations.

If Australia is to do its part in implementing this agenda and live up to its hefty obligations under the increasing number of international agreements it has ratified, it must be able to deliver on such agreements by implementing consistent national standards. In instances such as the transportation of hazardous waste, marine pollution, protection of the ozone layer and the atmosphere, separate state and Commonwealth strategies would be inadequate. Australia's experience as a federal country in becoming an active player in the global protection game is subsequently examined, but first we show how extensive the internationalization of its domestic environment policy has been. This international commitment has been manifest in a number of ways: institutional, educational, legal, and financial, with instruments ranging from agreements, conventions, and protocols to regulating international rights, obligations, and duties (Elser 1989: 221).

An important instance was the Labor government's full endorsement of the concept of ecologically sustainable development (ESD) put forward by the Bruntland Report (World Commission on Environment and Development 1987). In July 1989, the then Prime Minister, R. J. Hawke, announced immodestly, in what he called the "world's greatest environment statement," the establishment of an interdepartmental committee to prepare a paper on sustainable development (Hawke 1989). This was done, and, after endorsement by cabinet, nine working groups were set up to consider ESD in sectors of the Australian economy where competing uses of natural resources has created conflict (Commonwealth of Australia 1990; Harris 1991). In November 1991, the working groups presented their findings to cabinet, and these have been translated into various policy statements. While implementation has only begun and enormous difficulties remain, at least a start has been made in reorienting national policy making toward sustainable development goals.

Perhaps more concretely, Australia's commitment to international environmental standards can be found in legal instruments, such as the forty-three treaties and conventions relating to the environment which Australia has signed, ratified, or acceded to (see table 1). The most recent example is Australia's ratification of the biodiversity convention in June 1993. The then minister for the environment, Ros Kelly, claimed that "Australia has a special role to play in protecting our biodiversity as we are one of approximately 12 countries containing almost 70% of the world's species" (*Canberra Times* 21 June 1993). Australia is a contracting state to the Vienna Convention on the Law of Treaties, and the processes and procedures practiced by Australia in implementing treaties accord with the terms of this convention (Vienna Convention 1969).

The volume of multilateral and bilateral treaties to which Australia is a party reflects the ecological linkages between global ecosystems and domestic environmental problems, but raises problems of implementation because of the fragmented division of powers within the constitution. An initial phase of Commonwealth–state confrontation and court adjudication began to be replaced in the 1980s with more cooperative intergovernmental arrangements. These two phases are documented subsequently, but, first, we sketch the Australian constitutional division of powers which was tested by the new environmentalism.

Table 1. Conventions, Treaties, and Protocols.

General Environment
- Antarctic Treaty (signed by Australia 23.6.61)
- Convention Concerning the Protection of the World Cultural and Natural Heritage (17.12.75)
- Convention on the Conservation of Nature in the South Pacific (28.3.90)
- Convention on the Prohibition of Military or Any Other Hostile Use of Environmental Modification Techniques (7.9.84)
- Convention for the Protection of the Natural Resources and Environment of the South Pacific (18.9.90)
- South Pacific Nuclear Free Zone Treaty (12.12.86)

Coast/Marine Resources
- Indo-Pacific Fishery Commission Convention
- International Convention for the Regulation of Whaling (Amendment to the International Whaling Convention) (10.11.48)
- Convention on the Inter-Governmental Maritime Consultative Organization (17.10.74)
- South Pacific Form Fisheries Agencies Convention (12.10.79)
- Convention on Fishing and Conservation of the Living Resources of the High Seas (20.3.66)
- United Nations Convention of the Law of the Sea (10.12.82)
- Treaty on Fisheries Between the Governments of Certain Pacific Island States and the Government of the United States of America (2.4.87)
- Convention for the Prohibition of Fishing with Long Driftnets in the South Pacific (24.11.89)
- Convention on the Continental Shelf of Australia (10.6.64)

Toxic and Hazardous Wastes
- Protocol Relating to Intervention on the High Seas in Cases of Marine Pollution by Substances Other than Oil (5.2.84)
- South Pacific Nuclear Free Zone Treaty (12.12.86)
- Convention on Assistance in the Case of a Nuclear Accident or Radiological Emergency (23.10.87)
- Convention on Early Notification of a Nuclear Accident (23.10.87)
- Treaty Banning Nuclear Weapons Testing in the Atmosphere, in Outer Space and Under Water (12.11.63)
- Treaty on the Prohibition of the Emplacement of Nuclear Weapons and Other Weapons of Mass Destruction on the Seabed and the Ocean Floor and in the Subsoil Thereof (23.1.73)

Table 1. Conventions, Treaties, and Protocols. . . cont'd

- Convention on the Prohibition of the Development, Production and Stockpiling of bacteriological (Biological) and Toxin Weapons and Their Destruction (5.10.77)
- Protocol of 1978 Relating to the International Convention for the Prevention of Pollution from Ships (14.1.88)
- Amendment to the International Convention on the High Seas in Cases of Oil Pollution Casualties (5.2.84)
- International Convention on Civil Liability for Oil Pollution Damage (5.2.84)
- Convention on the Prevention of Marine Pollution by Dumping of Wastes and Other Matter (London Dumping Convention) (29.9.85)
- Protocol for the Prevention of Pollution of the South Pacific Region by Dumping (18.9.90)
- Protocol Concerning Co-operation in Combating Pollution Emergencies in the South Pacific Region (18.9.90)
- Convention on the Physical Protection of Nuclear Material (22.10.87)

Biological Diversity
- Convention on Wetlands of International Importance (RAMSAR) (12.12.75)
- Convention on International Trade in Endangered Species of Wild Fauna and Flora (CITES) (27.10.76)
- International Plant Protection Convention (27.8.52)
- Convention for the Conservation of Antarctic Seals (31.7.87)
- Plant Protection Agreement for the South-East Asia and Pacific Region (2.7.56)
- Convention on the Conservation of Antarctic Marine Living Resources (7.4.82)
- Japan-Australia Migratory Birds Agreement (1974)
- China-Australia Migratory Birds Agreement (1986)
- Convention on the Conservation of Migratory Species of Wild Animals (Bonn Convention) (1991) (22.10.87)

Air Quality
- Vienna Convention for the Protection of the Ozone Layer (17.8.89)
- Montreal Protocol on Substances that Deplete the Ozone Layer (22.9.90)

Biotechnology
- International Convention for the Protection of New Varieties of Plants (3.89)
- International Tropical Timber Agreement (16.2.88)

Constitutional Powers

The impact of such internationalization of environmental policy on domestic arrangements has been profound, with the national government claiming a larger role and this leading to bitter jurisdictional disputes with the states. By virtue of the section 51(29) external affairs power in the Australian constitution, the Commonwealth government has responsibility for negotiating and entering into international agreements affecting the environment. However, the Commonwealth government lacks direct plenary powers over the environment with the states having substantial jurisdictional claims in the area of resource management, as Bruce Davis points out:

> natural resources, utilization, land-use planning and nature conservation programs are all the prerogatives of the States, with the Federal role limited to suasion for common standards, research assistance of the provision of funds for some resource conservation activities. In addition, the Commonwealth jurisdiction includes federal sites and buildings within states and all Federal territories, including some off-shore islands and Antarctica. (1985: 2)

But, the Commonwealth does have a number of other constitutional powers which give it considerable influence over environmental policies of the states (Zines 1985). The section 51(1) trade and commerce power has been used to prohibit the export of minerals without the approval of the federal minister (*Murphyores* v. *The Commonwealth* 1976), and confers plenary authority on the Commonwealth to prohibit imports (Zines 1985). Under the section 51(20) corporations power, as the Tasmanian Dam case (*Commonwealth* v. *Tasmania* 1983) made clear, the Commonwealth may control, having regard to environmental considerations, all manufacturing, production, or extractive processes conducted by corporations for the purpose of trade. Most significant of all for our purposes, the Commonwealth's external affairs power, section 51(29), has been interpreted broadly to give the national government jurisdiction over international matters to which Australia is a party. As Mason CJ comments: "Entry of a property in the World Heritage List supported by the protection given by the Act, constitutes perhaps the strongest means of environment protection recognized by Australian Law" (*Queensland* v. *Commonwealth* 1988, 291, 296). Another Commonwealth avenue is the section 51(26) power to make laws with respect to the people of any race for whom it is deemed necessary to make special laws, which enables the Commonwealth to conserve a site which is of particular significance to people of aboriginal race. As well, the Commonwealth has extensive influence via fiscal provisions: section 96, which allows policy terms and conditions to be specified for grants to the states, and the spending power, sections 81 to 83, which enables expenditure for the purposes of the Commonwealth (Fowler 1991: 23). Finally, it should be noted that in instances where a Commonwealth and state law are inconsistent, by virtue of section 109 of the Constitution, the Commonwealth law prevails to the extent of that inconsistency. In sum, the practical reality in Australia is that the constitutional framework gives the states extensive jurisdictional powers over land-use management, but the Commonwealth still holds "most of the trumps" (Galligan and Lynch 1992).

Jurisdictional Battles

If the Commonwealth's environmental powers are extensive, they are by no means clear cut. With no specific environmental power as such, the area is a jurisdictional mine field. In this earlier phase, as the Commonwealth was increasingly drawn into environmental policy making, major controversies erupted as to the respective powers of the Commonwealth and state governments. In cases such as the extraction of mineral sands from Fraser Island (*Murphyores* v. *Commonwealth* 1976), the dam dispute in South West Tasmania (*Franklin Dam* case 1983), the pulp mill proposal in Wesley Vale Tasmania, the Lemonthyne and Southern forests inquiry in Tasmania (*Richardson* v. *Tasmanian Forestry Commission* 1988), the destruction of rainforests in Queensland and New South Wales, bauxite mining in the Jarrah Forests of Western Australia, and uranium mining in the Northern Territory, major public disputes arose which led to court battles and bitter political stand-offs between the two tiers of government (Galligan and Lynch 1992).

Such confrontation and judicial resolution were clearly less than ideal, and did little to clarify the precise legislative framework for environmental policy making and management. In the final analysis, the result of this either/or, develop or not develop approach was a tense, arms-length relationship between the states and the Commonwealth government. The order of the day was uncertainty, controversy, and suspicion with little likelihood of the state and Commonwealth governments cooperating to develop mutually conducive national standards for environmental protection. The absence of a systematic methodology and intergovernmental structures for dealing with environment and development disputes was costing the business community investor confidence, environmental groups peace of mind, and the state and federal governments votes. In terms of Australia's standing in the global community, state governments could seriously jeopardize the nation's capacity to enter into, and live up to, obligations under international treaties or conventions. Litigation before the high court was a most unsatisfactory way of proceeding, and some alternative means of achieving intergovernmental agreement had to be found. This earlier phase seemed to support the contention that federalism was not an appropriate structure for dealing with the new environmentalism.

New Intergovernmental Initiatives

Where constitutional jurisdiction is so divided between semisovereign governments, the appropriate way forward is not litigation, but working out cooperative arrangements and devising institutions and procedures which are effective and appropriate for a concurrent system of federal jurisdiction. Realization of this led to more enlightened attempts at intergovernmental coordination and the creation of new institutional arrangements for dealing with the environment in the late 1980s and early 1990s. The emerging pattern is one of increased Commonwealth government presence and leadership in environmental policy, but in conjunction with cooperative arrangements with the states (Bonyhady 1923; Barrie 1992). The assertion of leadership by the Commonwealth government in environmental matters quickened in the 1980s.

An earlier prototype of cooperative intergovernmental arrangements replacing jurisdictional squabbles was the Offshore Constitutional Settlement (OCS) introduced to offset the conflict which developed in the mid-1970s between the Commonwealth and the states as to their respective rights over offshore coastal jurisdiction. In 1973, the high court upheld the validity of the Commonwealth Seas and Submerged Lands Act 1973, which declared that the Commonwealth held jurisdiction offshore from the low water mark (Haward 1991). Prior to this decision, the states had assumed jurisdiction over the three-mile territorial seas and had managed the coastline accordingly. In July 1979, the Commonwealth and the six states and territories settled on a mechanism to improve the intergovernmental coordination of an Australian coastal policy. This mechanism came to be known as the OCS, which is embodied in two primary acts: the *Coastal Waters (State and Territory Powers) Act* 1980 and the *Coastal Waters (State and Northern Territory Title) Act* 1980.

The practical significance of the OCS is that each state the Northern Territory gained title to the seabed of the adjacent three-mile territorial sea. Moreover, by virtue of the *State Powers Act* (1980), a state can legislate with respect to activities beyond its territory if it can be shown that such laws are for the "peace, order and good government" of the state. The ultimate result is that a divided territorial sea has been created in which states have jurisdiction from the baseline to three miles and the Commonwealth has jurisdiction beyond. The *State Titles Act* (1983) effectively vests in the states the same rights and title to the property in the seabed and subsoil beneath these waters as the state has in its internal waters.

In the area of environmental policy, there has been a comparable transition from jurisdictional disputes between the Commonwealth and states to new institutional arrangements for working out more cooperative resolutions. An initiative designed to balance the green debate and instil a cooperative sentiment between the two tiers of government, was the establishment of the Resource Assessment Commission (RAC), in July 1989. Its role, according to its chairperson, Justice D. G. Stewart, was "to bring about a new level of rigour and sophistication to the Government's decision-making process related to resource use issues" (RAC 1991). The commission was charged with balancing competing interests between conservation and development after assessing the environmental, economic, industry, cultural, and social implications of major natural resources proposals. Although the RAC was a Commonwealth body, its act provided that state governments as well as interested parties be consulted. While the consultation process was not specified, the statutory requirement for cooperating with the states on important resource management issues was a significant statutory embodiment of cooperative federalism. Unfortunately, the RAC failed to win bipartisan political support or acceptance by powerful bureaucratic departments, and is being wound up at the conclusion of its current reference on the coastal zones.

More significant was the 1990–91 Special Premiers' Conference process, known as Hawke's "New Federalism," directed at practically improving intergovernmental arrangements through cooperation between the Commonwealth and the state governments on a range of issues (Fletcher and Walsh 1992). These included microeconomic reform, especially making the large public utilities and infrastructure like electricity, water, railways, and road systems more efficient, and devising national standards for areas like food packaging and heavy road transport (Galligan and Fletcher 1992).

The environment was also a key area singled out for attention. Prime Minister Hawke made a special plea to the states for cooperation: "the environment must increasingly become an area in which common ground and common purpose come to replace controversy and confrontation" (1990: 8–9). Policy areas included standardized national regulations for air and water quality, the Landcare program, management of the Great Barrier Reef Marine Park, and the Tasmanian World Heritage Area. In some of the areas, the states and the Commonwealth had already developed cooperative arrangements. Involvement of the states was necessary to implement the Commonwealth's more ambitious policy of ecologically sustainable development. Here, as in other areas, Hawke proposed that the best way forward was through working together on "commonly agreed environmental processes and guidelines" (1990: 8–9).

In the environmental area, there was considerable progress with an Intergovernmental Agreement on the Environment (IGAE), jointly worked up by teams of Commonwealth and state officials and signed in May 1992 (Galligan and Fletcher 1993). This was heralded by the minister for the environment, Ros Kelly, as initiating "a new chapter in relations between the Commonwealth and the States and Territories" (Kelly 1991).

The IGAE evidenced the commitment of the Commonwealth and state and territory governments to work cooperatively towards improving intergovernmental management of the environment. It set out broad statements regarding the responsibilities and interests of all three levels of government—national, state, and local—in the environment and a set of general principles to guide environmental policy. It also included nine schedules detailing the agreements on more specific areas: data collection and handling, resource assessment, land use and approval procedures, environment impact assessment, national environment protection measures, climate change, biological diversity, and the national estate (IGAE 1992).

The proposed structure of intergovernmental machinery for national environment protection is broadly similar to that in other New Federalism areas with a ministerial council, the National Environment Protection Council (NEPC), as the peak intergovernmental body. After final agreement at the meeting of the Council of Australian Governments in February 1994, NEPC is in the process of being formed and will be supported by both Commonwealth and state legislation. NEPC is to be constituted by a minister nominated by each government, with the Commonwealth minister likely to be the chair, and decisions made by a two-thirds majority of members. This ministerial council will be served by a staff of executive officers, probably on secondment from the Commonwealth and State Government Protection Agencies. While a major step forward in cooperative federalism, the IGAE and its associated ministerial council is as yet unfinished.

Noteworthy for our purposes was the recognition by Commonwealth and state governments that "environmental concerns and impacts respect neither physical nor jurisdictional boundaries and are increasingly taking on inter-jurisdictional, international and global significance in a way that was not contemplated by those who framed the Australian Constitution" (IGAE 1991: 2). This is evident in the designated role of the NEPC, which is to make national environment protection measures in areas of national significance which do not fall within discrete federal-state jurisdictional boundaries. They include ambient air quality; ambient marine, estuarine, and freshwater quality; general guidelines for the assessment of site contamination; environmental impacts associated with hazardous wastes; motor vehicle emissions; and the reuse and recycling of used materials.

The IGAE included acknowledgement by the states of the Commonwealth's responsibility for entering into international agreements concerning the environment. For its part, the Commonwealth is required to consult with the states before negotiating and ratifying any international treaty. The IGAE establishes a standing committee of both senior Commonwealth and state/territory officers to provide timely and coordinated assistance to the Commonwealth on the negotiation and implementation of international treaties. The consultation process requires the standing committee to

> identify treaty and other international negotiations of particular sensitivity or importance to states, and propose an appropriate mechanism for state involvement in the negotiation process; . . . monitor and report on the implementation of particular treaties where the implementation of the treaty has strategic implications, including significant cross-portfolio interests, for states; . . . co-ordinate as required the process for nominating state representation on delegations where such representation is appropriate. (RAC 1992)

One the basis of the new consultative process with the states, the Commonwealth has removed the need for federal clauses in international agreements. Previously, federal clauses were required to avoid the obligation of ensuring the implementation of national treaty standards consistently across the nation. The practical effect of a federal clause is that it can be used by the Commonwealth government as a mechanism to avoid the obligation of ensuring that all states comply with the mandatory provisions of a treaty. Federal clauses are now generally seen by the international community as avenues for federal states to avoid their full obligations as parties to a treaty. A residual proviso remains for treaties where it is clearly intended that the states will play a decisive role in implementation. For these, a "federal statement" may be included, provided this does not compromise Australia's obligations.

A further Commonwealth initiative is the establishment of its own special agency, the Commonwealth Environment Protection Agency (CEPA), in the Commonwealth department with responsibility for the environment. The federal government's purpose in establishing CEPA is to determine the Commonwealth's role in environmental protection and formulate national environmental policy. It was clear that the *ad hoc* approach which had previously characterized government decision making in resource management issues was ineffective and encouraged inertia in environmental management. CEPA's powers and functions are couched in terms of supervisory and enforcement provisions in existing Commonwealth legislation. Its tasks are to carry out research, develop and maintain indicators on the condition of the environment, monitor capability and performance, report on the state of the environment, and publicize environment protection issues (DASETT 1991: 11). This special Commonwealth environmental body will contribute submissions to the intergovernmental ministerial committee (CEPA).

Conclusion

These recent institutional innovations—the Resource Assessment Commission, the Intergovernmental Agreement on the Environment with its new National Environment Protection Council, and the Commonwealth Environmental Protection Agency—are indicative of Australia's emerging environmental management regime. Such institutional initiatives have a discernible tripartite pattern; internationalization of the environmental agenda and standards; increased national government presence and leadership in domestic policy making; yet cooperative intergovernmental arrangements to ensure state participation in national policy making and, more especially, its implementation. While individual institutions are at an early state and the Resource Assessment Commission is to be closed down, the emerging pattern is one of a stronger Commonwealth role in environmental policy making and monitoring, and more coherent and harmonious arrangements with appropriate state participation. The earlier Australian phase of confrontation between the Commonwealth and the states, *ad hoc* Commonwealth initiatives, and uncoordinated action among the various states is being replaced with more cooperative intergovernmental arrangements.

The Australian case study presented in the second half of the paper shows how an established federal system can handle modern environmental policy making. The pattern of responses demonstrates that the federal system can cope reasonably well in implementing international standards through appropriate intergovernmental arrangements. So much so that Australia is no longer relying upon federal clauses in becoming a party to international agreements. This is because the process of intergovernmental negotiation and implementation is sufficient to ensure prior consensus of the Commonwealth and state governments and subsequent joint implementation.

The internationalization of environmental policy making has shifted standard setting and rule making from the nation-state to international bodies. It is commonly observed that this process *ipso facto* diminishes the sovereignty of the nation-state. But, as argued in the first part of the paper, the concept of sovereignty does not sit well with federalism. That is because federalism entails two spheres of government, neither of which is sovereign, with powers divided between and among them. Therefore, adding an additional tier of policy making and rule setting is not uncongenial to such an already diffuse system.

In addition to the greater role for international bodies, the enormous expansion of the environmental policy field in recent years has increased the role of national and state governments within federal nations. Providing there are adequate institutional arrangements for ensuring cooperative action by national and state governments, there is no reason why federalism and environmental policy cannot be compatible.

References

Note: This paper draws heavily in parts from a consultancy report *New Federalism, Intergovernmental Relations and Environment Policy*, by Brian Galligan and Christine Fletcher (1993) commissioned by the Resource Assessment Commission, Coastal Zone Inquiry.

Barrie, D. 1992. *Environmental Protection in Federal States. Interjurisdictional Cooperation in Canada and Australia.* Discussion Paper No. 18, Federalism Research Centre, ANU, Canberra.

Bonyhady, T. 1992. *Environmental Protection and Legal Change.* New South Wales: The Federation Press.

Bryce, James. 1888. *The American Commonwealth*, Vols. 1–3. London: Macmillan.
Capling, A. and B. Galligan. 1992. *Beyond the Protective State.* Sydney: Cambridge University Pres.
Commonwealth of Australia. 1990. *Ecologically Sustainable Development.* Canberra: AGPS.
Commonwealth v. Tasmania. 1983. 158 CLR 1.
Department of Arts, Sport the Environment Tourism and Territories (DASETT). 1991. "Australian National Report to the United Nations Conference on Environment and Development." Paper prepared on behalf of the Australian Government (December).
Davis, Bruce W. 1985. "Federalism and Environmental Politics : An Australian Overview." In *Federalism and the Environment*, edited by R. L. Mathews. Centre for Research on Federal Financial Relations, ANU, Canberra.
Davis, S. Rufus. 1978. *The Federal Principle: A Journey Through Time in Quest of a Meaning.* Berkeley: University of California Press.
Diamond, Martin. 1961. "The Federalist's View of Federalism," in *Essays in Federalism*, edited by G. S. C. Benson, M. Diamond, et al. Claremont Men's College, Institute for Studies in Federalism.
Dicey, A. V. [1959] 1985. *Introduction to the Study of the Law of the Constitution.* London: Macmillan.
Elazar, Daniel J. 1984. *American Federalism: A View from the States.* 3d ed., New York: Harper & Row.
Elazar, Daniel J. 1987. *Exploring Federalism.* Tuscaloosa: University of Alabama Press.
Elser, P. (ed.) 1989. *The Conservation of Threatened Species and Their Habitat.* Canberra: Australian Committee for IUCN.
Fletcher, Christine. 1991. "Rediscovering Australian Federalism by Resurrecting Old Ideas," *Australian Journal of Political Science* 26: 79–94.
Fletcher, Christine, and Cliff Walsh. 1992. "Reform of Intergovernmental Relations in Australia: The Politics of Federalism and the Non-Politics of Managerialism," *Public Administration* 70 (Winter): 591–616.
Fowler, R. 1991. "Proposal for a Federal Environment Protection Agency." A report prepared for the Australian Conservation Foundation and Greenpeace Australia Ltd. January.
Franck, Thomas (ed.) 1961. *Why Federations Fail: An Inquiry into the Requisites for a Successful Federation.* New York: New York University Press.
Franklin Dam Case. 1983. 46 ALR 625.
Galligan, Brian. 1989. "Federal Theory and Australian Federalism: A Political Science Perspective." In *Australian Federalism*, edited by Brian Galligan. Melbourne: Longman Cheshire.
Galligan, Brian, and Christine Fletcher. 1992. (eds.) *Australian Journal of Political Science* 27, Special Issue, "Australian Federalism: Rethinking and Restructuring."
Galligan, Brian, and Christine Fletcher. 1993. *New Federalism, Intergovernmental Relations and Environment Policy.* Consultancy report commissioned by the Resource Assessment Commission, Coastal Zone Inquiry, Canberra.
Galligan, Brian, and Georgina Lynch. 1992. "Integrating Conservation and Development: Australia's Resource Assessment Commission and the Testing Case of Coronation Hill," *Environmental Planning and Law* (June).

Gerritsen, Rolf. 1990. "A Continuing Confession? A Comment on the Appropriate Dispersal of Policy Powers in the Australian Federation," *Australian Journal of Political Science* 25 (2): 228-40.
Gibbins, Roger. 1991. "Ideological Change as a Federal Solvent: Impact of the New Political Agenda on Continental Integration." In *The Nation-State Versus Continental Integration: Canada—North America—Germany—Europe*, edited A. Leslie Pal and Rainer-Olaf Schultze. Bochum: Universitätsverlag Dr N. Brockmeyer.
Goodin, Robert E. 1992. *Green Political Theory*. Cambridge: Polity Press.
Greenwood, G. 1976. *The Future of Australian Federalism*, 2d ed. St Lucia, Qld: University of Queensland Press.
Grodzins, Morton. 1966. *The American System: A New View of Government in the United States*, edited by Daniel J. Elazar. New Brunswick, NJ: Transaction Books.
Harris, S. 1991. "ESD: Implications for the Policy Process." Paper presented to the Royal Australian Institute of Public Administration Conference, Canberra, 9 December.
Haward, Marcus. 1991. "The Offshore." In *Intergovernmental Relations and Public Policy*, edited by B. Galligan, O. Hughes, and C. Walsh. Sydney: Allen and Unwin.
Hawke, R. J. L. 1989. Our Country Our Future—Statement on the Environment, AGPS, Canberra, July.
Hawke, R. J. L. 1990. "Towards a Closer Partnership." Speech delivered at the National Press Club, Canberra, 19 July.
Intergovernmental Agreement on the Environment (IGAE). 1991 (October).
IGAE. (Draft). 1992. (May).
Kelly, Paul. 1992. *The End of Certainty: The Story of the 1980s*. St Leonards, NSW: Allen and Unwin.
Kelly, R. 1991. "New Approaches to Environmental Issues." Paper presented at the Public Issues Dispute Resolution Conference, Brisbane February.
Krasner, Stephen, D. 1988. "Sovereignty: An Institutional Perspective," *Comparative Political Studies* 21 (1): 66-94.
Laski, H. J. 1939. "The Obsolescent of Federalism," *New Republic* (3 May): 367-69.
Mabo v. Queensland. 1992. Mimeo.
MacCormick, Neil. 1993. "Beyond the Sovereign State," *Modern Law Review* 56 (1): 1-18.
Murphyores v. Commonwealth. 1976. 136 CLR 1.
Queensland v. Commonwealth. 1988. 77 ALR 291, 296.
Resources Assessment Committee (RAC). 1991. Preface to *Kakadu Conservation Zone Inquiry, Final Report*, AGPS, Canberra, May.
RAC. 1992. Principles and Procedures for the Commonwealth-State Consultation on Treaties (January).
Richardson v. Forestry Commission. 1988. 62 ALJR 158.
United Nations General Assembly. 1989. Document A/C 2/44/L.86. 18 December.
Vienna Convention on the Law of Treaties. 1969.
Von Beyne, Klaus. 1988. "The Genesis of Constitutional Review in Parliamentary Systems." In *Constitutional Review and Legislation: An International Comparison*, edited by Christine Landfried. Baden: Nomos Verlagsgesellschaft.
Wheare, K. C. [1946] 1963. *Federal Government*, 4th ed. London: Oxford University Press.
World Commission on Environment and Development. 1987. *Common Future*. Melbourne: Oxford University Press Australia.

Zines, L. 1985. "The Environment and the Constitution." In *Federalism and the Environment*, edited by R.L. Mathews. Centre for Research on Federal Financial Relations, ANU, Canberra.

Ghosts of Federalism in the Soviet Successor States

Bohdan Harasymiw

Ostensibly, federalism was the principle of territorial division and cohesion of the former Union of Soviet Socialist Republics (USSR), as well as its principal component, the Russian Soviet Federative Socialist Republic (RSFSR). With the USSR's collapse as a discreet state, and its dismemberment into fifteen independent states, the question of the possibility of reunification in some new form of federation or confederation hovers over the heads of the political leaders of that formerly unified territory. This question arises because of the continued economic, strategic, and political interdependence of the parts of the former Union despite its *de facto* disappearance as a legal and political entity. Federalism also appears as a possible solution to the problem of internal integration of some of the individual successor states (for example, Russia) in the new post-1991 circumstances of independence, democracy, and self-determination. Even though Soviet federalism was a sham, can it now, nevertheless, be replaced—in all or part of the former USSR's territory—by some genuine forms of federalism? Can genuine federalism now be instituted anywhere in the former Soviet Union, and is it liable to survive? The ghosts of empire and of federalism past are haunting the former Soviet Union, both inhibiting and encouraging decision makers in their search for new institutional forms or the restoration of old ones; the outlines of post-Soviet arrangements are equally ghostly.

In his 1975 essay on the subject, William Riker defines federalism as:

> *a political organization in which the activities of government are divided between regional governments and a central government in such a way that each kind of government has some activities on which it makes final decisions.* (1975: 101; original emphasis)

The two governments, as is commonly accepted, are independent and coordinate. There is no ideal division of responsibilities between the two, but, rather, federations can range from extremely loose alliances to extremely centralized states. In the one case, the minimal federal arrangement, "the rulers of the federation can make decisions in only one restricted category of action without obtaining the approval of the rulers of constituent units" (Riker 1975: 102). In the opposite, the maximal, "the rulers of the federation can make decisions without consulting the rulers of the member governments in all but one narrowly restricted category of action" (102). This definition of federalism helps us avoid looking for an Aristotelian ideal and reminds us that a variety of types is to be expected. If federalism has these essential features, then it should be possible to recognize it in the context of post-Soviet constitution making.

Almost any circumstances in which constitution makers face the problem of reconciling unity with diversity have usually been considered—at least potentially—appropriate for the adoption of federalism. More precisely, Riker argues, insofar as the conditions historically conducive to such arrangements are concerned,

> federalism is a constitutional bargain among politicians and the motives are military and diplomatic defense or aggression. Riker's sole conditions are:
> 1. A desire on the part of politicians who offer the bargain to expand their territorial control by peaceful means, usually either to meet an external military or diplomatic threat or to prepare for military aggrandizement.
> 2. A willingness on the part of politicians who accept the bargain to give up independence for the sake of the union either because they desire protection from an external threat or because they desire to participate in the potential aggression of the federation (Riker 1975: 113–14).

Following Birch, Riker acknowledges that the threat in such cases may be internal rather than external. These conditions not only bring the parties together initially, but their presence determines the survival of the federation:

> In every successfully formed federation it must be the case that a significant external or internal threat or a significant opportunity for aggression is present, where the threat can be forestalled and the ag-

gression carried out only with a bigger government. This is what brings union at all and is the main feature, the prospective gain, in both giving and accepting the bargain. At the same time there must be some provincial loyalty so that the bargain is necessary, that is, it must be necessary to appease provincial rulers (1975: 116).

Federalism is only possible when there is a bargain, a question of territorial control, a threat to survival, or else an opportunity for expansion, and strong provincial loyalties. The preservation of unity and diversity may be an effect of federalism, but it has its genesis in a rational bargain in which something is given up and some other thing gained, and there is some advantage to all parties.

Riker examines thirty-five federations, successful and unsuccessful, formed between the eighteenth century and 1970. He found that his theory is borne out in every instance, and demonstrated that the two stipulated conditions are not only correlates of federalism, but logically necessary factors. In addition, he reported that previous political association between states correlated with successful federalism, but was not necessary (1975: 117-27). Owing to its economy and persuasiveness, his theory can serve well to assess the likelihood of the (re)establishment of federalism on the territory of the former Soviet Union. Naturally, all of the USSR's main components, the union republics, have the experience of political association, externally as well as internally, so we can discount that factor. Riker's theory directs our attention to the following critical factors.

A bargain. This suggests that a federal agreement cannot be imposed, but must be negotiated. An imposed or coerced agreement, even if it embodies other features of federalism, such as division of powers, cannot be expected to survive or to operate as a true federal arrangement. "Failure and break-up are much more likely to occur when the establishment of the federation has not been completely voluntary and spontaneous" (Hicks 1978: 11).

Provincialism. There must be a distinctive provincial identity or independence which requires protection. In the case of the former Soviet Union, this has been met hitherto by the provision of ethnonational territorial divisions. Some divisions are still valid; while some are no longer regarded as being so.

Threat or opportunity for expansion. Is there an external military threat, or an internal security threat, that would motivate combining independent states into a federal union? Is there an opportunity for expansion?

Federalism. The proposed or newly created union must satisfy the criteria of a minimally federal organization, as opposed to being merely a unitary arrangement with autonomy conferred on the localities by the centre at its own discretion.

Were these conditions present in either the former Soviet Union as a whole or some part of it, or within any of its individual components, the former union republics, at time of this writing (mid-1993)? The success of federalism has been studied by Riker's student, Jonathan Lemco (1991), and earlier by Thomas Franck (1968) and his colleagues. Lemco examined forty-four federations that have existed over the past two centuries (thirty-two of them since 1945), compared their conditions in light of numerous theories of federalism, and measured the relationship between these conditions and the political stability of the subject federations. He found a significant correlation (not a causal relationship) between political stability and: (1) the degree of centralization (the more centralized, the stronger the central government, the more likelihood of stability); (2) the number and size of component units (many small units are better than a few large ones; an exceptionally large unit amidst small ones spells trouble); (3) an effectively operating two- or multi-party system; (4) the existence of a military or economic threat, which can enhance the national federal government's legitimacy; (5) the absence of ethnoterritorial units and of religious cleavages; (6) a modern society, but not a rapidly modernizing one; and (7) elites who assess the benefits of federation as outweighing its costs (Lemco 1991: 160 and *passim*).

In amplification of the latter point, Thomas Franck (1968: ch. 5), on the basis of studying four failed federations (East Africa, Central Africa, Malaysia, and West Indies), concluded that: first, commonalities are useful, but not necessary, for survival (in the cases in question, neither their British colonial heritage nor the presence of economic cooperation was able to save them); secondly, the main cause of failure was a lack of commitment to the idea of federalism itself: it has to be present at the outset and generated or nurtured thereafter; and, finally, "federations are apt to fail when they are justified to the participants only in terms of immediately realizeable practical advantages" (182). These observed generalizations can serve as guideposts to assessing the survivability or revivability of federalism on the territory of the former Soviet Union.

USSR and CIS

It is not the purpose of this paper to analyse the genuineness of federalism in the USSR or the RSFSR as it existed up to 1991, nor why the Soviet Union disintegrated, but rather to look forward from the present situation and assess the likelihood that a federal organization might take root there out of the rather incoherent conditions of chaotic independence that now exist. It may well be that the involuntary nature of the union, the removal of the external military threat (the ending of the Cold War, and the collapse of communist rule in eastern Europe), and the collapse of the Communist Party of the Soviet Union—and especially of its centralized control over personnel through the notorious *nomenklatura* system (Lemco 1991: 79)—constitute three of the critical reasons for the dissolution of the Soviet federation. And it may also be that the integrity of the Russian federation is similarly being undermined now. This paper's orientation is more in the direction of the future instead of the past; prospect rather than *post mortem* is the focus here.

No neat dividing line can be drawn between the end of the USSR and the post-Soviet order: a legacy of leftovers overlaps, and business begun in a previous era was carried over into the other. In particular, mention must be made of Mikhail Gorbachev's ill-fated Union Treaty, which was to have replaced the highly centralized Soviet constitution with a much more decentralized arrangement, while still retaining a central government. Opposition to this document's final incarnation impelled the unsuccessful coup of August 1991. Since the previous November, successive drafts of the treaty have given more power to the republics as a condition of their agreement. The Union Treaty was, effectively, a repudiation of the existing Soviet federation, and would have suddenly changed it from extremely centralized to extremely decentralized (or peripheralized, in Riker's terminology); it went too far for some people, not far enough for others. The idea of a Commonwealth, or loose association of states, as a replacement for the USSR, as well as the relative strength of appeal among the fifteen Soviet republics of such an organization or devolution of power, began to take shape early in 1991, long before the collapse of the Soviet Union. These attempts to prop up the old order are relevant to the post-1991 situation.

Of the fifteen union republics of the Soviet Union, the three Baltic republics of Estonia, Latvia, and Lithuania have to be excluded from any consideration of a possible post-Soviet federation. (Lithuania's independence was declared in 1990 on the basis of their illegal incorporation into the USSR fifty years earlier, was unsuccessfully challenged by Moscow using embargo and armed force, reiterated in 1991, and finally recognized by the USSR State Council in early September 1991.) Estonia, Latvia, and Lithuania withdrew from the organizational structure of the USSR in the course of 1991, have not taken part in the activities of the Commonwealth of Independent States (CIS), and are reorienting themselves in terms of international contacts principally towards Germany and Scandinavia. There are, therefore, only twelve potential candidates for a federation of Soviet successor states.

Not all of the twelve are equally interested in a federation, just as they were not all uniformly enthusiastic about the Union Treaty or the Commonwealth. Alexander Rahr summarizes the situation in early 1991:

> In January [1991], in response to the Soviet military crackdown in the Baltic republics, El'tain and the leaders of Ukraine, Belorussia, and Kazakhstan signed a quadripartite agreement to demonstrate firm republican resistance to the attempts of the center to preserve its hegemony by force. This document laid the foundations for the commonwealth agreement signed in Minsk at the end of the year. (1992: 9)

The commonwealth idea of a loose association of independent states was gestating at the very same time as the Union Treaty was being successively modified into a very decentralized federation, or perhaps confederation. In the version published in March 1991, the Union Treaty basically gave the republics exclusive jurisdiction over two fields: taxation and natural resources. The centre was to have jurisdiction over a wide range of activities, but since the setting of policy in these areas was also to be a joint or concurrent responsibility of the centre and the republics, its exclusive jurisdiction was severely narrowed to such matters as

> the declaration of war and the conclusion of peace; . . . . The approval and execution of the union budget; [and] the management of space research, unionwide communications and information systems, geodesy, cartography, meteorology, and establishment of standards.
> (FBIS 141MAR08)

In other words, the centre would have been very much a creature of the constituent republics and largely under their control, a situation at the opposite pole from the then existing USSR in terms of federal arrangements. But even this was not acceptable to all the republics remaining in the Union. In April 1991, only nine republics met with Gorbachev to discuss this version of the treaty; by August, only seven were said to have been ready to sign (*RFE/RL Research Report* 3 January 1992: 9; 1 January 1993: 38). In the fall of 1991, after the coup, Gorbachev attempted to revive the Union Treaty, but

Ukraine's refusal to participate, let alone to sign, and the Ukrainian President Leonid Kravchuk's rejection even of confederation, consigned that project to oblivion (*RFE/RL Research Report* 3 January 1992: 37). The Commonwealth of Independent States, built around a core of the three Slavic republics, was agreed to by all except Georgia, and this has "replaced" the USSR and the Union Treaty.

Could the CIS grow over or be made over into a federation? Could at least some former republics of the USSR refederate? The answers are no and yes. From the beginning, as Ann Sheehy says,

> the treaty setting up the commonwealth was a compromise, with Ukraine regarding the CIS only as a civilized means of divorce and its membership in it as strictly temporary, while Russia wanted a closer, more permanent association. Belarus and the other eight republics that joined the commonwealth two weeks after its creation also had their own agendas. (*RFE/RL Research Report* 1 January 1993: 37)

As a consequence, "the first year of the existence of the Commonwealth of Independent States (CIS) was marked by serious doubts about whether the new body was viable," let alone its being transformable into anything like a federation (*RFE/RL Research Report* 1 January 1993: 37). At the outset, Georgia did not join the CIS, which left eleven states in the alliance; although Azerbaidjan's president did sign the treaty, its ratification was unanimously rejected by the Azerbaijani parliament on 7 October 1992. Of the ten remaining adherents of the CIS treaty, only seven (the same ones who had been ready to sign Gorbachev's Union Treaty in August 1991) signed the charter of the CIS in January 1993, temporarily leaving out Ukraine, Moldova, and Turkmenistan (*CDSP* 17 February 1993: 5-9).

The charter of the CIS formalizes its coordinative and consultative activities on behalf of the member states and establishes an organizational structure apparently patterned after the European Community (for the text of the draft and accompanying organization chart, see *Holos Ukrainy* 27 January 1993). It says explicitly that the "Commonwealth is not a state and does not possess supranational powers" (Article 1). In spite of this, Moldova's "President Mircea Snegur said in early December 1992 that the draft CIS charter was a step toward recreating a new 'center' and stated that Moldova would not sign it even if the republic had to pay a high economic price" (*RFE/RL Research Report* 1 January 1993: 37). The rule of unanimity gives each member state a veto over proposed cooperation schemes, and thus safeguards independence, but once an agreement has been reached every state would presumably be inextricably bound and would then have its sovereignty curtailed. It is this to which Moldova and Ukraine apparently object, and why some feel that the charter is a reintroduction of the old empire. But is it federalism?

Neither the Charter nor the practice of the member states during the first full year of its existence, nor objective circumstances, suggest that the CIS is a federal arrangement of government. Nor is it likely to evolve into one and survive. In essence, the Commonwealth is an alliance woven together by a series of treaties—over two hundred were signed by its members' heads of state and heads of government in 1992 (*RFE/RL Research Report* 1 January 1993: 38). Its purpose is to harmonize policies among the member states, but the mechanism of harmonization involves a surrender of sovereignty by the states to the CIS rather than a bargain in which there is mutual gain. In fact, practically nothing has been handed over by the member states, certainly not defence, and "there has been little sign of the CIS states coordinating their foreign policy" (*RFE/RL Research Report* 1 January 1993: 38). The Commonwealth is really just a forum for cooperation (Adams 1993). Despite their interdependence, economic cooperation through the CIS actually declined rather than increasing. One might try to argue that the CIS could grow over into a federal organization, but at present the conditions for this are simply not conducive. First, there is no external military or diplomatic threat facing the full ten member states or even the inner seven (although there are internal ones), and no visible opportunity for expansion or dominion that would be enhanced by pursuing it in association rather than separately. Secondly, there is certainly the provincialism, all of these states having declared independence in 1991 and having since sought to establish separate customs, trade, and currencies, but this is complicated by the as yet unresolved question of citizenship, so that the situation in this respect is confusing; not all former republics of the USSR—even CIS members—are equally willing to give up their independence. And finally, there is no separation of areas of activity as between the CIS and member states; there is on paper and in practice no federal government—the Ukraine will not tolerate it, nor will Moldova. The fact that some of the very states of the former Soviet Union which do face serious threats to their security—Moldova, the Ukraine, Georgia, Azerbaidzhan, and Turkmenistan—are the least supportive of the

CIS makes it very doubtful the Commonwealth could be turned in a federation.

Returning to the criteria which Lemco and Franck enumerated earlier, several facts are apparent. The elites have shown no commitment to the idea of federalism (at best they have spoken of confederation [Adams 1993: 8]), and they are motivated by practical considerations of a need for coordination (principally economic, to which even the Ukraine has agreed), rather than of re-creating a new nation. A centralized supranational government is unlikely to develop, given the premium each state places on sovereignty; this is especially true of the Ukraine, which means that a federation of the CIS would have to go ahead without it, and the dominance of Russia would quickly destabilize any genuine federation. Given that there is no external military threat to the CIS members, the economic threat comes from within in the form of the command economy, which cooperation and coordination within the Commonwealth will only exacerbate rather than alleviate. And, the commonality of the Soviet experience is no assurance that a federated CIS would survive. Greater integration of CIS member states has been proceeding and will likely continue to do so, but much of it goes on outside the Commonwealth in the form of bilateral and multilateral treaties and alliances; a confederal structure for the CIS is more probable than federalism.

The Russian Federation

As defined by its 1978 constitution, the Russian Republic was administratively divided into sixteen autonomous republics, six territories (*kraia*), forty-eight provinces (*oblasti*), the cities of Moscow and Leningrad which were directly under the RSFSR government, five autonomous provinces within the territories, and eleven autonomous districts within either territories or provinces (Feldbrugge 1979: 289-90). The principle of federalism applied only to the relationship between the centre and the ethnonational autonomous republics (which were, in turn, further subdivided into the other, smaller ethnonational units). The two principal cities and the forty-eight provinces, on the other hand, which were purely administrative units as opposed to ethnoterritorial, were not in a federal relationship with the centre, but a purely municipal one. The constitution given to the RSFSR government, among others, assigned the following powers, which bore on the activities of the constituent autonomous republics:

♦ establishing the procedure for the organization and operation of republic and local organs of state power and administration;

- conducting a unified socioeconomic policy and directing the economic system of the RSFSR;
- formulating and confirming state [economic] plans . . . and the state budget of the RSFSR; . . . directing the implementation of the state budgets of the autonomous republics;
- establishing . . . the revenues . . . of the RSFSR;
- directing the branches of the national economy;
- establishing the procedure for using the land, mineral wealth, the forests and the waters; protecting the environment;
- directing housing and municipal utilities, trade, and public catering, services, . . . housing construction, . . . amenities of the cities, . . . and railroad construction and transport;
- directing public education, cultural and scientific organizations, . . . health care, physical culture and sport. (Feldbrugge 1979: 292)

Article 78 stated that "outside the limits of the rights of the USSR and the RFSFR, an autonomous republic independently resolves questions within its jurisdiction." Was this a federation?

The 1978 constitution did not provide a specific list of the activities exclusively reserved to the autonomous republics. Article 79 stated, however, that

> an autonomous republic participates in the resolution of questions within the jurisdiction of the RSFSR and the USSR. . . . The autonomous republic ensures integrated economic and social development within its territory, facilitates the exercise within its territory of the authority of the USSR and the RSFSR, and implements the decisions of the . . . USSR and the RSFSR. . . . With regard to questions within its jurisdiction, an autonomous republic coordinates and supervises the activities of . . . organizations of union and republic (RSFSR) subordination.

This leads to the conclusion that the autonomous republics were intended to be extensions of the RSFSR government, and may have had some small area of independent activity in the sphere of cultural policy, but this type of federation was extremely centralized. It is hard to imagine a sphere of competence that was independent of the USSR and RSFSR governments, except undertakings of extremely limited and local significance.

It is against this background of a highly centralized, or minimal, federalism that the current controversies within Russia about its internal structure, and about whether it is disintegrating or not, have to be interpreted. If the constitution of 1978 prescribed a norm, then the slightest departure from it could be regarded as an alarming explosion. In reality, Russia is only now moving towards federalism, not away from it.

The alarm over the integrity of Russia stems from the widespread demands on the part of the thirty-one autonomous units for ethnonational sovereignty and independence from the centre, from the uncertainty about an appropriate territorial structure for the Russian state, as well as from the uncertainty generated by the long delay in producing a new Constitution (Walker 1992). In the meantime, the Federal Treaty (not to be confused with Gorbachev's Union Treaty for the ill-fated USSR) signed in March 1992 (*CDSP* 29 April 1992: 15–16), and intended to serve as the part of the new constitution for Russia dealing with organization of the federation, should be reassuring as to the practical (in contrast to the rhetorical) likelihood of separatism dismembering Russia. The Federal Treaty basically gives Russia's central government jurisdiction over the following matters: the constitution; federal territorial structure; citizenship and civil and minority rights; federal institutions and property; federal development policies; a single market, monetary regulations, and banking; federal budget and taxes; power generation and transport and communications; foreign policy; foreign economic relations; defence, security, and borders; judicial system; application of federal laws; meteorology and standards; honours; and the federal civil service.

It gives joint responsibility to the federal and (formerly autonomous) republic governments for: conformity of republican constitutions and laws with their federal counterparts; protection of rights, ensuring legality, law and order, and public safety; use of resources; education and science generally; coordination of public health and social security; disasters; republic taxation; administrative, labour, family, land, housing, water, and forest law; subsoil resources and environmental protection law; the bar; small ethnic communities; and principles of local self-government.

The republics are specifically given only the residue from the above lists as well as the right to participate in international relations, but their control over resources is yet to be negotiated with the federal government. By implication and deduction, it would appear that the following matters are left more or less to the exclusive sphere of activities of the republics: language; higher education; culture; commerce; tax collection; the republican budget;

and republic and municipal institutions. The Federal Treaty provides for a genuine, if modest, federalism.

The fact that eighteen of the twenty relevant ethnoterritorial units of the RSFSR signed the Federal Treaty should give reassurance that, despite the separatist rhetoric, nearly all republics are willing to make and stick with the bargain. Siberia, in particular, is much too economically dependent for any of its components to attempt independent survival politically (*RFE/RL Research Report* 16 October 1992: 6-14; *CDSP* 29 April 1992: 9-10). The controversy over the refusal of Chechnya and Tatarstan, especially the latter, to sign the treaty is little more than a tempest in a teapot, although Russian politicians and academics have been referring to it as the very death knell of Russia, because the separation of Tatarstan would leave a hole in the middle of Holy Russia (*CDSP* 22 April 1992: 6-8; 14 October 1992: 1-6; 25 November 1992: 15-16; *Pravda* 13 February 1993). All that is necessary to accommodate Tatarstan is some form of special status, much like Québec enjoys within Canada, and which would give that republic a more federal relationship to the centre than the other republics have (*CDSP* 29 April 1992: 6-8).

There are other factors which may still undermine the present agreement. One is that the legitimacy of the signers of the Federal Treaty is questionable (Walker 1992: 15). They were elected to their positions before the fall of the communist system, and it is not clear if they are committed to democracy. Another factor is that the republic boundaries are far out of line with the ethnic composition of their populations, which makes the present ethnoterritorial organization of the RSFSR seem likely to be temporary. According to the 1989 census, in only six of the thirty-one relevant ethnic units (republics, provinces, regions) of the RSFSR were the indigenes a majority; Russians made up over 50 percent of the population in eighteen of thirty-one units (*CDSP* 26 June 1991: 8). Even in Tatarstan, the most vociferously independentist republic, Tatars comprise barely 48.5 per cent of the population. It would be possible for Moscow to use the instrument of referendum to pare down the ethnonational territories, but at the risk of further inflaming interethnic hostilities.

Will the Russian Federation last? Regardless of its internal configuration, which may continue in its present form and which may evolve gradually towards a predominantly nonethnic territorial division, the conditions for federalism are favourable. Russians comprise over 80 percent of the population of the RSFSR (81.5 percent, to be exact, according to the 1989 census [*Vestnik statistiki* 1990: 72]). Some 25 million of their brethren live in the former non-Russian republics of the USSR. Russian politicians, including Boris Yeltsin himself, have expressed concern for those fellow-Russians in the "near abroad" and endorsed Russia's responsibility to them. Here is a clear motive for aggression or expansion. Russia's expansion is very much feared by politicians in the Baltic states, the Ukraine, and Georgia, not to mention Moldova. The only restraint on such behaviour is Russia's membership in the Conference for Security and Cooperation in Europe, which obliges her to respect existing borders. As to the necessity for bargaining between centre and constituent units, Yeltsin himself opened wide the doors to this element of federalism by telling the Komi, Bashkir, and Tatar local elites, in the autumn of 1990, to "take all the sovereignty you can swallow" (cited in Walker 1992: 5). Although many regional leaders have been acting on this advice and demanding greater sovereignty, it is significant that they seem to see it in an all-or-nothing, rather than a bargaining, sense. Indeed, there is no bargaining culture or tradition in Russia; the tendency is to conceive of politics in exclusively dichotomous terms, in this case, centralism or separation. At least one can say that, unlike the CIS, there is a federal government in place in the RSFSR, which will likely last for some time yet and may help assure the federation's survival. There is also, with exceptions like Chechnya and Bashkortostan, a commitment on the part of elites to the idea of federalism, even if the local leaders see a much more decentralized federation than do Yeltsin and others at the centre. On the negative side, in terms of trends towards instability, it must be recognized that the degree of centralization in Russia is decreasing, and the presence of strong nationalist sentiment in several ethnoterritorial units is increasing.

The only part of the RSFSR which is liable to break off from the RSFSR and to form its own federation is the cluster of territories along the northern Caucasus mountains, in (or to) the south of Russia: Adygeia, Karachaevo-Cherkessia, Kabardino-Balkaria, northern Ossetia, and Chechen-Ingushetia. Threatened from one side by Russia, and on the other by Georgia, these peoples seem to be in a classic position to bury their differences and to combine in a federal union to survive (*CDSP* 28 October 1992: 5–8). Forcible incorporation of these peoples into the Russian federation will not work, and one, the Chechens, have already indicated their refusal to cooperate by not signing the Federal Treaty and by not participating in the referendum held on 25 April 1993 (*RFE/RL Research Report* 7 May 1993: 1).

Thus, the prospect for Russia is as a federation of unaccustomed looseness. Economic dependence (as in the case of the Siberian territories) will keep some of its units subordinate and loyal to the centre in Moscow. Certain others, where nationalism is strong (for example, Tatarstan) or where there is a perceived opportunity for economic self-sufficiency based on control over natural resources and their direct marketing abroad (like the Republic of Sakha [formerly Yakutia]), will continue to resist the central government and will demand more powers (*RFE/RL Research Report* 9 April 1993: 8). A few are already acting independently of the central government. The purely administrative (non-ethnoterritorial) provinces of European Russia are now demanding the same powers as the twenty-one ethnoterritorial autonomous republics (*CDSP* 21 April 1993: 27). This is a positive development from the point of view of encouraging a stable federal system, as it would increase the number of units of the federation to around ninety and dilute the power of the ethnoterritories. Given this dispersion or fragmentation, as well as the absence of an effective party system and its unlikely appearance in the near future, the chances of a strong, centrally directed federalism are less than those of a looser federation. But a loose federation is better than no federation at all, if that is a major concern.

Federalism in Other Parts of the Former Soviet Union

In those states of the former USSR where there are, at present, ethnic tensions or outright fighting, and states either did not join the CIS or else did not sign the charter, some consideration ought to be given to the possibility of federalism as a solution to, or preventer of, conflict. Estonia, for example, has pockets of Russian population, especially in its eastern regions. Establishment of a federal district for these people is not likely because it would formalize an irridenta claimable by Russia; Estonia has little enough territory to be thinking of giving any away. Estonia's leaders are not in a mood to bargain with their Russian inhabitants (*RFE/RL Research Report* 12 June 1992: 15–17). Lithuania has pockets of Polish settlement, but, again, a federal solution is being resisted because this might altogether undermine the state's existence.

There is an interesting combination of factors, favorable and inauspicious, for federalism in the Ukraine. The Ukraine has significant numbers of Russians in its eastern and southern regions, as well as Hungarian and Ruthenian minorities in the west (*RFE/RL Research Report* 7 February 1992: 17–23). Some talk has gone on about the adoption of federalism so as to recognize the distinctiveness of these areas, but the draft constitution makes no mention of federalism (*Holos Ukrainy* 17 July 1992: 4–15), possibly because politicians fear this as a preliminary step to the dismemberment of the Ukraine or its at least partial reabsorption by Russia. Actually, the Russian threat is an ambiguous one. Apart from nationalistic rhetoric on the part of some Russians, incorporating the economically disadvantaged rustbelt of eastern Ukraine (Donbas) or the outrightly economically unviable retirement haven of the Crimea by Russia is impractical. It would be a liability rather than a gain for Russia. On the other hand, instead of resisting the idea of federalism lest it lead to secession (a fear which does have some basis), members of the Ukrainian political elite should consider the Russian threat as a means of strengthening and ensuring the survival of a federal Ukraine. In fact, conditions in the Ukraine seem favourable for the creation of a stable federal system: first, there is an external threat in the form of encroachment by Russia and Romania, as well as the fighting in Moldova. Secondly, the federation would likely be made up of an appropriately large number of units (some twenty-five) of roughly equal size. Thirdly, the minority ethnic territories would be few in number (perhaps six at most), which should not greatly destabilize the federation. Autonomy has already been granted Crimea, which indicates the possibility of accommodation of ethnocultural demands within a common Ukrainian state. Fourthly, following the Soviet experience, the national government is still highly centralized. And finally, there is (in a certain sense) a modern society. Thus, the major element lacking in the Ukraine for the creation of a federation, despite the presence of favourable objective conditions, is a commitment to the federal idea by the political leaders whose tradition leads them to equate survival with centralism.

Moldova, with its separatist "Dniester Republic" in the northeast, and its Gagauz enclave in the south, might be a candidate for the federal solution, the more so as it is threatened from one side by absorption into Romania, and, from the other, into Russia (a long-distance confederation?) or the Ukraine. Secessionists have, in fact, proposed either a federal or confederal system for Moldova (*CDSP* 14 April 1993: 21). But no one is in a mood to bargain, and so Moldova may be dismembered and remembered only as a mistake (*RFE/RL Research Report* 1 January 1993: 12-16). No one is in a mood to bargain in the three Transcaucasian republics, either. In Georgia, Shevarnadze has been accusing Russia of aiding the Abkhazian and Ossetian separatists, and since the Russians have, in fact, been doing this there is no basis for a bargain between the three sides. In Azerbaidjan, there is no prospect of bargaining with the Armenians of Nagorno-Karabakh because the latter insist on independence, in which they are at odds with the state of Armenia. The three states will not consider federating because their fears about federalism are so different: Russia, Turkey, and Iran. Fighting, not federal bargaining, is the mood in the southern tier of the former Soviet Union.

Conclusion

Outside of Russia, and beyond the half-dozen states closely associated with her in the CIS, the conditions for the establishment and survival of federalism are meagre to the point of being academic. Federalism does not, it seems, have a ghost of a chance. Even in the inner circle of the Commonwealth, as within Russia, these conditions are not altogether favourable. Russia, together with Belarus, Kazakhstan, Kyrgyzia, Uzbekistan, and Tadzhikistan, could still reform the rump of a Soviet empire rather than evolve toward federalism. Russia may well devolve into a patchwork neighbourhood of alliances, treaties, and "special statuses" instead of the closer association that was characteristic of the RSFSR in the simpler, more boring Soviet era. As Canadians well know from their addiction to it, federalism is a solution to boredom (although an overdose as with any drug induces a catatonic state); it is not a cure for chaos.

References

Adams, Jan S. 1993. "Will the Post-Soviet Commonwealth Survive?" An Occasional Paper from the Mershon Center project entitled Assessing Alternative Futures for the United States and Post-Soviet Relations. Columbus, Ohio: Mershon Center, Ohio State University (April)
Current Digest of the Post-Soviet Press, 26 June 1991 to 21 April 1993.
Foreign Broadcast Information Service (141MAR08). 1991. *USSR: Revised Draft Union Treaty Published*. PM0803203191 Moscow IZVESTIYA in Russian 9 Mar 91 Union Edition.
Feldbrugge, F. J. M. (ed.) 1979. *The Constitutions of the USSR and the Union Republics: Analysis, Texts, Reports*. Alphen aan den Rijn, The Netherlands, and Germantown, Maryland: Sijthoff & Noordhoff.
Franck, Thomas A., et al. 1968. *Why Federations Fail: An Inquiry into the Requisites for Successful Federation*, edited by Thomas A. Franck. New York: New York University Press; London: University of London Press.
Hicks, Ursula K. 1978. *Federalism: Failure and Success*. London and Basingstoke: Macmillan Press.
Holos Ukrainy, 17 July 1992 and 27 January 1993.
Lemco, Jonathan. 1991. *Political Stability in Federal Governments*. New York: Praeger.
Pravda. 13 February 1993.
Rahr, Alexander. "El'tain Eclipses Gorbachev as Hard-line Coup Fails," *RFE/RL Research Report*, 3 January 1992.
Radio Free Europe/Radio Liberty. 1992–1993. *RFE/RL Research Report*. Munich.

Riker, William H. 1975. "Federalism." In *Handbook of Political Science, Volume 5*, edited by Fred I. Greenstein and Nelson W. Polsby. Reading, MA: Addison-Wesley.
Vestnik statistiki, 1990, no. 10:72.
Walker, Edward W. 1992. "The New Russian Constitution and the Future of the Russian Federation," *Harriman Institute Forum* 5 (June).

Aboriginal Self-Government and Treaties: A Discussion

Leroy Little Bear

Aboriginal self-government, within the recent past, is a topic that has been heatedly debated in Canada. The debate usually revolves around questions such as what is self-government?; what does it look like?; how is it structured?; how is it going to operate and function?; who is going to pay for it?; what powers will it have?; are Indians ready for it? This discussion paper will attempt to put in perspective another issue that arises whenever aboriginal self-government is a topic of discussion: what is the relationship between treaties and self-government? Are treaties a basis for self-government? Are treaties the source for self-government? But, before engaging in discussion on self-government and treaties, I would like to present some general observations about 'government.'

Cultures or group life-ways do not manifest themselves solely in observable customs and artifacts: there is more to social and cultural phenomenon than immediately meets the eye and ear. "In sum, the way of life that is handed down as the social heritage of every people does more than supply a set of skills for making a living and a set of blueprints for human relations. Each different way of life makes its own assumptions about the ends and purposes of human existence, about ways by which knowledge may be obtained, about the organization of the pigeonholes in which each sense datum is filed, about what human beings have a right to expect from each other and the gods, about what constitutes fulfillment and frustration." In other words, each society has what may be called a philosophy, an ideology, or a world view. This philosophy, of necessity, results in a different paradigm: a different way of looking at things, a different way of analyzing and synthesizing information and a different way of organizing and governing the social collective.

Government is that institution that all societies have for the governing of the social collective. A particular government will be based on a combination of factors: the societal philosophy and world view, ecological and environmental factors, and normative values and customs of the society. Consequently, how a government is structured and how it operates cannot be disassociated from paradigms that arise from philosophy, norms, and the environment. Government is a process that evolves and not a thing that simply comes into existence. It is a process for the orderly day-to-day functions of a society. It prescribes and circumscribes rules for the relations between members of the society, relations with outsiders, and relations with the environment, and allocates resources among the members of society. Questions to the effect of how is aboriginal self-government going to look?; how is it going to operate?; what powers is it going to have?; and so on, imply an ignorance of aboriginal cultures and the creation of a rather artificial body remote from the ethos of the people that it is supposed to serve.

The important issue in my opinion is the philosophical and legal basis upon which aboriginal self-government is based and not the structural, operational, and functional aspects of government, which are best left to each First Nation. Philosophically, the differences between white society and aboriginal society are well documented in the "Report of the Task Force on the Criminal Justice System and its Impact on the Indian and Metis People of Alberta":

> The underlying premises of any culture are the result of a combination of several factors, including the worldview and values of that culture. The nature of the underlying premises of White society can be characterized as "linear and singular," and "specialist and product oriented." Linear thinking is very well illustrated by Western European concepts of time. Time is conceptualized as a straight line. It is like a river flowing toward the self and flowing on past. What is immediately around the self is the present. What is behind the self is the past. The future is upstream. But one cannot see very far upstream because of a waterfall which serves as notice that one cannot predict the future. This straight line is objectified by White society as quantity, as lengths made of units. A length of time is envisioned as a row of similar units. For instance, a day is a unit, and therefore, separate and different from other units. The consequence is that each day is a different day; each day is a new day. Another ramification of thinking about time in

this manner is that time flows in one way only. Once a day-unit goes by, it will never return. Wasting and making up time combined with values that speak to productivity result in ideas about the efficient use of time. (Canada 1991: 9-2-9-5)

Linear thinking lends itself to a singularity of view. Implicit is the idea that a line leads only to one thing. Ramifications of this idea are beliefs that there can be only one god, only one true answer, one and only one way. Horizontal and hierarchical chronologies are still other outgrowths of the linear and singular worldview.

Every society has positive and negative sanctions; rewards for living according to the prescriptions of the culture and ostracism for deviations from the prescriptions. Positive cultural prescriptions that result in rewards, recognition, and prestige are called social values. Values are usually part of the implicit and unstated part of the culture. The values that arise out of a linear/singular worldview will differ markedly from a holistic/cyclical worldview. A linear view implies a number of things. A line can be divided into units; a line has two opposing ends; a line is singular in direction; a line can be horizontal or vertical. Using these characteristics of a line, a number of social values implicit in linear thinking can be illustrated. Categorizing, dichotomizing, and reducing to smaller units are examples of the divisibility of a line. The opposing ends of a line leads to either/or modes of thought: good/bad, saint/sinner, big/small, fast/slow, new/old, day/night.

In terms of value judgements, good is preferred over bad, saint over sinner, faster over slower, bigger over smaller, and newer over older. The singular nature of a line leads to values that imply only one answer, one true way, and so on. Hierarchical orders are the result of a line in a vertical position. The consequences are values that prefer higher over lower, the leader over a commoner.

A linear/singular worldview leads towards specialist and product orientation. The singular nature of a line results in a singular identity. Personal identification is drawn from a specialty such as lawyer, teacher, doctor, mechanic, and so on. If people cannot apply a label of some kind to themselves, they are a 'nobody' in terms of social status. The movement from A to B to C on a line orients one toward achievement of a goal or the achievement of a product.

Language is one of the systems an observer can use to detect consistent trends and patterns. In other words, language, to a large extent implicitly embodies the worldview and values of a culture. For instance, English reflects the linear worldview. It is a language that has a bias for nouns or identification. Identification complements categorizing and dichotomizing, and the notion of 'thing' or product. One can conclude that English is noun-rich, but action-poor.

In contrast to white society's linear/singular worldview, the Indian and Metis worldviews can be characterized as cyclical/holistic, generalist, and process oriented. The cyclical/holistic view looks at time in terms of cosmological cycles and patterns and not in terms of an artificial creation of time units. Cosmological cycles are generally imperceivable in terms of change. Consequently, time at the functional operative, day-to-day level is not considered dynamic, and therefore, is not an important referent. The holistic view leads to an implicit assumption that everything is interrelated. Interrelatedness leads to an implicit idea of equality among all creation. Equality is brought about by the implicit belief that everything—humans, animals, plants, and inorganic matter—has a spirit. Anthropomorphic factors are not important because metamorphosis readily occurs. The common denominator is the spirit.

The cyclical/holistic view can be described as 'looking at the forest as opposed to the trees.' Implicit in the cyclical/holistic view is generalism and constant motion. In other words, there is a bias toward generalist knowledge and process. This arises out of the slow and imperceivable, but continuously changing patterns in the cosmos and the interrelationship of all creation.

Similar to the reflection of western European values in the culture of white society, the cyclical/holistic view embodies values that are implicit reflections of the worldview. The cyclical aspect leads to respect for cycles, phases, and repetition. A circle can be viewed as a whole. It has no beginning or no end, but it can be viewed as going round and round, not unlike the cyclical patterns of the cosmos. Repetitive patterns do not lead to goal orientation as they would in a linear view. Rather, they focus on the process. Implicit is the belief that if the process is followed, a product will happen.

When a circle is viewed as a whole, implicit convictions arise that, in the case of a society, the whole or the group is more important than a part or the individual. Being part of the group is better than being alone. The whole, combined with interrelatedness, results in values suggesting harmony and balance. Implicit in cycles and wholeness is generosity and sharing; everyone shares and shares alike. No one should be more important, wealthier, or different from everybody else.

Aboriginal languages, like other languages, are repositories for many implicit convictions, as Benjamin Whorff states:

Every language contains terms that have come to attain a cosmic scope of reference, that crystalize in themselves the basic postulates of an unformulated philosophy, in which is couched the thought of a people, a culture, a civilization, even an era. Most metaphysical words in Hopi are verbs, not nouns as in European languages.

Here, Whorff points out the process orientation of the Hopi language in comparison with the noun- or product-oriented English language. Blackfoot and Cree are not unlike Hopi. The categorizing process in most aboriginal languages classifies almost all things as animate. Inanimate categories are nearly nonexistent. If most things are animate and if all things have a spirit, then humans can relate to not just other humans, but also to animals, plants, and even inorganic matter.

The basic foundations—those rules of a culture that are dominant in the control of the behaviour of the members of a society—are worldview and value constituted. The underlying premises of white society can be articulated as follows:

God created the universe, the earth, and everything in it and on it.
God created humans in His own image and gave them dominion over everything.
God had a chosen people that He blessed to show the true way for all others.
Creation is divisible.
Individuals are more important than the group. Nations exist to protect
and provide for individuals.
Property is individually ownable, including land.
Knowledge is the learning of skills for a comfortable living.
Accumulation of wealth is a sign of success.
Social order is hierarchical.
The earth and everything in and on it is for the benefit of man.

The underlying foundations of Indian/Metis culture can be stated as follows:

The Creator made everybody, as equals, including humans, animals, plants, and inorganic life.
Everybody is interrelated with everybody.
Existence consists of energy and is expendable.

The energy quotient of creation is rechargeable through ritual.
Man is subordinate to, and a mere part of creation.
Other-than-human beings have knowledge that humans do not have.
Attainment of the knowledge of other-than-human beings is power.
Harmony and balance brings about happiness, order, beauty and health.
The group is more important than the individual.
Aggressive tendencies bring about disorder and imbalance.
All land and resources belong to the group.
Individual property is private but should be generously shared.
Individuals are important and should be given a lot of freedom.
Disorder is corrected through rehabilitative and restorative action.
Everything in the universe and on earth is alive and has a spirit.
Anthropomorphic aspects are not important.
Metamorphosis occurs readily.

The above premises, even though they are not exhaustive, are sufficient to point to differences between aboriginal and white culture.

The above philosophical differences results in a government for white society that is hierarchically structured, where power is divided among several units, and is operated according to 'the rule of law,' with a belief that everything other-than-human is for the benefit of humans. In contrast, aboriginal governments are horizontally structured, where power is shared by the whole, law is applied contextually, and balance and harmony are taken into consideration with all creation.

Legally, the relationship of aboriginal self-government and treaties will depend on the context within which the relationship is examined. For the purpose of this discussion, the writer will examine three contexts. The relationship between First Nations and Canada from an aboriginal perspective: the relationship between First Nations and Canada from a Canadian perspective; and a confederation perspective.

The Aboriginal Perspective

The basic premise of the aboriginal perspective is that First Nations are outside of the Canadian constitution framework, but with a unique relationship with Canada consisting of aboriginal and treaty rights. Treaties, pursuant to this view, are agreements between two or more sovereigns. Generally, treaties are agreements about specific matters and not all encompassing. This view of treaties is not unlike the view of treaties in international law. The Vienna Convention on the Law of Treaties defines a treaty as "an international agreement concluded between States in written form and governed by international law, whether embodied in a single instrument or in two or more related instruments and whatever its particular designation" (Article 2[1] [a] Vienna Convention). The aboriginal view of treaties finds support in the writings of John Locke. Native governments of the New World were characterized by Locke as independent states under (aboriginal) "kings" or "rulers" and those who had the supreme power of making laws in European countries are to the Indians simply "men without authority." Locke argued that when Indian nations entered into treaties (what he called "treaty federalism" or "treaty Commonwealth") with the American nations, those treaties and the bonds they established were limited to specific purposes rather than being comprehensive subordination of Indians' will to the will of non-Indians. This is his so-called principle of contractual treaty of commonwealth.

The view of treaties by aboriginal people as agreements between nation-states also finds support in the annuity arbitrations between the Dominion and Ontario governments concerning the Robinson treaties and *Connolly* v. *Woolrich* case of 1867. In the annuity arbitrations, the Solicitor General of Canada, Hon. J. J. Curran made the following statement:

> We contend that these Treaties are governed by international, rather than municipal law. They were made with the tribes under the authority of the Sovereign, and the faith of the nation was pledged in dealing with those annuities. The Crown is a trustee in those matters, and occupies a special relationship towards those Indians, and is bound to watch over their interests and enforce their rights, and will not be allowed to set up its own laches as a defence against these claims. All these claims are safeguarded in a manner that is quite a different manner from any claim that would arise between two subjects of Her Majesty who might come before any Court to have their matters adjudicated upon. (Department of Indian Affairs 1897)

In the *Connolly* v. *Woolrich* case, the court, in response to the contention that the presence of British subjects in Athabaska country and the Royal Proclamation of 1763 had displaced native law, said the following:

But admitting, for the purpose of conceding to the Defendant all that can be granted, that, in 1803, the Athabaska district was included within the western limits of the Hudson Bay territories, still that portion of the Common Law of England which would prevail there, had a very restricted application; it could be administered and enforced only among, and in favour of, and against those "who belonged to the Company or were living under them." It did not apply to the Indians, nor were the native laws or customs abolished or modified, and this is unquestionably true in regard to their civil rights. It is easy to conceive, in the case of joint occupation of extensive countries by European and native nations or tribes, that two different systems of civil and even criminal law may prevail. History is full of such instances, and the dominions of the British Crown exhibit cases of that kind. The Charter did introduce the English law, but did not, at the same time, make it applicable generally or indiscriminately; it did not abrogate the Indian laws and usages. The Crown has not done so. Their laws of marriage existed and exist under the sanction and protection of the Crown of England, and Mr. Connolly might bind himself as well by that law, as by the Common Law of England. It is still further contended that, by the treaty of Paris, in 1763, by which all the French possessions on the continent of America were ceded by France to Great Britain, the North-West was brought, not only under the dominion of England, but the common law of the realm was *ipso facto* introduced into the country. As a matter of fact and of public law, the treaty in question effected on such change in the laws of the territory. It will be observed that between 1670 and 1763 nearly one hundred years had elapsed, and during that period the French colonists and French trading companies had made settlements and established trading posts as far as the Rocky Mountains; that these countries were in the occupation of the French, and that no change could take place in their laws, or in the Indian usages, except by the express will of the conqueror, or of the sovereign to whom the cession was made. I find in the proclamation in pursuance of that treaty, dated 7th October 1763 the following clauses:

> And we do further declare it to be our royal will and pleasure, for the present, as aforesaid, to reserve under our sovereignty, protection, and dominion for the use of the said Indians, all the land and territories not included within the limits of the territory

granted to the Hudson's Bay Company; as also all the land and territories lying to the westward of the sources of the rivers which fall into the sea from the west and north-west as aforesaid; and we do hereby strictly forbid, on pain of our displeasure, all our loving subjects from making any purchases or settlements what ever, or taking possession of any of the lands above reserved without our especial leave and license for that purpose first obtained.

There is nothing to be found in this, or in any subsequent proclamation, abolishing or changing the customs of the Indians or the laws of the French settlers, whatever they may have been; nothing which introduced the English common law into these territories. When Connolly went to Athabaska, in 1803, he found the Indian usages as they had existed for ages, unchanged by European power or Christian legislation. He did not take English law with him, for his settlement there was not preceded by discoveries made either by himself or English adventurers, nor was it an uninhabited or unoccupied territory. This pretension of the Defendant, therefore, that, to the exclusion of the laws and customs of the natives, the common law of England prevailed at Rat River in 1803, or at any subsequent period, must be over-ruled, and in doing so the Court may remark that it was not competent in any case for Mr. Connolly to carry with him this common law of England to Rat River in his knapsack, and much less could he bring back to Lower Canada the law or repudiation in a bark canoe. *(Connolly v. Woolrich* 1867)

Mention is made of these supports found in history and law for the contention by First Nations that treaties signed with them should be looked at from a nation-to-nation perspective to show that the contention is not spurious but does have a basis in law and fact. The implications the contention has for self-government and treaties are:

1. Treaties are specific agreements about peace and friendship and/or land. Treaties have nothing to do with self-government. Self-government arises from aboriginal nationhood. The only relevance treaties have is that they are acts of nations.
2. The Royal Proclamation is declaratory recognition of the nation-to-nation relations between first nations and Great Britain.

3. SECTION 91(24) of the Constitution Act of 1867, SEC. 25, SEC. 35 of the Constitution Act of 1982, and other constitutional provisions such as the Natural Resources Transfer Agreements are arrangements internal to Canada as to its relationship with First Nations. In other words, Canada is basically saying through these constitutional sections "This is how I will carry out my relations with First Nations."
4. The Indian Act *should be* the administrative aspect of the treaty relationship.

The Canadian Perspective

The basic premise of the Canadian perspective is that Indians are Canadian citizens with some justification for a special legal status due to historical factors. The underlying *modus operandi* is parliamentary supremacy. Parliamentary supremacy holds that you cannot circumscribe or limit the sovereign without his/her permission. Parliamentary supremacy is exemplified and well illustrated by the lack of hierarchy in law. In other words, though the labels such as constitutional law, statutory law, regulatory regimes, and executive orders are used to label different types of laws, so long as Parliament passes it, it is law. In many cases, this approach resulted in regulations overriding fundamental aboriginal and treaty rights (for example, the Baker Lake case 'superseded by law' and provincial fishing regulations overriding treaty rights to fish). This all encompassing Parliamentary supremacy has resulted in the present legal regime as regards Indians.

Prior to 1982, the legal regime as regards Indians arose from SEC. 91 (24) of the Constitution Act, 1867. SEC. 91 (24) was the enabling clause for the Indian Act. Indian treaties and aboriginal rights were of minor significance because citizens cannot enter into treaties with their government. As a consequence, treaties were by and large extinguishing instruments of Indian rights. According to the *St. Catherine's and Lumber Co.* case (1888), the Indian interest in land is a mere "personal and usufructuary right, dependent on the goodwill of the sovereign." In other words, Indians never had complete title to their territory. The effect of a treaty is to remove the personal and usufructuary (beneficial) interest that acted as a burden on the title of the Crown making the Crown's interest complete. Consequently, one can conclude that prior to a treaty being signed, the basis of the relationship is the continuing existence of the personal and beneficial interest in land and SEC. 91 (24). But once a treaty is signed, the personal and beneficial interest is exchanged for a reserve and other promises, but the main and continuing basis for a relationship is SEC.91 (24) and the Indian Act passed pursuant to it. Accordingly, under the Canadian perspective, treaties, just as under the aboriginal perspective, have little relevance for self-government. The only source for self-government is a statutory one: the Indian Act.

Since 1982, with the patriation of the Canadian constitution, the Canadian perspective has to some extent been modified, but not radically. Prior to 1982, there was no entrenchment of rights in the Canadian constitution, but since then Parliament has agreed to some limitations on its supremacy to the extent of the Charter, and specific to Indians, SEC. 25 and 35. An important point to make is that prior to 1982, even though Canadians thought they had rights, they really did not. Everything was at the goodwill of the sovereign. It has only been since patriation that Canadians can legitimately claim rights against their government. The notion of 'rights' only makes sense from within the Canadian perspective, but not from the aboriginal perspective with respect to Canada. The agenda between nations is relations, while the agenda between citizens and governments is rights. We want to emphasize this point because most people who engage in discussion about these matters speak of everything in terms of rights.

Generally speaking, in spite of the fact that the term "collective rights" has come into common usage, rights belong to individuals and not to governments. Governments do not have rights: they have power and sovereignty. Speaking of self-government on the basis of rights is, in fact, putting it in the context of citizen-government relations and not in the context of nation-to-nation.

In conclusion to this section, two further observations are worthy of note. First, an Indian band, more or less, is a federal municipality if looked at from the point of view that a municipal government is a delegated form of government that owes its existence to a higher level of government. From this point of view, a band and its government owes its existence to the federal government through the Indian Act not unlike a city that owes its existence to a provincial government through municipal legislation. Secondly, jurisdiction is a matter of division of powers between two or more governments. Jurisdiction makes sense only if one is talking from within the four square corners of a constitutional framework. Nations do not talk jurisdiction between each other, they talk treaty and other international mechanisms. The point to be made is that arguing about jurisdictional matters with regard to aboriginal self-government is really speaking from within the Canadian perspective.

The Confederation Perspective

The basic premise of this perspective is that First Nations are outside of the Canadian constitutional framework, but will now join the union either as a separate order of government or as a province. If First Nations become a province then their constitutional position will be the same as any province and will operate through section 92 of the Constitution Act of 1867. If First Nations formed a third order of government then they would operate under a newly created set of powers that would most likely be a blend of sections 91 and 92. The Confederation perspective implies that the *quid pro quo* for joining the union are aboriginal and treaty rights and sovereignty. The major concern for First Nations in this context are, or should be, 'terms of union.'

A variation on this model is a constitutional upgrading process. In other words, starting from the Canadian perspective, i.e. Indian Act government, the same result could be achieved as the Confederation model if Indian bands were constitutionally upgraded to provincial status or third order of government. Some ramifications of this perspective are:

1. Treaty and aboriginal rights will be *quid pro quo* for confederation. Treaties will not have much relevance as regards Indian government except only as a bargaining chip for favourable terms of union.
2. Indian Act and most case law as it exists in the Canadian perspective will disappear because the basis of the relationship will now be SEC. 92 or third order of government. The present legal regime found in the Canadian perspective is based on Indian Act, treaties, aboriginal rights, and so on, but that would disappear under this context.
3. An interesting note to conclude with is that the Charlottetown Accord attempted to achieve a new relationship between Canada and the First Nations somewhere along the line of a confederation model, by recognizing the inherent right aboriginal people have to establish their own governments and recognizing those governments as one of three orders of government within Canada.

Conclusion

Aboriginal self-government is an issue that has been heatedly debated in government and aboriginal circles in the past few years. Most discussions fail to focus on the basic philosophical and legal foundations, but, instead, focus on the structural and functional aspects of self-government. The structure, functions, and powers will depend on the culture and ethos of a particular society. Legally, a government's structure, power, and functions will depend on its source of authority. From an aboriginal perspective, the source of authority for government lies in the aboriginal nationhood of First Nations and is not accorded by any other authority. Treaties do not have much relevance insofar as the authority to form governments except as indicators that treaties are acts of nations. The Canadian perspective assumes that aboriginal people are citizens of Canada and therefore, subject to the legal regime of Canada. Self-government means Indian Act. Treaties, as extinguishing documents of aboriginal rights, do not have much relevance with regard to self-government except as checks on the power of Parliament because of SEC. 25 and 35 of the Constitution Act of 1982. In the confederation perspective, the authority to form government based on the inherent sovereignty of First Nations will become the *quid pro quo* for joining the union. In this context, treaties will be one of the bargaining chips for entering and becoming part of the union, but will not directly affect the form, structure, powers, and functions of government.

References

Connolly v. Woolrich. 1867. 1 CNLC 70.
Department of Indian Affairs. 1897. From the records of the Federal-Provincial Arbitrations (Unsettled Accounts Arbitration), Indian Claims, Robinson Treaties, Vol. 5 (12 January).
St. Catherine's and Lumber Co. 1888. 14 A.C. 48 (J.C.P.C.).

COMMENTARY

Beyond Gloom and Doom: Federalism, Citizenship, and Political Change

Linda Trimble

Introduction

When reading the papers written for the third session of the Future of Federalism Conference, which was titled "Contemporary Challenges to Federal Structures," I was struck by the view of federalism offered by "outsiders" to the study of Canadian politics. The papers written by Brian Galligan and Georgina Lynch (Australian political scientists) and Bohdan Harasymiw (a Canadian who studies the Soviet successor states) represented federalism as a complex, flexible, and responsive governmental structure. Both saw federalism as integral to the solution of grave problems; environmental degradation in Australia, and incipient violent ethnic and national conflict in the former Soviet Union. On the other hand, the participants who are students of Canadian politics (Leroy Little Bear, who made a presentation about aboriginal peoples in Canada, and Roger Gibbins, who offered several comments during the discussion period), argued that federal structures and processes are inherently artificial, inflexible, and exclusionary. It is in this vein that the forces discussed by panel members were conceptualized as challenges to federal systems.

Three forces with the potential to shape federal systems were discussed. The first, traditional territorial politics, includes regional, geographic, and linguistic cleavages. The second is aboriginal self-determination. While territorial in nature, the quest for aboriginal rights, land claims, and self-government has not yet been accommodated within existing federal structures, or adequately articulated within federalism discourse. The third factor is clearly nonterritorial; this force includes the aspatial politics of environmentalism, feminism, human rights, and peace activism.

These three forces can be seen as challenges to federalism or as opportunities for federal states, depending on the situation and one's point of view. I will argue that the English-Canadian political-science tradition is distinguished by a "gloom-and-doom" tradition, which sees federalism as a fragile construct, propped up by elites, and intolerant of conflict and multiple identities.[1] The gloom-and-doom perspective holds profoundly conservative assumptions about the amount of competition and diversity the political system can accommodate. Therefore, within this perspective, both new and old conflicts and identities are viewed as challenges, and even as threats, to national unity and political survival. I will contest the gloom-and-doom position by arguing that the three forces identified as challenges to federalism can alternatively be seen as important instruments of, or catalysts for, change and innovation in federal states. In particular, feminism and other social movements offer new, and valuable, conceptions of citizenship, conceptions which are perhaps more easily articulated and realized in federal systems than in unitary systems.

The Gloom-and-Doom Tradition

The gloom-and-doom tradition in Canadian political science is best illustrated by the following sample of textbook and monograph titles drawn from the English-Canadian literature:

Must Canada Fail?
One Country or Two?
Bleeding Hearts . . . . Bleeding Country
Divided Loyalties
Canada in Question
Unfulfilled Union
Canadian Federalism: Myth or Reality?
And No One Cheered
Disruptions
Conflict and Unity
Canada and the Burden of Unity
The Roots of Disunity

---

1. I hasten to add that neither Roger Gibbins nor Leroy Little Bear are quintessential gloom and doomers; in fact, to my knowledge, Roger Gibbins is generally quite optimistic about the future of federalism in Canada. However, during the Future of Federalism conference, both took the view that federalism cannot cope with new or old (but emerging) political identities and movements.

The tradition is invariably gloomy; studies of federalism and the constitution interpret new and old forces, ideas, and conflicts in a negative light. One of the most striking examples of such pessimism is *And No One Cheered*, a collection of articles written after the patriation of the constitution in 1982. The book is ominously dedicated "to our children, who will live with the consequences" (Banting and Simeon 1983). The gloom-and-doom tradition is premised on the assumption that, in Canada, the federal experiment is doomed. Indeed, Canadian political scientists have been predicting, or musing about, the disintegration of the country for many years, as the above titles illustrate. For example, Garth Stevenson asserted, at an academic post-mortem on the Meech Lake Accord in 1990, that Canada lacks "the necessary degree of social, economic and political integration to support the institutions of a federal state" (cited in Smith and Courtney 1991: 9–10).

The gloom-and-doom persuasion is premised on the belief, summarized by Ed Black, that Canada lacks a clear and strong pan-national identity; "the most conspicuously missing ingredient in this political system has been any sign of an overarching nationalism" (1975: 1). Political integration is seen to require a "clearly established national identity or, . . . a higher allegiance (Canadian for example) prevailing over all others" (Orban 1991: 83). The persistence of dualism and regionalism are seen to be largely responsible for Canada's integration problem. Dualism, the presence of "two sociological nations" within the Canadian state,[2] divides political loyalties. Moreover, unity is threatened by the persistence of Québec nationalism and the movement for sovereignty-association; in this context the word "crisis" is often used.[3] In the introduction to *Must Canada Fail?*, Richard Simeon wrote:

> This is not an optimistic book . . . however much good will there is, the fissure in the Canadian communities may be too deep to be bridged, and one of the communities may decide to seek its own independence as a sovereign state. Disintegration is no longer simply a possibility, as it was when the predecessor to this book, *One Country*

---

2. Lord Durham's report on the situation in British North America after the rebellions in 1837 summarized the problem as "two nations warring the bosom of a single state." See also Resnic (1991: 19–32).
3. See, for instance, "The Anatomy of Conflict: The Task Force on Canadian Unity," abridged in Blair and McLeod (1993: 141).

or Two? was published in 1971. It may not be a probability yet, but it is not far from it. (1977*a*: 1)

Regionalism is also regarded as inherently dysfunctional: "If the interests and/or the values of one or several important regions are too distinct, or even of a clearly conflictive nature when compared to those of the national majority, this phenomenon could lead to a rather serious disequilibrium" (Orban 1991: 83). Federal-provincial conflicts, typified by the Alberta-Ottawa 'oil wars' of the early 1980s, are cause for considerable anxiety among gloom and doomers.[4]

While dualism is perceived as the seam which could split Canada apart, it is also seen as the glue which holds the country together. John Deutch, one of the pioneers of the Canadian political science tradition, quoted former Ontario premier Leslie Frost in this regard:

> French-English partnership, stretching back to the days of 1763, has been of the utmost value to both. If it had not been for this, probably our English-Canadian culture would have long ago been absorbed into the United States. Conversely, the partnership has meant that the French-Canadian culture has been preserved. My view is that anything we do should be calculated to strengthen and preserve the partnership, and to avoid its break-up, which could be disastrous to the Canadian way of life. (1971: 2)

The original Canadian social contract, between the French and the English, is essential to Canada's survival, but this contract is perceived to be so fragile that it must be protected from the forces of change, be they new sources of identity or challenges to elite accommodation. For this reason, the gloom-and-doom tradition is troubled by regional identities and cleavages. Regionalism has been described as a myth (Careless 1991: 24–32), and as a backlash against Québec:

> Indeed it is possible that much of the disenchantment with the present federal system in many parts of English-speaking Canada is not at

---

4. See Young, Faucher, and Blais (1988: 136–63), for a critical analysis of this tendency in the gloom-and-doom persuasion.

bottom regionalism at all, but a backlash against the burdens of accommodation with French-speaking Canadians. (Mallory 1971: 400)

Those who see regionalism as a reality argue that it is not a reflection of social and economic diversity but, rather, a by-product of federal institutions, which construct political identities along territorial lines (Simeon 1977*b*; see also Gibbins 1980). Some observers say regionalism is "in decline" (Gibbins 1985: ch. 4); most see regional differences as fixable. Garth Stevenson (1989), for instance, laments the forces of decentralization and promotes a strong central government. Many political scientists prescribe intrastate federalism (strengthening national institutions such as the Senate) as a tonic for uppity premiers and alienated periphery-dwellers.

The gloom-and-doom tradition is premised on a view of citizenship which cannot accommodate multiple identities. While Québec nationalism poses a threat to the development of a pan-Canadian identity, it is clearly an enduring feature of Canadian political life, one which cannot be denied or described as a myth. The gloom-and-doom tradition holds that while a split personality is difficult to manage, multiple allegiances will tear Canada apart. Regional identities, aboriginal political communities and other psychological communities (for example, based on gender, ethnicity, environmentalism) are viewed with trepidation, and even perceived as antithetical to federalism. According to David Smith and John Courtney, "the past decade introduced new constitutional questions, new constitutional actors, and a new constitutional norm in the form of the Charter. The effect has been *inherently antifederal, as federalism has traditionally been understood in Canada*" (Smith and Courtney 1991: 8, emphasis added).[5]

Solutions for Canada's integration problems are sought at the elite level—via such measures as intergovernmental conferences, cooperative federalism, and institutional reform. Further, it is often stated, or implied, that only elites can foster integration and that too much citizen participation is inherently destabilizing.[6] For example, in an 1990 article, Peter Russell observed that the Charter has fostered the desire for a more participatory form

---

5. Alan Cairns makes a similar argument in *Charter versus Federalism* (1992).
6. As John Meisel put it in "Bizarre Aspects of a Vanishing Act," students of Canadian politics must be aware of "the importance, in any examination of party responses to cleavages, of the relation between elites and the mass publics. The former are normally more open, less bigoted, and, naturally, more active in searching for compromises" (1975: 271).

of constitutional politics. Yet he cautioned against widespread citizen involvement in constitution making, arguing that constitutional reform requires compromises which can only be reached through elite accommodation: "A more democratic process of constitutional politics may push . . . [the] difference between the constitutional values of English and French majorities closer to the surface" (1990:259). Stevenson said much the same thing, after the demise of the Meech Lake Accord:

> Quebec after the Quiet Revolution began to challenge its position within Confederation and to demand a renegotiation of its terms. Nonetheless, our traditions of consociational elite accommodation seemed to make this possible and thus to preserve Confederation through incremental changes. The Meech Lake Accord was the culmination of this approach, and its failure is thus highly significant. (cited in Smith and Courtney 1991: 259)

For gloom-and-doom proponents, "salvation by constitution" is our only hope.[7] The patriation agreement of 1981, which did not have Québec's support, inspired a sense of urgency among students of constitutional politics which was raised to a fever pitch by the failure of the Meech Lake Accord. Participants at a Meech Lake *post mortem* argued that the lessons from Meech Lake must be learned, and learned quickly because "there will be no further chance" (Smith and Courtney 1991: 12). There was another chance, but the Charlottetown agreement was soundly rejected by Canadian voters, when put to a referendum in October 1992. If constitutional politics can be compared to baseball, gloom and doomers are most likely saying "three strikes—Canada's out."

Beyond Gloom and Doom

Obviously, Canada persists, and even thrives, notwithstanding decades of gloomy predictions by political and academic elites. The late Donald Smiley wrote, in the introduction to *The Federal Condition in Canada*: "In retrospect it appears that I, and most other observers of Canadian affairs, very much over-estimated the strength of Quebec nationalism and pro-

---

7. Ed Black uses this phrase as a section heading in *Divided Loyalties* (1975: 231).

vincialist influences elsewhere in the country and very much under-estimated the capacity of the system to respond effectively to such divisive pressures" (1987: ix). I think Smiley was half right; Canadian political science has underestimated the resilience of the system. But Québec nationalism, provincialism, and other sources of identity and conflict have not been underestimated; rather, their impact has been misinterpreted and misrepresented. The gloom-and-doom tradition is based on a conservative assumption about the amount of conflict and diversity the Canadian political system can accommodate.[8]

Gloom and doomers assume that the traditional politics of language and territory, and regional economic conflict, are essentially disruptive and destabilizing. Indeed, students of federalism see federal-provincial cooperation as the Canadian equivalent of the holy grail. This is a strange argument for political scientists to make, given that politics is about who gets what, where, and when. In other words, politics involves power, conflict, communication, and decision making, and as Albert Breton observes, "in some areas, cooperation is *not* an efficient principle of social organization and . . . is less efficient than competition, essentially because cooperation can easily degenerate into collusion, conspiracy, and connivance, and that is not necessarily good!" (1988: 286).

Federal structures are chosen, and designed, to reflect and accommodate various sources of diversity and conflict. It is true that the societal schisms which inspire federal states may threaten them, but is it not possible that geographic and linguistic cleavages provide bases of innovation and change? After all, social change occurs when conflicts and differences are voiced and debated. Territorial and linguistic cleavages can provide opportunities as well as challenges. It seems to me that traditional sources of diversity and conflict (dualism and regionalism) have benefited Canadian society and Canadian political life to a much greater extent than academics and political leaders like to admit. Québec nationalism has certainly broadened and enriched political debate in Canada. It has attenuated the individualizing thrust of lib-

---

8. Not all students of federalism fall into the gloom-and-doom category. For instance, Roger Gibbins notes the concern in the literature about "the integrative capacity of the Canadian political system, for its capacity to knit together often disparate regional and linguistic communities into a national whole." He responds to this concern with an optimistic observation: "Although the Canadian political community has been confronted with an array of very difficult problems, the national community has endured and prospered" (1985: 5).

eralism by promoting the group consciousness of a linguistic community. Québec nationalists in the 1960s and 1970s spoke of decolonization and employed terms like domination and oppression, revolution and liberation, thereby adding important and dramatic words to Canadian political discourse. Likewise, for the group consciousness of feminists, "nationalism provided women with a political vocabulary with which they could analyze their oppression" (Lamoureux 1987: 51).[9]

Regionalism has also stimulated change and progress. Western alienation has provided fertile soil for new political parties (the Progressives, Social Credit, the Cooperative Commonwealth Federation of Canada [CCF]/New Democratic Party [NDP] and, most recently, the Reform Party) with novel, and sometimes bizarre, ideas. Significant policy innovations have been developed at the provincial level, including the oft-cited example of universal health care. Last, but not least, regional and linguistic differences offer Canadians a vibrant and diverse cultural experience, as fans of Céline Dion, Kashtin, Rita MacNeil, W. O. Mitchell, k. d. Laing, Emily Carr, Bill Reid, and CODCO will attest.

Everything Old is New Again

The gloom-and-doom tradition, which is common to both political and academic elites, tends to obscure nonterritorial identities, cleavages, and conflicts. John Porter recognized this thirty years ago:

> The major themes in Canadian political thought emphasize those characteristics, mainly regional and provincial loyalties, which divide the Canadian population. Consequently integration and national unity must be a constantly reiterated goal to counter such divisive sentiments. . . . The question which arises is whether the discord-unity dialogue has any real meaning in the lives of Canadians, or whether it has become, in the middle of the 20th Century, a political technique of conservatism? (1965: 369)

While traditional federalism discourse continues to act as a conservative break on the articulation of nontraditional identities and ideals, aboriginal

---

9. Lamoureux also notes that nationalism "has always held a misogynous view of women" and argues that feminists must critique nationalism's concepts.

politics and social-movement politics are gaining limited recognition. Aboriginal self-government and the politics of environmentalism, feminism, peace, and human rights have been around for a very long time, but only recently have they made their way onto the (official) political and academic agenda.

Not surprisingly, given the gloom-and-doom tradition's focus on federalism and the constitution, mainstream political science did not hear these political voices until aboriginal and equality rights were enshrined in the Charter of Rights. They are suddenly legitimate by virtue of being "constitutionalized" (see Cairns 1991, ch. 4: 108-138). According to F. L. Morton, there are now "two different constitutions battling for control of the Canadian state" (1992: 299). On the one hand, there is the old constitutional order, "the constitution of governments, federalism, and French-English dualism," which is designed and renovated by political elites (299). On the other hand, there is the new constitutional order inspired by the Charter; it speaks of individual rights and freedoms, aboriginal rights, multiculturalism, equality, and democracy. This characterization places the new/old politics in opposition to federalism—as the title of Alan Cairns's latest book, *Charter versus Federalism* (1992), indicates. Women, aboriginal peoples, and other previously marginalized groups are characterized as "Charter Canadians," consumers of rights, and as otherwise unconnected to the larger federal/constitutional order.

As Jill Vickers points out, this is both inaccurate and condescending (1991: 18). Women, aboriginal groups, visible minorities, and the disabled have been knocking on the door of the "old constitutional order," indeed the established political order, for several decades. Yet "aboriginal peoples and women are the new kids on the constitutional block, not permitted to be in the neighbourhood until recently and still treated with suspicion by the long-time residents" (Greshner 1991: 223). The new constitutional kids on the block are not simply rights bearers and greedy rights seekers; they are citizens who have an interest in and a commitment to fair and effective policy making, to federal structures which facilitate the expression of both diversity and commonality, and to representative and democratic political institutions.[10] Women recognize that the "division of powers, and the represen-

---

10. It is generally assumed that those who identify as women, first nations people, as visible minorities or differently abled, focus on their particular circumstances and cannot see "the

tativeness of institutions of government, like the Senate, are issues which will determine whether and how women come to enjoy equality in the conditions of our lives" (Day 1991: 95). Yet the constitutional participation of the women's movement goes well beyond discussion of gender equality. During the most recent discussions of constitutional reform, which culminated in the Charlottetown Accord, the National Action Committee on the Status of Women (NAC) lobbied strenuously for recognition of the inherent right to self-government for First Nations, for special status (in the form of asymmetrical federalism) for Québec, and for democratic reforms to the Senate, such as election of senators by proportional representation.

So why the fuss? In Canada, the unspoken assumption among those who resist discussion of the problems and demands raised by feminists, aboriginal peoples, and others, is that we cannot even deal with the original sources of conflict, and if we pile additional problems onto old cleavages, dire consequences will ensue. Critical social movements are, according to Warren Magnusson, open, experimental, innovative, and oriented towards dialogue and change (1990: 527). That they are viewed as fundamental challenges to federal systems is indeed telling and, to my mind, disturbing. Is federalism, as a political arrangement, so rigid, static, and impermeable that it cannot accommodate new cleavages, new discourses, and new demands for change? In a word, no. There is nothing about the nature of federalism—which is simply an arrangement which divides power and jurisdiction between governments—which prevents the democratization of political institutions and the emergence of creative politics.

The new/old politics raise another matter of concern to students of Canadian federalism; they question traditional ways of thinking about the nation state. As Galligan and Lynch point out in their paper, aspatial politics transcend geographic boundaries by articulating global concerns and demanding international solutions. On the other hand, the new/old politics emphasize democratic action within smaller political communities. As a result, social movements may ultimately "de-centre the state" (to borrow Magnus-

---

big picture." But how can people generalize without understanding where and how they are rooted? Joanne St. Lewis said this much more eloquently than I am able to; "As a black woman I must be able to reach a point where I can generalize from the particularity of my experience and make contact with some part of the universal, some aspect of my community's experiences, some part of the broader social and political framework. *This is a critical part of having voice."* (1991: 65, emphasis added).

son's phrase). Because aspatial politics promote identities which transcend, or crosscut, the territorial communities on which federal structrues are based, Gibbins believes social movements will, ultimately, "corrode" fedrealism (see Gibbins's article in section 2). Is this really the case? Galligan and Lynch posed this question in their paper, and they said the answer, with respect to environmentalism and federal politics in Australia, is no. In fact, they argued that federal structures can cope with the new environmentalism and, indeed, federal institutions and processes are uniquely capable of accommodating demands for solutions to problems like environmental degradation. They believe aspatial politics have the potential to shape federal practices in the twenty-first century. In other words, the new/old politics may improve rather than disrupt federal structures.

Towards an Inclusive Definition of Citizenship

I mentioned earlier that the gloom-and-doom tradition holds a narrow view of citizenship. According to Richard Vernon, traditional political-science discourse sees model citizens as people "with a single overriding object of loyalty" (1988: 3). Moreover, model citizens would be willing

> to set particular interests aside when necessary. They are supposed to attach importance to their membership in a political community, at the expense sometimes of their membership in families or professional or regional communities; and they are supposed to define their own interests, at least in certain contexts, in terms of the interests of the political community to which they belong. (3–4)

Vernon notes that federal citizens have two official loyalties—federal and provincial. And Canadians have many unofficial loyalties. Yet the gloom-and-doom perspective is premised on the belief that divided loyalties are problematic; we can not be good Canadian citizens if we have other interests, identities and allegiances.

Such a view is unrealistic, exclusionary, repressive, and perhaps even undemocratic. It is unrealistic because it decontextualizes people. We do not become citizens in the abstract; indeed, it is through our particular interests, our family and community ties, that we learn the rights and responsibilities of citizenship. We learn to care for the broader political community because we learn how to care for each other, first in the family, then as peers, playmates, friends, neighbors and colleagues.[11] In other words, our particular interests are essential to the development of the qualities of good citizens, which include "self-sacrifice, responsibility, concern for shared goals" (Vernon 1988: 10).

The definition is exclusionary because it asserts that full citizenship is only possible if one loyalty overrides all other attachments. Therefore, in this light, Québec nationalists, environmentalists, first nations people, feminists, and so on, pose threats to the larger constitutional order. The idea of a homogeneous federal citizenship is also repressive. It requires people to suppress the ideas and visions which connect them to others, which make them whole, and it asks people to exercise their citizenship in a language which is not their own. As Gabriel Garcia Marques said: "The interpretation of our reality through patterns not our own serves only to make us ever more unknown, ever less true, ever more solitary" (cited in Razak 1991: 40).

Finally, the 'one Canada' view of citizenship is not particularly tolerant of democratic participation. When citizenship requires the repression of subnational loyalties, it disempowers many people and serves as a barrier to their self-actualization. Those who are not allowed participate on their own terms are effectively disenfranchised. True citizenship, argues Virginia Sapiro, "entails the liberty, even the responsibility, to share in the governance and the political life of a community. . . .Those who are governed but do not govern are not citizens but subjects" (1984: 7). Those who participate in their own fashion enrich the political system. For instance, the creative potential of aboriginal politics is evidenced by the non-partisan, consensus-based legislative system in the North West Territories, where aboriginal peoples comprise the majority of the population (see White 1991).

The women's movement is undertaking the arduous, but necessary, task of saying goodbye to the universal woman. While women share a core of oppression, differences among and between women are striking, and politically salient. The movement has realized that if we continue to simplify and universalize women's experiences, we deny "the privilege of skin, class, age, heterosexuality, and physical and mental ability," with harmful consequences (Razak 1991: 39, 41). Recognizing difference is not easy; in fact,

---

11. "No man becomes a great patriot without first learning the closer loyalties and learning them well: loyalty to the family, to the place he calls home, to his province or state or county." (Roderick Haig-Brown, cited by George Woodcock 1983: 333).

it is a painful, heart-wrenching and time-consuming endeavor. The women's movement welcomes this process, however, because it will enrich and empower us all.

Likewise, the Canadian community will become stronger if and when we learn to acknowledge and appreciate expressions of diversity. One positive feature of a federal system, as Vernon notes, is that, at the very least, dual loyalties are built into the symbols and structures of government. Federalism enhances citizenship because it divides civic loyalty (1988: 11). Vernon applauds Proudhon's assertion that "citizenship is compatible only with multiple loci of attachment," and notes this is more likely to occur in a federal system: "To the extent that 'the federal principle' leaves open the question of priority, permitting individuals to balance one attachment against another, it permits more scope, Proudhon believes, for self-determination" (10).

This is not simply a matter of theory, or lofty ideals. To deny the political and social value of human relationships and commitments is to deny those forces which animate and bind our communities. Donna Greshner also points out that forcing people to repress identities and choose between communities causes great harm:

> I suggest we keep aboriginal women in the forefront of our minds as we think about the constitution. First, they remind us, simply by who they are, that everyone has multiple identities at one and the same time and all the time. Their treatment by government for decades—the injustice of section 12(1)(b) of the Indian Act by which they were told they could either be Indians or mothers and wives in the family of their choice—illustrates shamefully that it is unrealistic and profoundly damaging to force people to select one facet of their identity. . . . If we want a unified Canada, our search must be for methods of governance that permit and foster multiple identities, as federalism once did and may do still. (1991: 223)

Conclusion

Traditional territorial cleavages, aboriginal self-determination and the aspatial politics of environmentalism, human rights, feminism and other postmaterialist values, have all been regarded as threats to federalism. I have argued that federalism may be more flexible and adaptable than many political scientists, and political elites, admit. Gibbins and Little Bear said, during the discussion period following this session, that federalism is an artificial construct which must be constantly articulated, defended and explained. But what is created and articulated can be rearticulated and reconfigured. Federal structures can be 'home grown.' They can, if we expand our understanding of citizenship and if we are vigilant in our pursuit of democratic representation, be based on the cultures and belief systems of the people they serve.

References

Banting, Keith, and Richard Simeon, (eds.) 1983. *And No One Cheered.* Toronto: Methuen.
Black, Edwin R. 1975. *Divided Loyalties.* Montreal: McGill-Queen's University Press.
Blair, R. S., and J. T. McLeod, (eds.) 1993. *The Canadian Political Tradition,* 2nd ed. Scarborough: Nelson Canada.
Breton, Albert. 1988. "Competition and Cooperation in the Canadian Federal System." In *Perspectives on Canadian Federalism,* edited by R. D. Olling and M. W. Westmacott. Scarborough: Prentice-Hall.
Cairns, Alan. 1991. *Disruptions.* Toronto: McClelland and Stewart.
Cairns, Alan. 1992. *Charter versus Federalism.* Montreal: McGill-Queen's University Press.
Careless, J. M. S. 1991. "The Myth of the Downtrodden West." In *Crosscurrents: Contemporary Political Issues,* edited by Mark Charlton and Paul Barker. Scarborough: Nelson Canada.
Day, Shelagh. 1991. "Constitutional Reform: Canada's Equality Crisis." In *Conversations Among Friends/Entre Amies,* edited by David Schneiderman. Edmonton: Centre for Constitutional Studies.
Deutsch, John. 1971. Introduction to *One Country or Two?,* edited by R. M. Burns. Montreal: McGill-Queen's University Press.
Gibbins, Roger. 1980. *Prairie Politics and Soceity: Regionalism in Decline.* Toronto: Butterworths.
Gibbins, Roger. 1985. *Conflict and Unity.* Toronto: Methuen.
Greshner, Donna. 1991. "Commentary." In *After Meech Lake: Lessons for the Future,* edited by D. Smith and J. Courtney. Saskatoon: Fifth House Publishers.
Lamoureux, Diane. 1987. "Nationalism and Feminism in Quebec: An Impossible Attraction." In *Feminism and Political Economy,* edited by Heather Jon Maroney and Meg Luxton. Toronto: Methuen.
Magnusson, Warren. 1990. "Critical Social Movements." In *Canadian Politics: An Introduction to the Discipline,* edited by Alain Gagnon and James P. Bickerton. Peterborough: Broadview Press.
Mallory, J. R. 1971. *The Structure of Canadian Government.* Toronto: Macmillan.
Meisel, John. 1975. *Working Papers on Canadian Politics,* 2nd ed. Toronto: McGill-Queen's University Press.
Morton, F. L. 1992. *Morgentaler* v. *Borowski: Abortion, The Charter and the Courts.* Toronto: McClelland and Stewart.

Orban, Edmond. 1991. "Constitution and Regional Cleavages: A View from Québec." In *After Meech Lake: Lessons for the Future*, edited by D. Smith and J. Courtney. Saskatoon: Fifth House Publishers.

Porter, John. 1965. *The Vertical Mosaic.* Toronto: University of Toronto Press.

Razak, Sherene. 1991. "Issues of Difference in Constitutional Reform: Saying Goodbye to the Universal Woman." In *Conversations Among Friends/ Entre Amies*, edited by David Schneiderman. Edmonton: Centre for Constitutional Studies.

Resnic, Philip. 1991. *Toward a Canada-Quebec Union.* Montreal: McGill-Queen's University Press.

Russell, Peter. 1990. "The Charter and the Future of Canadian Politics." In *Canadian Politics: An Introduction to the Discipline*, edited by Alain Gagnon and James T. Bickerton. Peterborough: Broadview Press.

Sapiro, Virginia. 1984. *The Political Integration of Women.* Urbana: University of Illinois Press.

Simeon, Richard, (ed.) 1977a. *Must Canada Fail?* Montreal: McGill-Queen's University Press.

Simeon, Richard. 1977b. "Regionalism and Canadian Political Institutions." In *Canadian Federalism: Myth or Reality*, 3rd ed., edited by J. Peter Meekison. Toronto: Methuen.

Smiley, D. V. 1987. *The Federal Condition in Canada.* Toronto: McGraw-Hill Ryerson.

Smith, David, and John Courtney, (eds.) 1991. Introduction to *After Meech Lake: Lessons for the Future.* Saskatoon: Fifth House Publishers.

St. Lewis, Joanne. 1991. "Conversations: A Talking Circle." In *Conversations Among Friends/ ntre Amies*, edited by David Schneiderman. Edmonton: Centre for Constitutional Studies.

Stevenson, Garth. 1989. *Unfulfilled Union*, 3rd ed. New York: Gage.

Vernon, Richard. 1988. "The Federal Citizen." In *Perspectives on Canadian Federalism*, edited by R. D. Olling and M. W. Westmacott. Scarborough: Prentice-Hall.

Vickers, Jill. 1991. "Why Should Women Care About Constitutional Reform?" In *Conversations Among Friends/Entre Amies*, edited by David Schneiderman. Edmonton: Centre for Contitutional Studies.

White, Graham. 1991. "Westminster in the Arctic: The Adaptation of British Parlimentarism in the Northest Territories," *Canadian Journal of Political Science* 24, no. 3 (September): 499–523.

Woodcock, George. "Confederation as a World Example." In *And No One Cheered*, edited by K. Banting and R. Simeon. Toronto: Methuen.

Young, R. A., Philippe Faucher, and André Blais. 1988. "The Concept of Province-Building: A Critique." In *Perspectives on Canadian Federalism*, edited by R. D. Olling and M. W. Westmacott. Scarborough: Prentice-Hall.

V: TRANSFORMATIONS IN FEDERAL STRUCTURES

The European Community: Is it a Supranational State in the Making?

Gretchen M. MacMillan

The European Community (EC) is *sui generis*.[1] It is not just an international organization; it is also not a federal state. In many ways it is as it has been throughout most of its existence in a state of flux. The present state of the EC might make the possibility of future integration seem unlikely. There could be less integration and more intergovernmentalism in the future. On the other hand, the degree and type of integration may move in new directions and the EC might become more of a supranational state, if not quite a federal state. Given the evolution of the EC, it would be unwise to rule out such growth and development.

The emphasis in this paper will be on the possibilities of further integration and the creation of a supranational state among the member-states and future member-states of the EC.[2] This paper is divided into three sections. Initially, there will be an examination of EC development up to and including the Maastricht Agreement, with a special emphasis on the issues of intergovernmentalism and federalism. This will be followed by an examination of those aspects of the agreement which would aid or abet the creation of an European political community, which would be necessary if the

---

1. In my study of the EC and its development I have been greatly helped over the past three years by my students in Political Science 561—the Governments and Politics of the European Community. I would like to take this opportunity to thank them for their insights and observations on this organization. This paper was originally written and presented before the completion of the ratification of the Treaty on European Union. At that time, the official name of the European Community was changed to the European Union. I will however refer to the European Union (as it became in October 1993) as the European Community. The change in title does not in any way change the conclusions in this paper.
2. There are many studies of the EC and its development. See, in particular, Keohane and Hoffman (1992); Laffan (1992); Urwin (1991).

EC is to become a supranational state. The final section will examine how integration in the EC might achieve legitimacy in the European political community that does not yet exist.

There is no doubt the European Community is at a crossroads. The euphoria following the agreement between the heads of state and government that resulted in the Treaty on European Union at Maastricht in December 1991 was replaced with doubt and uncertainty with the Danish rejection of the agreement in June 1992, and the impact on the Exchange Rate Mechanism (ERM) and Economic and Monetary Union (EMU) of the devaluation of several EC member-state currencies in the fall and winter of 1992–93. These developments, along with high unemployment, the impact of the current recession, the costs of German unification, the rise of right-wing nationalism, and the failure of the leaders of the EC to agree on a common approach to the ethnic wars in the former Yugoslavia, give cause for concern.

However, the process toward closer integration has not been completely halted. Ten member-states ratified the agreement before the second Danish referendum in June 1992 overturned the May 1992 referendum. The agreement has also been ratified by the British House of Commons. The Schengen Agreement, which provides for closer cooperation on law enforcement, visa policy, and immigration, among other things, has expanded beyond the inner six. The internal market agreed to under the Single European Act (SEA) came into effect on 1 January 1993. Discussions have begun with Austria, Finland, Sweden, and Norway about their possible admission to the EC.[3]

Some of the difficulties confronting the EC today are products of the experiment's success; some are the result of the changes that have occurred in Europe after 1989 and the collapse of the Soviet Union and its empire; some have occurred because of the growing awareness among citizens of what the experiment may mean for the individual state and society. While these developments might limit the overall agenda of closer political and economic union among the member-states of the EC, none are likely to bring the experiment to an end. Until this point in its evolution, development and integration has been driven by the member-state executive-dominated EC institutions such as the European Council, the Council of Ministers, and the

---

3. Treaties of accession have since been signed with these four states. They must now be ratified by the citizens of each of the new states as well as the European Parliament and the present twelve member-states' legislatures.

quasi-civil service EC executive European Commission. However, the response to the Treaty on European Union (to give the Maastricht Agreement its proper name) indicates that future successful integrative development will have to take place in a more societal oriented framework.

Intergovernmental Organization and European Integration

The European Community had its origins in the desire of certain European political leaders to prevent a reoccurrence of the two world wars that had torn Europe apart in the first half of this century. The dream of the European leaders who created first the European Coal and Steel Community (ECSC), in 1951, and the European Economic Community (EEC), in 1957, was much grander than a trade and customs union.[4] They envisaged a political and economic union which would ensure future peace among the warring European states.

The EC as a political unit creates difficulties for students of political institutions and public policy because it is more than just an international organization but it is not quite a nation-state (see Wallace 1983). Its institutional framework and policy process includes both Community institutions and national governments (see Bulmer 1982-83). From the beginning, the EC's institutions were given control over selected areas of economic policy among the member-states, and have possessed a degree of autonomy and sovereignty not true of any other international organization. It is for this reason that the term supranational rather than international is usually applied to the EC.

This has complicated the examination of EC integration by academic observers who have attempted to develop appropriate conceptual frameworks.[5] Most of the approaches on integration can be divided into two broad categories—the idealists and the realists (for more discussion, see Wallace 1982-83: 64). Idealists (often functionalists and neofunctionalists) believed that the nation-state would eventually wither away and be replaced by

---

4. The European Coal and Steel Community was created by the Treaty of Paris, in 1951. The agreement was between France, West Germany, Italy, Belgium, Luxembourg, and the Netherlands. These same six states signed the Treaty of Rome, in 1957, which created the European Economic Community and Euratom. The United Kingdom, Ireland, and Denmark joined in 1973, Greece in 1981, and Spain and Portugal in 1986.
5. For an example of the literature on the EC and integration, see Pentland (1973); Taylor (1983; 1989).

a single united Europe.[6] Realists (including intergovernmentalists and interdependent theorists) have been less willing to accept the eventual demise of the nation-state.

I would argue that some configuration of the nation-state will survive. Institutional inertia and the vested interest of state political actors, along with the national identity associated with particular states and the political legitimacy that regimes and governments derive from this identity, are all factors influencing its survival. Given the dominance of the executive and member-state executive-dominated institutions in policy formation and implementation and in the furthering of integration, the EC will likely continue in the foreseeable future as a form of intergovernmentalism with federal overtones, or as federalism with intergovernmentalist overtones (Wallace 1983; Pinder 1985-86).

What is meant by intergovernmentalism and federalism in the context of the EC? The term "intergovernmentalism" can be used in two ways in reference to the EC.[7] The first use of the term refers to the mechanisms used by the member-states to prevent the institutions of the Community from operating in ways that contravene their interests. In this sense, it carries many of the aspects of the term associated with it in international relations. In other words, it refers to a type of decision making in which control remains in the hands of the units. It also emphasizes the role of the nation-state in the Community (see, for instance, Hoffman 1982-83). The second way in which the term is used emphasizes the policy component of the term. Given the domestic content of much of this policy, the term reinforces the mechanisms by which the units of a federal state play a significant role in the decision-making and policy process in the central institutions (see Bulmer 1982-83).

In the EC, both terms are applicable. At the same time, the degree to which the terms are used also reflects the degree to which one is willing to see the EC as a peculiar international organization; an unique federal organism; or *sui generis* a supranational state in the making. If the EC is an international organization, then clearly the first definition of the term would be given preference, but if it is a federal organism, the second definition

---

6. For the "withering away of the nation-state," see Wallace (1982-83: 64). For functionalist and neofunctionalist approaches, see Lindberg (1963). For idealists, see Hoffman (1982-83).
7. For a discussion of some of the various terms used in examining the EC, see Laffan (1991: 1-21, and more specifically 11-13).

might be more appropriate. However, if the EC is examined as a supranational organization then it can be concluded (as it is here) that both play an important role. These roles have been important at different times and sometimes simultaneously.

The role of intergovernmentalism in the first meaning of the term is best seen in the creation and function of the European Council, while the second meaning of the term is best seen in the ongoing functionings of the Council of Ministers and Committee of Permanent Representatives (COREPER). The provisions for cooperation in the areas of foreign and defence policy and home affairs and justice in the Treaty on European Union provide an example of a combination of the two meanings. Meetings held by ministers and representatives from the commission under these sections of the treaty are outside the provisions of the Treaty of Rome and their decisions are non-justiciable by the European Court of Justice. To that extent they are therefore meetings of ministers in a quasi-international organization meeting. This is particularly reinforced in the first area of responsibility, which deals with foreign and defence policy issues. This is less evident in the second set of meetings, which deal with issues traditionally associated with the powers and responsibilities of the member-states at the domestic level.[8]

Intergovernmentalism in the second meaning also includes the idea that the decision making at the Union level is a complex interwoven tapestry of member-states interests and union interests that need to be taken into account in examining decision making at this level. At this level, intergovernmentalism shifts away from an emphasis on the Union level to one which includes the national governments as well. What it often did not emphasize was the profusion of links that existed across the member-states themselves, as well as the ones that existed between the member-states and the Union. Some have argued that the use of the term interdependence catches the complexities of these linkages and the limits and constraints that might exist on states' activities better than does the term intergovernmentalism (see Laffan 1992: 22). This term also includes the limits that might exist on a state's activities, not only as a member of the Union, but also of other international organizations such as General Agreement on

---

8. See Title V, "Provisions on a Common Foreign and Security Policy," and Title VI, "Provisions on Cooperation in the fields of Justice and Home Affairs," in The Treaty on European Union.

Tariffs and Trade (GATT), North Atlantic Treaty Organization (NATO), and the United Nations (UN).

Intergovernmentalism is not the only term that creates difficulties for those who examine the development of the Community. Federalism, while explaining much of the policy process of the Community, is a term laden with emotive meanings that upset many individuals in the member-states of the EC. On the one hand, the EC is clearly not a federal state. The powers over coercive force remains with the member-states. Although the sovereignty of the member-states has clearly been compromised and the recognition of the authority of the European Court of Justice decisions by both member-states' executives and judiciaries have gone a long way to creating the legal federal framework, the member-states still retain the right to opt out of the Union.

At the same time, the Community fits the more classic definition of federalism in that there are two separate sets of government operating in the same territory in which the laws of the central unit take precedent over the laws of the units where there is conflict in shared areas of competency. However, the Community is not a classic federal state. To a great extent, the term "executive federalism"—developed by Donald Smiley to explain federal-provincial relationships in Canada—gives us a better framework to look at developments in the EC. Smiley defined this as "a system of government which is executive dominated and within which a large number of important public issues are debated and resolved through the ongoing interactions among governments" (1987: 83). This phenomenon of executive federalism reflected changes in attitudes toward the nature of the proper relationship between the two levels of government within Canada. In classical federal units, the process of power distribution can be described as interstate federalism. In interstate federalism, there is a constitutional distribution of powers, duties, and financial resources between the federal and provincial governments which allows the two orders of government to operate independently of each other in their own spheres of influence, while also providing a framework to maintain relations between the two orders of government (Smiley and Watts 1985: 4). When conflict arises in a federation primarily organized along these lines it is usually dealt with through a system of intergovernmental relations and organizations.

Alternatively, federal units may organize themselves in slightly different ways in which the interests of regional units, "are channelled through and protected by the structures and operations of the central government" (Smiley and Watts 1985: 4). In this system, conflict is usually managed through the institutions of the central government. This is referred to as intrastate federalism.

In spite of the differences between the EC and more traditional federal states, the policy-making process as it now exists can be described as federalist in so far as it possesses two distinct levels of government, each with defined constitutional authority operating within the same territory, and that in certain defined areas under the constitution/treaties the laws of the central institutions are supreme over the laws of the component units.[9]

While there were political and economic reasons for the sovereign states who created the EC to agree to a diminishment of their sovereignty, only a few idealists truly believed that this would provide the framework for a new state. Certainly, some members of the member-states' political elites were not interested in creating even a federal Europe. Following the Luxembourg Crisis in the mid-1960s, power shifted away from the European Commission to the member governments themselves through the Council of Ministers and COREPER (see Hayes 1984; Hayes-Renshaw et al. 1989-90). The member-states assumed the key roles in policy and decision making in the EC through the use of their veto power in the Council of Ministers, which allowed them to hold on to their state sovereignty and to protect their national interests through increased intergovernmental decision making.

Yet even so, there were still many conflicts that could not be resolved through the existing Community institutions. This prompted the leaders of the member-states to seek other mechanisms to deal with system-wide problems. An increased emphasis was placed on the role of the executive agencies at the centre and on mechanisms that brought the executives of the centre and parts together. This led to the creation and growth of the supranational role of the European Council of the Heads of Government and State in the EC (see Bulmer and Wessels 1987).

This process in the EC, which has been defined as "the 'pooling' and 'mixing' of national sovereignty with Community powers" (Bulmer and Wessels 1987: 10), has been described as cooperative federalism. This can be defined as a system in which the two levels of government have become integrated to the extent that both levels of government play a role in policy making because the two levels are unable to carry out their tasks alone, as

---

9. For similarities and differences between Canadian and EC models of federalism, see MacMillan (1991; 1994).

the tasks they must fulfil go beyond their individual institutional, constitutional, and economic resources. Weakness in institutional frameworks, therefore, gave rise to executive dominance and intergovernmentalism. This in turn led to the creation of a summitry mechanism to handle conflicts that could not be resolved by any of the established constitutional mechanisms. It also resulted in a system that emphasized the preservation of regional and state interests as well as regional political actors.

The shift to the extra-constitutional framework of the European Council from the Commission reduced the centripetal influences of the EC's institutions, even as it became the engine of closer integration. While the Commission was in eclipse in the early 1980s, it regained a certain prominence under the leadership of Jacques Delors, however, the role of major decision maker in the EC remains the European Council. This role has been reinforced by the changes introduced in the SEA and the Treaty on European Union.

By the early 1980s, the EC, preoccupied with budgetary problems and agricultural surpluses, appeared moribund. Although several reports had been commissioned by the European Council on how further unity might be achieved, most were accepted, tabled, and forgotten. The Community was widening with the admission of Greece, Spain, and Portugal, but not deepening. In 1984-85, this stagnation began to shift with the introduction of the process that would lead to the creation of an internal market by 1992. Not surprisingly, given the central importance in the EC of the Franco-German axis, a central role was played by French President Francois Mitterand and West German Chancellor Helmut Kohl. An intergovernmental conference was held to negotiate the changes to the treaties that were required to bring about closer relationships and provide the groundwork for the internal market. The changes incorporated into the SEA were agreed to by the twelve states in 1985.[10]

The process of reaching decisions on what might be referred to as the constitution of the EC—changes in the treaties—demonstrates the complexity of interaction among the executives of the member-states. The series of intergovernmental meetings and special committees struck to consider issues of political integration and constitutional change were initiated by members of the European Council. This body made decisions regarding the implemen-

---

10. For a discussion of events and reports leading up to the SEA, see Moravcsik (1992); Murphy (1985).

tation of discussions, while the actual wording of any agreements were agreed upon through the mechanisms of the Council of Ministers. Following approval by heads of government and state, the SEA was submitted to the parliaments of each of the member-states. In two states, Denmark and Ireland, it was necessary to hold national referendums.

Following the implementation of the SEA, the EC appeared to be moving to closer economic integration. In 1989, the European Council had already agreed to the setting up of an intergovernmental conference (IGC) on economic and monetary union, to be held in December 1990. Thus the move towards economic and monetary union had already begun before the full implications of the Soviet collapse in eastern Europe were apparent. In April 1990, at a special European Council in Dublin, French President Mitterand and German Chancellor Kohl introduced the idea of moving towards closer political union as well. At the October 1990 European Council, in Rome, it was decided that an IGC on political union would also begin in December 1990. The final agreement between the member-states worked out in these intergovernmental conferences would be signed by the member-states at the European Council meeting in Maastricht, the Netherlands, in December 1991.

The Maastricht Agreement and the Democratic Deficit

The rotating presidency of the European Community for 1991 fell to the small member-states of Luxembourg and the Netherlands. They had the responsibility of shepherding the agreements on economic and political union to their completion in December 1991.[11] The major issues dealt with in the IGCs and the meeting at Maastricht itself centred on different visions of what closer political and economic union really meant. There were clear differences in the degree of willingness of the member-states to establish a federal basis of the Union. The idea of a "Union with a federal goal," which existed in most drafts of the treaty, was removed from the final version at the insistence of the British. Instead, the leaders agreed to a statement that their goal was to create an ever closer union among the peoples of Europe. Combined with this emphasis on union among the peoples of Europe was also the principle of subsidiarity, which promised that decisions would be taken as

---

11. For background to the intergovernmental conferences, see Keatinge (1991).

close to the people as possible (Title One, Article A of the Treaty on European Union).

The issue of just what would fall under the competency of the Union was a major debate during the IGCs. It is summarized in the two radically different concepts of the EC as either a living tree in which all institutions and policies come out of one entity (the Dutch version), or as a series of pillars supporting a common roof—separate institutions all supporting a single entity (the Luxembourg version). This latter version, summarized in the Luxembourg Draft Treaty of June 1991, provided the basis for the final agreement. The living-tree version was introduced in the Dutch Draft Treaty put forward in October 1992, and had the support of the Commission, but was rejected by all the other states except the Netherlands and Belgium. The living-tree version, if it had been adopted, would have moved the Community closer to being a true federal state as it would have brought foreign and defence policy, along with internal affairs and justice, within an area of shared competency between the Community and the member-states.

The Luxembourg Draft Treaty set out areas of shared competency along with those of the Community under three pillars. The powers of the European Community itself under the Treaty of Rome, along with the new provisions for European Economic and Monetary Union created one pillar, which would be under the auspices of the EC institutions and justiciable by the European Court of Justice (ECJ). The other two pillars would involve EC institutions, but would primarily be the responsibility of the member-states and nonjusticiable by the ECJ. These were the provisions on European Political Cooperation and foreign and security issues and the provisions on home affairs and judiciary issues. In the Dutch Draft Treaty, these would have all been brought under the auspices of the Treaty of Rome, although the powers of the member-states to introduce and initiate policy in foreign and security issues and home affairs and judicial issues would remain dominant. It is not surprising that this degree of federalism was rejected by so many of the states.

The concept of union along with that of subsidiarity provide parameters for future development within the EC. At the highest level of the EC institutions, this will be based on intergovernmentalism and federalism. If it is to work, however, it must be based and seen to be based on a political community with a stake in its future. At the moment this does not exist. But are there possibilities within the Maastricht Agreement that might lead to the creation of such a community in the future?

Two mechanisms considered by many observers as important for creating this necessary political community are subsidiarity and a common European citizenship. Subsidiarity is a principle that has become important in the evolution of the EC over the past few years. While its roots go back to Aristotle and Thomas Aquinas, its more modern use is associated with Catholic social teachings and particularly the 1931 Papal Encyclical, *Quadragessimo Anno*.[12] It initially meant that, wherever possible, tasks should be left to the individual or family or private institutions and not the state. In the EC, it has come to mean that in the divisions of public authority policies should be carried out by the level of government best suited to do so. The implication is that this will be the lowest level of government, but in some cases it may well be the highest level of government.

There is broad agreement among the member-states on the significance of subsidiarity. The growth of the EC and particularly the role of the Commission along, with the increased use of weighted voting, has led to some concern among the member-states over the centralization of power and authority in Brussels. This tension between closer integration and maintenance of sovereignty is a concern for all states, although, clearly, this creates more difficulties for some states than for others. However, it is fair to say that all states are concerned about any move toward the creation of a single unitary state. Subsidiarity and its inclusion in the body of the treaty would make it justiciable before the ECJ, a move which all member-states approve. However, while subsidiarity is seen by many states such as the United Kingdom and Denmark as a mechanism to ensure the continuation of the power and authority of their state legislatures, it might also provide support to devolution to lower levels of government such as the Lander in Germany and to regions in countries such as Spain, Italy, or Belgium.

Furthermore, the Commission is overburdened with administrative and policy-making tasks. If the number of areas that the Commission is to be responsible for either entirely or as shared with the member-states increases, then some new system might be needed to harmonize legislation without necessarily creating new laws. At the same time, there has been an increase in devolved government in many member-states, including Spain, France, Italy, Belgium and of course the example of the Federal Republic of Germany. The concern by some subunits, especially the Lander in Germany, of being submerged into a centralizing EC was assuaged somewhat by the clause

---

12. For a discussion of subsidiarity, see Laffan (1991: 32-36).

on subsidiarity. Subsidiarity needs to be reinforced as well because of the concern over the "democratic deficit" in the Community as well as issues of the legitimacy and authority of EC institutions.

Another important component in the treaty relating to the development of a Union society is the idea of citizenship and equal treatment of the citizens of the Community. The equal treatment of citizens of one part of the Community with those of another, as far as possible in the right to vote and to stand for public office, would certainly expand the federalist basis of the Community. The present model of reciprocal rights and privileges that exist between the Republic of Ireland and the United Kingdom could well provide an excellent example for the Community to follow in the future.[13]

The issue of citizenship is central to the idea of statehood. As Moxon-Browne (1992) points out, there are two approaches to the basis of the prerequisites of an European Community citizenship. The one links it to nationality and to the political authority that has sovereignty over that person. Since there is no political entity called the European Community that possesses this authority over individuals living in the area covered by the European Community, there can be no such thing as a European Community citizenship. The other approach is that while there may not be a political entity called the European Community which possesses a society, it is in the process of creating a society. This society is anchored in such things as the legal norms established by the ECJ. It is further developed by individual citizens of the member-states who use the EC institutions "to exert leverage against their own governments" (Moxon-Browne 1992: 4). The act of a citizen trying to influence government is central to the role of a member of society in the polity. Identification with the Community is necessary if political union is to be achieved. This can be achieved, he argues, by making the European Parliament a truly representative and functioning body within the EC; by expanding the social policy of the EC so that it is truly community-wide in impact; and in the creation of community-wide symbols and emblems that people can identify with. The issue of citizenship is connected as well with the entire issue of the legitimacy of the authority of the institutions of the EC.

The changes proposed to the institutions of the EC in the treaty were in part meant to expand their legitimacy in European society. Many of the

---

13. For citizenship, see Moxon-Browne (1991); for the UK and Irish Republic, see MacMillan (1992a).

areas of competency included in the treaty have been part of the EC's responsibilities since the Treaty of Rome. Yet the number of areas in which the EC would have competency or shared competency raises the issue of just how successful would the Community be in actually implementing them. The Community's success in developing common policies in the areas already under their competency is limited. The concern therefore that any expansion of the Community's competency is mere window dressing has to be taken seriously.

Some issues included in the Treaty of Rome, 1957 were: free movement of goods; agriculture; free movement of persons, services and capital; transport; common rules in the areas of competition, fiscality, approximation of legislation; economic policy; social policy, education, vocational training, youth; and the European Investment Bank. Under the Single European Act, 1985, several more areas were added, including economic and social cohesion, research and technological development, and the environment. The Treaty on European Union amended some of these areas of competency. The most significant were the changes made in the section on economic policy which set out the parameters of economic and monetary union. The areas added under the treaty included culture, public health, consumer protection, trans-European networks. Most of these are shared areas of responsibility. In other words, the initiation and development of legislation by the Commission in all of these areas will involve the member-states.

If the EC is to overcome the opposition of those who see its' decision making as secretive, nondemocratic, and executive-driven, then it must ensure that its' institutions are accountable to the people of Europe. There is no doubt about the difficulty in developing processes that might explain how twelve countries with different cultures and nine languages can maintain their distinctiveness and, at the same time, come together to make binding decisions. However, the EC lacks any central executive responsible either to the community electorate or to a community parliament and while this has been rectified to some degree by the Union Treaty, the basis of decision making remains an elaborate and intricate system involving both nationally elected and non-elected officials.

The most significant aspect of change in the EC's institutions was the increased role of the European Parliament (EP). Given that it is the only EC institution elected directly by the people of Europe, an increase in its role in lawmaking would help rectify the lack of responsibility of the leadership of the Community to the people of Europe. This lack of responsibility became more apparent following the introduction of direct elections by the people of Europe in 1979. Not surprisingly, it was members of this new, directly elected Parliament that first raised the issue of a lack of democratic accountability within the EC. In the early 1980s, members of the EP called for a People's Europe (see Lodge 1989*a*; 1989*b*). In both the SEA and the Treaty on European Union, provisions were made to increase the voice and authority of the Parliament over the content of EC legislation. However, it is still true that most of the power remains with the Commission and even more so in the Council of Ministers and the European Council.

The power of the EP has been the subject of much debate among the member-states. The small states see an increase in the powers of the EP as a threat to their own powers in the Council of Ministers. For other states, especially the Federal Republic of Germany, this lack of democratic accountability is a very important consideration. For other states, such as the United Kingdom and Denmark, the question of any derogation of the sovereignty of their own parliaments is highly suspect.

The question of the legislative powers of the European Parliament also involves the nature of voting in the Council of Ministers. In the Council of Ministers, there two methods of voting—weighted voting and unanimity. The traditional method of voting was by unanimity. This resulted in many long discussions and negotiations before the Council agreed on any issues. While the Treaty of Rome provided for weighted voting, it was not used on a regular basis until the SEA. The decision to pass all the implementing legislation needed to complete the internal market by weighted voting increased the recognition of its value. It has been extended under the Maastricht Agreement to include nearly all policy areas within the competency of the EC.

The increase in the competency of the Commission and the Council of Ministers only makes the problem of the democratic deficit and the legitimacy of the acts of the Community more apparent. Under Article 189 of the Treaty of Rome, the Council and the Commission can make regulations, issue directives, take decisions, and make recommendations or deliver opinions to the member-states on issues within their competency. The regulations are equivalent to laws and require the approval of the Council of Ministers and the European Parliament which make up the legislature of the EC. Clearly, the Council of Ministers as the body representing the states has abrogated to itself most of the political power over the process. Under the Treaty of Rome, the EP had the right to be consulted but could not stop legislation being approved. Changes were made, at least as far as the budget was concerned, after 1979, when the EP required a veto over the EC budget. Under the SEA, they were given increased powers in some areas of policy with the introduction of the method of cooperation in voting, which allowed them a say in some legislation, although the Council of Ministers could overturn their veto. A further change introduced in the Treaty on European Union called codecision would also increase their powers in certain areas of decision making.

The role the EC would play in the everyday life of the peoples of Europe was not really taken into account by the founders. Given the idea that the EC was a peculiar international organization, this was probably understandable. However, it is clearly more than an international organization. It does make domestic policy decisions which affect the daily lives of all Europeans—thus the concern about the lack of accountability of the Community's institutions to the people of the Community. At the same time any increase in direct accountability of the Community to the people of Europe only leads towards an increased federalism.

It is not just the domestic impact of the EC that is important in making the institutions of the EC more accountable to the people of Europe; there is increased cooperation in areas of foreign policy as well. While these issues of high politics remain in the competency of the member-states, the Treaty of Rome does assign to the European Community, and more specifically the Commission, the responsibility of negotiating all trade agreements between the member-states and third parties. This authority of the EC does not extend to foreign policy. Yet, an important part of the definition of the modern state is its competency in the area of relations with other states (foreign policy) and its ability to protect its people and territory from external and/or internal attack. From this perspective, the European Community is not a sovereign state. At the same time, the integrative process has advanced to the point where issues of foreign policy and matters of security and defence cannot be left to chance. Issues of foreign policy have been subject to closer cooperation since the creation of European Political Cooperation (EPC) in the early 1970s. But while the member-states gave foreign policy a status in the SEA, under Title III, they left it deliberately outside the boundaries of the Treaty of Rome. The issues of defence and security do not even exist within this framework.

Issues of defence have been excluded, in large part, because that has been the wish of the member-states. The neutrality of Ireland, combined with the membership of the others in NATO, allowed them to use the former's neutrality as an excuse for not debating defence issues. The collapse of communism, followed by the Gulf War, created an environment in which these issues could be examined from a new perspective. The fiasco of the EC response to the Gulf War led the members to reconsider their defence capacity and, more particularly, the role of defence including the use of the Western European Union (WEU) as a defence arm of the EC. This question has become even more significant in relation to the break-up of Yugoslavia. Here, the differences among the states has made it difficult for the EC to develop a coherent and effective policy.

The Treaty on European Union was from the beginning a dramatic undertaking by the member-states of the EC. It would be less than fair to indicate that most states had some reservations regarding parts of the agreement. The issues became more apparent in the months following the initial agreement at the Maastricht European Council. Many of the issues in the treaty were more promises of what the member-states would do rather than agreements on what they were going to do. Already, some modifications have been made both to dates on implementation, such as those set out for the introduction of EMU and other requirements as regards issues such as citizenship for the Danes. However, for most political actors there is no denying their commitment to the process. If it is to have the same support among the citizens of the Community then the provisions increasing the legitimacy and accountability of the EC institutions will need to implemented.

To this point, the development and integration of the EC has largely been at the instigation of the political actors in the member-states. Actors in the EC institutions have played important roles in this integrative process, especially the ECJ whose decisions have advanced the sovereignty claims of the EC and established the autonomy of the EC in its areas of competency. These institutions lack legitimacy within member-states societies. The EC itself has no political community. It has been dependent for its existence upon the agreement among state actors. If it is to become even a supranational state, it will require its own political community. The Treaty on European Union does provide, in theory, the framework for such a development, but can it overcome the objections of both the member-states and their own political communities in turning this into reality? Can a European nationality be created on top of, or in place of, the regional identities already in place? Is it necessary to do so?

The Legitimacy and Sovereignty of the European Community

If the institutions of the EC are to be effective and legitimate in the societies of Europe, then they will need to acquire better mechanisms of accountability among these societies. At the same time, these societies are confronted with major changes as a result of the major shifts in production and deindustrialization along with increased regionalization and citizen participation and their disillusionment of the political process in these western European societies. This is also strongly influenced by the globalization of their economies and their increased integration into the European Community. All of these changes will have major effects on the nature of the nation state.

I would argue that it might well lead to the reemergence of a community framework similar to the patchwork quilt of medieval Europe. However, this time instead of all authority and sovereignty deriving from God to imperial (temporal) and papal (spiritual) suzerains and then downwards through kings and bishops to nobles and priests and merchants and peasants, authority will be derived from the people and move upwards through municipalities, regions, and provinces to states and suprastates. Therefore, if a new state emerges out of the EC, it would probably be a supranational state that would see new definitions of sovereignty and legitimacy as applied to state power. The supranational state structure, which would leave certain questions of responsibility vague or in the hands of the member-states, is likely to be more acceptable to the people of Europe than is a move to a more federal system which would increase the power of the centre at the expense of the units in areas of foreign policy, defence, or even culture and language.

It is my contention that the concept of sovereignty of the people possesses the potential to allow the diffusion of power throughout a whole series of layered institutions and that, as a result, it would be possible to revamp power and authority among these institutions. It could provide a framework within which a fair amount of decentralization could occur, along the lines of subsidiarity already outlined in the EC documents including the Maastricht Agreement, while at the same time making allowance for the possible centralization that might occur as a result of economic globalization. While it does appear that economic globalization will probably lead to increased centralization of economic decision making, it is not clear that political centralization need follow.

Two major issues confronting the EC as a supranational organization are the issues of sovereignty and legitimacy. The issue of sovereignty primarily affects the member-states, and the issue of legitimacy as a reflection of societal response affects the EC institutions and member-states' societies.

Is the EC a sovereign legal entity?[14] Each member-state agreed to the transfer of some of their sovereignty to the European Community institutions in signing the treaties of Rome and Paris, their own acts of accession, the Single European Act and the Treaty on European Union, indicating their willingness to accept the supremacy of EC law over municipal law in the areas designated to be under the control of the supranational institutions. They have, for the most part, incorporated articles that insure the supremacy of EC law (or directives) over municipal law into their municipal law and often into their constitutions as well. To that extent then, the EC is "endowed with sovereign rights, the exercise of which affects Member States and also their citizens" (cited from the European Court's decision in *Van Gend en Loos*, Case 26/62).

As a result, the legal sovereignty of the member-states is already compromised by the laws governing their present membership. However, as the member-states have the right to leave the EC, they are still the ultimate depository of sovereignty within the EC. Furthermore, the coercive forces of the state, which can be defined as the ultimate power, are still under the control of individual member-states. To that degree, the acceptance of the laws of the EC is voluntary and there are no coercive forces available to the EC to compel member-states to accept its decisions.

Some of the concerns raised about the Maastricht Agreement centre on the need to protect the economic, social, and cultural life of the societies of the member-states from external threats. While some states like the United Kingdom and Denmark see the EC as the major threat to this identity, other EC member-states like Italy and Spain are having this identity attacked from below.[15]

While the influence of nationalism has increased in the EC member-states, there is still a sense that, having confronted the worst excesses of nationalism in this century, they have pulled back from the abyss and adopted other approaches to resolving conflict—one of which is the EC itself. Modern technology and communications systems, along with the increasing commitment by the industrial states to forms of free trade, are also threats to this kind of

---

14. For a discussion of the EC and sovereignty, see MacMillan (1992*b*).
15. The UK does have an internal issue in which its identity is in question and the EC is seen as a possible answer. This is the question of the future of Scotland.

national sovereignty. To that extent then, the sovereignty of all states could be described as semisovereign.[16]

There is no doubt that alternatives to the nation-state have gained some popularity in certain parts of the EC. The EC itself does provide an alternative mechanism in which some groups and regions (such as Scotland in the United Kingdom, and Catalonia in Spain) feel they might be able to protect their own distinctive culture and language while sharing in the greater wealth and security provided by an institution like the Community. It comes down to the source of authority of the institutions of government. The source of the sovereignty which the state can exercise over society in democracies has come to be seen as deriving from the people, although in some democracies it is centred in specific institutions, such as parliament.

The evolution of state-societal relationships in western Europe since the 1500s can be examined as an attempt to answer the question, where is the locus of authority in the state? This has centred more specifically on the locus of sovereignty, whether it is a prerogative of institutions such as parliament or executive or the people themselves. If the people agree on the exercise of authority by the institutions that govern them, the institutions acquire legitimacy; if they disagree, then a crisis occurs. Illegitimacy can be defined as the "improper use of authority for the system" (Pye 1972: 136). It can arise as a result of several developments, but the most significant one here is that which develops from a conflicting or inadequate basis for authority.

At some point, members of a society can and usually will assert their right to be heard. This is true in all political systems, but it is a central point in democratic systems in which the legitimacy of the institutions of government, and perhaps even the state itself, is dependent on the willingness of the citizenry to accept the authority of the institutions and the political actors who run the institutions. If the EC is to be legitimate in the states and regions of the Community, it must at some point deal with the issues that make a state responsible to the members of society and allow them to judge the effectiveness, capacity, and rightness of the state and its institutions. Even while, as I have pointed out, this is likely to be best achieved through the creation of a supranational state, it is also apparent that the process must be similar to that which occurs in a federal state where the central unit must compete

---

16. See Bulmer and Patterson (1989-90). This thesis fits into the idea of interdependence rather than strict intergovernmentalism as well (see also Laffan 1991; Hoffman 1982-83).

for the loyalty of the citizenry with the subunits. While we take such a situation for granted in most federal states, the process is not always complete as the Canadian example currently demonstrates, and as other examples such as that of the United States have demonstrated in their evolution.

Therefore, if the integrative process in the EC is to be legitimate in the hearts and minds of the Europeans, a sense of community with loyalties to the EC supra-state based in Brussels needs to be created. While the aim would be to make the EC's institutions legitimate among the people of Europe, it may have other results as well. It may have an effect on the member-states themselves as power is dispersed downward into the regions and localities through the principles of subsidiarity and regional responsibility. This may weaken the bureaucracies of Brussels but it may also have the same effect on the member-states themselves.

If a European political community is to be created, mechanisms to overcome the centrifugal forces of the nation-state and replace them with a new integrated Europe will need to be developed. Yet, in spite of the aim of political union in the Treaty on European Union and the inclusion of a Union citizenship, the very history of Europe makes it highly unlikely that a single cultural, political, or even linguistic community is ever going to develop. Even without further expansion, the twelve states possess nine official languages between them, not to mention different legal systems, administrative traditions, and institutional frameworks. Therefore, closer union will still require a mixture of the intergovernmentalism and federalism it already possesses.

The survival of the nation-state as the basic unit in the EC will make the building of a single political community difficult, but not impossible. However, I think it more likely that what will survive will be a mixture of regions and states within the broader framework of the EC. This is even more likely if the Community expands not only to include Austria, Sweden, Norway, and Finland, but also Poland, Hungary, the Czeck Republic, and Slovakia.

Until recently, the concept of an unified Europe was not an important issue on the agenda of any of the member-states' societies (Slater 1982–83). In large part, this was probably because most of the major issues on the EC agenda have been economic or economically linked and not cultural or linguistic. As political union has become a more significant part of the integration process, the issues of sovereignty of the member-state and democratic legitimacy have also grown in importance (Moxon-Browne 1992).

Is it necessary that legal, political, and popular sovereignty be identical and indivisible? In federal states sovereignty is divided. Legal sovereignty is vested in the national state and not its component parts. But popular and political sovereignty is divided. However, this does not indicate where political and popular sovereignty are located. Most federal units were created because the component parts were not willing to give over complete sovereignty to the central government. There can be a combination of both legal sovereignty and divided political and popular sovereignty within the state. The difficulty for most European states and administrative frameworks, including that of the EC itself, is that they have little experience of federalism but a great deal of experience of centralized government.

Conclusion

This paper examines the development of the European Community within the context of the question if it is a supranational state in the making. The answer very briefly is both yes and no. A move away from the achievement of the internal market within the framework of the present political and constitutional framework is highly unlikely. To that extent, it already is a supranational organization. The achievement of this status has been, for the most part, the accomplishment of the member-states' political elite and, more specifically, their executive leadership. The dominance of state actors in the integrative process to this point can be explained in part by the nature of the issues involved, including free trade and regional security and in part by the strong state tradition present in the founding states of the EC.

If it is to move onwards from a supranational organization to a supranational state, then the institutions will have to acquire a more wide-based sovereignty both internally and externally, and the institutions will have to acquire legitimacy among the citizens of the member-states. More specifically, there will need to be a political community to give its allegiance to the European Community and not just to the member-states. To this point in its evolution, much of the emphasis has been on issues of free trade, internal market, and regional security. In the future, issues of democratic deficit, subsidiarity, and citizenship are likely to be more significant. This is mostly because of the concern of citizens about the direction of the integrative process as a result of the Treaty on European Political Union. This issue, usually summarized under the heading of the democratic deficit, is in part the result of the success of the EC project. If it is to become a supranational state then it must resolve the conflict of sovereignty between the nation states and the supranational institutions, and if the supranational institutions are to be successful in acquiring this sovereignty, they must acquire legitimacy in the hearts and minds of the citizens of the member-states.

References

Bulmer, S. 1982-83. "Domestic Politics and European Community Policy Making," *Journal of Common Market Studies* 12:349-63.
Bulmer, S., and W. Patterson. 1989-90. "West Germany's Role in Europe: 'Man-Mountain' or 'Semi-Gulliver'?" *Journal of Common Market Studies* 28:95-117.
Bulmer S., and W. Wessels. 1987. *The European Council*. London: Macmillan.
Hayes, F. 1984. "The Role of COREPER in EEC Decision-Making," *Administration* 32:177-200.
Hayes-Renshaw, F. et al. 1989-90. "The Permanent Representatives of the Member-States of the European Community," *Journal of Common Market Studies* 28:119-37.
Hoffman, S. 1982-83. "Reflections on the Nation State in Western Europe Today," *Journal of Common Market Studies* 21:21-37.
Keatinge, P. (ed). 1991. *Political Union*. Dublin: Institute for European Affairs.
Keohane, R. O., and S. Hoffman (eds). 1992. *Decision-Making and Institutional Change in the European Community*. Boulder: Westview Press.
Laffan, B. 1991. "The Governance of the Union." In *Political Union*, edited by P. Keatinge. Dublin. Institute for European Affairs.
Laffan, B. 1992. *Integration and Co-operation in Europe*. London: Routledge.
Lindberg, L. N. 1963. *The Political Dynamics of European Integration*. Stanford: Stanford University Press.
Lodge, J. 1989a. "The European Parliament—From Assembly to Co-Legislature: Changing the Institutional Dynamics. London: Pinter.
Lodge, J. 1989b. "Social Europe: Fostering a People's Europe." In *The European Community and the Challenge of the Future*, edited by J. Lodge. London: Pinter.
MacMillan, G. M. 1991. "Is the European Community a Viable Model for Canada?" In *Defence of Canada: Constitutional, Economic and Security Dimensions*, edited by R. P. Tychonick. Occasional Papers, Strategic Studies, University of Manitoba.
MacMillan, G. M. 1992a. "The Referendum, the Courts and Representative Democracy in Ireland," *Political Studies* 40:67-78.
MacMillan, G. M. 1992b. "The Nation-State and the European Community: The Impact of Membership on State Sovereignty." In *The Nation State Versus Continental Integration*, edited by L. Pal and R-O. Schultze. Bochum: Brockmeyer.
MacMillan, G. M. 1994. "Canadian Executive Federalism and European Community Summitry." In *The European Community, Canada and 1992*, edited by G. M. MacMillan. Calgary: Faculty of Social Sciences.
Moravcsik, A. 1992. "Negotiating the Single European Act." In *Decision-Making and Institutional Change in the European Community*, edited by R. O. Keohane and S. Hoffman. Boulder: Westview Press.
Moxon-Browne, E. 1991. "The Legitimacy of the Union." In *Political Union*, edited by P. Keatinge. Dublin. Institute for European Affairs.

Moxon-Browne, E. 1992. "The Concept of European Community Citizenship and the Development of Political Union." Paper presented at the ECPR Joint Sessions at the University of Limerick.

Murphy, F. 1985. "The Single European Act, Parts I and II," *The Irish Jurist* 20:17–42; 239–63.

Pentland, C. 1973. *Integration Theory and European Integration*. London: Faber and Faber.

Pinder, J. 1985–86. "European Community and Nation-State: A Case For a Neo-Federalism?" *International Affairs* 62:41–54.

Pye, L. 1972. "The Legitimacy Crisis." In *Crises and Sequences of Political Development*, edited by L. Binder. Princeton: Princeton University Press.

Slater, M. 1982–83. "Political Elites, Popular Indifference and Community Building," *Journal of Common Market Studies* 21:69–93.

Smiley, D. 1987. *The Federal Condition in Canada*. Toronto: McGraw-Hill.

Smiley, D. V., and R. Watts. 1985. *Intrastate Federalism in Canada*. Toronto: University of Toronto Press.

Taylor, P. 1983. *The Limits of European Integration*. New York: Columbia University Press.

Taylor, P. 1989. "The New Dynamics of EC Integration in the 1980s." In *The European Community and the Challenge of the Future*, edited by J. Lodge. London: Pinder.

Urwin, D. 1991. *The Community of Europe: A History of European Integration since 1945*. London: Longman.

Wallace, W. 1982–83. "Europe as a Confederation: The Community and the Nation-State," *Journal of Common Market Studies* 21:57–92.

Wallace, W. 1983. "Less than a Federation, More than a Regime." In *Policy-Making in the European Community*, edited by H. Wallace, W. Wallace and C. Webb. Chichester: John Wiley and Sons Ltd.

Federalism and the Postsocialist Experience of Eastern Central Europe

Victor V. Kuvaldin

In the twentieth century, eastern Europe (including the European part of the former Union of Soviet Socialist Republics) was destined to become an experimental ground for the idea of federalism. Situated in the centre of the huge Eurasian continent, at an intersection of nations, cultures, and civilizations, the region is distinguished by a complex and colourful ethnic palette. A mottled mosaic of peoples occupy the nations of the region, nations which over the centuries have often changed their boundaries and the composition of their peoples. These people accumulated a broad range of both positive and negative experiences in their interaction with one another. Under such circumstances, ethnic and national attitudes became both a force for change and a barrier that resisted change.

Unlike western Europe, where the nation-state began to emerge as early as the Middle Ages, multiethnic conglomerates prevailed in the eastern part of the continent until the twentieth century. The disintegration of Soviet imperial domination over eastern Europe, and the recent emergence of democratic regimes in the region, have presented the formidable challenge of identifying and establishing new forms of the state within which different nations and peoples are able to coexist effectively. Both processes of democratization and state formation have been long and painful ones in the area, and it remains to be seen whether federalism will be able to survive as a meaningful political and administrative structure against the countervailing force of naturally integrated communities.

The prospects for federalism appear especially dismal in the case of eastern Europe, including the former Soviet Union. Three federations which have endured for most of the twentieth century—Czechoslovakia, Yugoslavia, and the USSR—collapsed one after another within a few years. More than two dozen states emerged from those federations, states founded primarily on the principle of nationality. Nations which have been living in a state of comparative harmony for much of the century are in the process of dissolution. In many of these states, which are not distinguished by ethnic homogeneity, conflicts between the various nationalities which comprise them threaten to destroy their political and economic viability. The bloodshed in Yugoslavia, one of the main seats of modern civilization, has become a tragic epitaph to the idea of federalism. The situation in eastern Europe is all the more depressing when compared with the continued integration of western Europe, notably with the adoption, in January 1993, of the Maastricht Agreement. Thus, the two parts of the European continent appear to be moving in opposite and, perhaps, incompatible directions.

Given these recent developments, what are the prospects for building future states on the ashes of the former socialist camp? Will the eastern part of the continent need to adopt the same models as the western—that is, to first create purely national states, and then to seek some form of unification?

The significance of these questions transcends regional concerns. The vitality of federalism and its relevance to the contemporary world are at issue. No less important is the geopolitical aspect. Attempts to reshape borders along nationality lines will be fraught with conflict, and the shocks are already in the process of destabilizing a major territory in the centre of the Eurasian continent, with potentially disastrous effects on the world community.

The causes of the present dislocations are deep-seated and profound. Of the three federations considered here—Czechoslovakia, Yugoslavia, and the Soviet Union—all were relatively young federations by European standards, largely the creatures of World War I, which brought about the collapse of the three major empires on the continent—Austria-Hungary, Russia, and the Ottoman Empire.

It is difficult to assess the extent to which the multinational eastern European states were restrained by the historical burden of their imperial pasts. There is little doubt that the relations between the 'titled' ethnic groups (for example, Russians, Czechs and Serbs) and their 'younger brethren' were far from idyllic. There is little basis to believe that they were countries with developed democratic traditions—with the possible exception of Czechoslovakia. It would be equally unfounded to classify those states as empires with the traditional division into metropolis and colony. Rather, those states tended to be kindred nations connected by common historical traditions and cultural ties.

The socialist regimes established in those countries following the two world wars tended to freeze ethnic conflicts without resolving them, leaving them as festering problems to be unleashed with radical alterations in the political and international regimes. The socialist regimes endured beyond the end of such classical empires as the British, French, or Portuguese, but they did not resolve the problems of nationality, even though they may have appeared to have been resolved because of the absence of open conflict. It was this veneer of peaceful coexistence in eastern Europe, prior to the end of the 1980s, that made the explosion of nationality conflict, as the socialist states collapsed, seem so sudden and violent. Yet, any careful analysis would demonstrate that the roots of such conflict lie not in the specific state model, but in a profound systemic crisis in all spheres of the former social order. The new order was unable to sustain the unprecedented challenges to tradition.

The transformation of eastern Europe involved centripetal and centrifugal forces. In eastern European and in the western republics of the former Soviet Union, a change in the system meant not only a transformation in ideology and political orientation, but also a significant geopolitical shift. An orientation toward the East gave way suddenly—almost overnight—to an equally one-sided orientation toward the West. The aspirations of some of the more developed regions of the former socialist countries to 'return to Europe' as soon as possible evoked powerful forces that sought to break free of existing state structures and institutions.

If states which appeared strong, at first glance, were unable to survive the transition to a new order, there was virtually no capacity for interstate economic and military-political alliances to weather the storms of change. An immediate death sentence was pronounced on the Council of Mutual Economic Assistance and the Warsaw Pact when the socialist model of development was obviously unable to survive. The fracturing of long-standing institutions and relations contributed to the creation of a geopolitical vacuum, as, for instance, between the new Russia and a united Germany, and it remains undetermined how that vacuum will be filled.

The political, economic, and sociocultural rupture of the old regimes established the necessity to build a new order from the ruins. It may well be premature to speak of the victory of democracy in the former socialist states, but there is little doubt that many of them are moving toward democracy. Free elections, freedom of speech, protection of the civil and political rights of individuals, the principle of a division of governmental powers, and the need for independent courts are gradually entering the lives of the former totalitarian regimes.

Democratization of the social order brought about a sharp ideological and political differentiation in eastern Europe. A rich political palette emerged from a previously monotonous political landscape. Yet, eastern Europe is not monolithic, and the winds of change are less forceful in some countries than in others. It seems that an invisible line has crossed the eastern European subcontinent. If in Poland, Czechia, and Hungary the right wing and centrist parties dominate, in Slovakia, Romania, Bulgaria, and Serbia the former communists retain strong positions. In the new states formed from the remains of the Soviet Union, the old nomenclature has, with a few exceptions, retained the levers of power. In the postsocialist era, such variations within eastern Europe derive from a complex set of factors steeped in the historical differences among the countries of the region, including the distinctions between western and eastern Christian traditions and their corresponding cultural differences.

On the economic level, there is a shift everywhere from command to market economies, but the velocity of change, the institutional basis of transformation, and the results achieved to date vary considerably from one country and area to another. These variations are underscored by the 1992 review conducted by the European Bank for Reconstruction and Development (EBRD), which found a wide divergence among the experiences of the postsocialist states.

In the shift to market economies that is taking place in eastern Europe, there is an evident leading group of nations, represented by the former Czechoslovakia, Poland, and Hungary. The countries not only began at different levels of economic development, but also used different strategies in undertaking their transition to free market structures. Poland emphasized financial stabilization and employed so-called shock therapy. The main component of the Czechoslovakian model was rapid and massive privatization, which was accomplished through vouchers issued to the entire population. One of the factors that contributed to the collapse of the Czechoslovakian federation was conflict between the leaders of Czechia and Slovakia over approaches to the economic transformation; that conflict became especially pronounced following the parliamentary elections of June 1992. If the Czechs tended toward a more rapid shift toward a free market, the Slovakians preferred a slower transformation with a continuation of a high degree of state regulation and control. In the case of the Hungarian reforms, major features of the program have been the government divestment of state properties through auctions, the attraction of foreign capital, and the increased production of goods for export. In the estimate of the EBRD, these countries have already passed through the lowest point of their economic crises and entered a stage of stabilization. In Czechoslovakia and Hungary, the current account in convertible currencies and the gross international reserves are growing, and the external debt is decreasing. To date, Poland's financial relations with foreign countries have not stabilized, although there has been improvement (EBRD 1992: 42, 48, 66). Problems of course remain, including unemployment, which was generally unknown in the socialist regimes. In October 1992, for instance, the level of unemployment in Prague was 0.3 percent, in Czechia 2.5 percent, and in Slovakia 10.4 percent (40).

These three central European countries deserve particular attention because they have made significant strides in the establishment of democratic institutions and market economies. It is recognized that the most vital prerequisite for success with their reforms is the accomplishment of a high degree of political stability, based on a broad social consensus and a common vision of the future.

The accomplishments of the advanced industrial countries are especially visible against the backdrop of the postsocialist world. This is most striking in such southeastern European countries as Albania, Bulgaria, and Rumania. In 1992, those countries experienced a sharp and prolonged decline of between 7 and 11 percent in the real gross domestic product (GDP). Average consumer prices grew by no less than 100–200 percent. Their current accounts in convertible currencies and their external debt are growing; the gross international reserves in convertible currencies are reduced for the region (except Bulgaria). Officially, the unemployment level has reached two digits (10–16 percent, although there is no data available for Albania). The real figures are likely much higher than official statistics (EBRD 1992: 72, 75, 78, 86).

The countries of southeastern Europe are experiencing problems in other areas as well. Population growth has effectively ended in Rumania, Albania, and Bulgaria, and there is a net outflow of peoples from those countries. For instance, in 1992, an estimated 4,000 persons left Albania each week, which is more than 0.1 percent of the nation's population (EBRD 1992: 70). The International Migration Organization reported that at the end of 1992, 71 percent of Albanians, 18 percent of Russians, 20 percent of Bulgarians, and 21 percent of Ukrainians were prepared to leave their countries for the West for economic reasons (International Migration Organization 1993: 4).

The postsocialist countries of southeastern Europe have tied their hopes for economic development to the rapid expansion and modernization of the agricultural sector, where private entrepreneurship has made more significant gains. In Albania, almost three-quarters of the cultivated lands have now been transferred to private ownership. In Bulgaria, 45 percent of all agricultural production takes place on the 15 percent of land that is privately owned.

In the former Soviet Union, reform efforts have faced an equally difficult situation. The four largest republics—Russia, Ukraine, Bylo-Russia, and Kazakhastan—possess the bulk of the former Soviet Union's territory, natural resources, and population, and produce most of the manufactured goods of the former republics. Under economic reform, production in a number of areas has fallen off markedly, with rates of production in various sectors in those republics declining between 14 and 20 percent. The prices for 1992 also rose, again by an estimated 13 to 25 times. Government deficits vary from 6 to 30 percent of the gross national product (GNP) in the republics; government finances are in disarray; trade relations are chaotic, and the flow of foreign investment is very weak (EBRD 1992: 92, 99, 104, 118).

To a large extent, these problems derive from the determined but nonetheless unconsidered and inconsistent actions of the Russian leadership; such a situation has significantly increased the price of reforms for the population, and dissipated the otherwise positive effects of reform. One consequence of such difficulties has been to narrow the base of support for reforms and to shift more initiative to the opponents of change. Increasingly, for many people the primary objective has become mere survival.

It is also evident that a widening gap has emerged between the rate of economic transformation in Russia and the other former Soviet republics. This is particularly striking in the critical area of privatization. According to official estimates, over 20 percent of the Russian population worked in the private sector in Russia at the end of 1992. In Bylo-Russia, by contrast, almost all enterprises remain in the ownership of the state, not including agriculture, where individual farms account for almost 25 percent of total production. In Ukraine, also by contrast, the private sector produces only 2-3 percent of the GNP. In Kazakhastan, 13-15 percent of the total number of employed people work in the privatized sector of the economy, excluding the agricultural sector, although that 12-13 percent is composed primarily of work collectives which have become the owners of their enterprises.

The postsocialist world is caught on the horns of a major dilemma. On the one hand, the general economic, political, and social crises in the region impede any effective steps toward integration. There is a high degree of inertia concurrent with the considerable momentum of the dissolution of existing structures. Each nation appears to be attempting to cope with its problems in isolation, relying on its own resources. At the same time, it is practically impossible to return to, or maintain, an isolated existence. In this interdependent world, success is determined by coordinated concepts and concerted action, and this simple truth is gradually paving the route to more integrated and effective social and political planning.

In contrast to the past, however, new forms of interaction are derived from individual and group interests, not *a priori* state schemes. Solutions increasingly derive from the objective needs of social development, not ideas which are artificially imposed from above. This trend is particularly reflected in the cooperative development of energy; the transport, production, and processing of oil and natural gas which has been taking place in post-Soviet territory. Such key republics as Russia, Bylo-Russia, and Kazakhastan have demonstrated their interest in developing closer economic ties in this area as well as in military relations.

At the same time, central and eastern European countries have indicated an understanding that they are best served by closer integration with their neighbours and economic partners. They have contemplated various subregional forms of cooperation, such as the Alps-Adriatic, Vysehrad Triangle, Balkan community, Baltic forum, or means of developing unofficial cooperation amongst the Danube states. Despite different motives, dynamics, concrete forms of implementation, and actual results, the subregional interaction models have much in common. The intention to avoid the so-called trap of nationalism has been a major factor promoting various cooperation projects among central and eastern European nations. There is also a definite aspiration to secure themselves against the possibility of resurgent post-Soviet totalitarianism.

The present necessity to balance the interests of all eastern European participants is at the heart of the cooperative approach, especially the common striving for a return to Europe, gradually reorienting external ties toward western European states and collective organizations. From this perspective, cooperation in central and eastern Europe is regarded as a 'preparatory school' on the long road to the implementation of the geopolitical megaproject for a single Europe.

Secondly, there is much interest in large-scale projects which cannot be contemplated by one nation. Thirdly, there remains a historically and psychologically explicable apprehension by some nations of being in the shadow of a unified Germany, and an aversion toward re-experiencing German-Austrian pressures or Hungarian irredentism. An additional factor that ties the nations and peoples of central and eastern Europe are the commonality of their centuries-old cultural and historical traditions.

The scale of subregional cooperation is rather extensive. It includes energy transport, telecommunication information systems, ecology, tourism, science, culture, and ethnic relations. The development of integration at the basic level is greatly facilitated by the fact that European regional cooperation is a traditional and well-conceived form of interaction among the nations of the region.

Among the many initiatives that have been undertaken in this area, two deserve special consideration because of their potential significance. The first was the initiative of V. Havel, president of the then Czechoslovakia, who sought to establish a tripartite alliance of Czechoslovakia, Hungary, and Poland. Havel advanced the concept in a speech of 30 January 1990 to the Polish parliament. Havel emphasized the need for a coordinated effort by the three neighbouring mid-European states as part of their pursuit for re-integration into Europe. The president advanced the idea of a "mini-COMECON" within the framework of the Council for Mutual Economic Assistance, which still existed at that time. Havel's overtures found favourable response. Following intense and protracted negotiations among the Czech and Slovak republics, Poland and Hungary in the course of 1992, late in the year, the parties reached agreement for the establishment in stages of a free trade zone, which came into force on 1 January 1993. This marked an important step toward regional integration.

Another no less graphic example of the efforts at integration that have been occasioned by the breakup of the socialist world was the attempt by Italy, the former Yugoslavia, Austria, the former Czechoslovakia, Hungary, and Poland to resolve a wide range of economic, political, and cultural issues that had plagued their relationship. To that end, in early August 1990, after concluding meetings held in Venice, they established a cooperative organization.

The coincidence in timing between the establishment of the central European and the Venetian groups was the result of several factors. Both cooperative and integrationist efforts derived from several factors. Both initiatives emerged from the same 'tectonic' shifts in the centre and north of the continent. But during the six months between the two events, the number of participants increased and the nature of the venture underwent a significant change. This time it was a joint effort of the former socialist countries and such representatives of the Western world as Italy (a NATO and European Economic Council [EEC] member) and Austria (a European Free Trade Association [EFTA] member on the waiting list for EEC membership). This mutual intention to bridge the gap that divided Europe during the Cold War represents the single most important dimension of the new integrationist movement in the collective effort to resolve the acute problems of the post-socialist world.

New emerging structures have vividly embodied the dream cherished by many eastern Europeans—just to become Europeans in as short a time as feasible. On another and more cultural plane, the Rome-Warsaw axis has reaffirmed the importance of the invisible border between western and eastern Christianity. Trying to accentuate their difference from other participants in the former socialist community and emphasize their European orientation, Hungary, Czecho-Slovakia, and Poland have sought to emphasize that they belong to central Europe, which in their view also includes Denmark, Belgium, the Netherlands, Luxembourg, Germany, and Austria.

Unfortunately, the implementation of the projects of the Central European Initiative has been paralysed by the protracted Yugoslavian crisis. Waiting for more favourable circumstances, the initiative's working groups of experts are, in the interim, attempting to establish the groundwork for the future.

Some former socialist nations have already made a beginning in their longer term objective of returning to full involvement in Europe. Hungary, Czechia, Slovakia, Poland, Rumania, and Bulgaria have become associated members of the EEC under Article 238 of the Treaty of Rome, and have concluded trade agreements with it. Similar accords facilitating access to West European markets have been signed with seven states, all members of the EFTA (excluding Bulgaria, which anticipates joining in the course of 1993). Nonetheless, it is anticipated that these nations will remain in this state of purgatory for some time because of the prior claim to membership in the EEC by Turkey and the EFTA countries.

In spite of the short-lived euphoria that swept through parts of Europe with the collapse of the old order in eastern Europe, it has become evident to many that the restoration of European unity will be an ongoing and frequently difficult process. Compared with western Europe, all postcommunist nations, including the more prosperous and stable ones, live in a different historical phase. The so-called lost half-century of socialist construction was superimposed on the premodern economic, political, legal, and cultural institutions and values of eastern European nations, most of which had yet to undergo the capitalist transition. As a result, there was a significant gap between the stage of development in those nations, in all spheres of life, and the nations of western Europe. It has thus been a difficult process to forge overnight modern democracies with free enterprise economies from the former totalitarian regimes that were tied to the Soviet system.

An additional problem has been that western European countries have not hastened to embrace their eastern brethren. Undoubtedly, western Europe is greatly interested in democratization and stabilization in the postsocialist regimes. Western Europeans have logically placed their highest priority on their own economic and political problems, and are unwilling to risk retarding western European integration through a diversion of energies and funds to the eastern European problems. The West has also been reluctant to include the eastern European subcontinent in its system of defense and collective security. The EEC Commission has demonstrated a preference to concentrate on deepening the degree of integration among its members, rather than expanding its membership. On the other hand, the West has supported the new governments both in tangible and philosophical terms. For instance, in 1992, western investments in the former socialist countries increased, demonstrating growing confidence in the investment future of the region. There has also been progress in relations with the Council of Europe (CE), whose mandate includes the issues of humanitarian cooperation. Hungary and Czechoslovakia, and later Poland, became full members of the CE in the early 1990s, one of the major admission criteria being free elections with party platforms.

The most acute difficulty facing the area is the integration of states which were former enemies into the western collective security system. The eastern European nations found themselves in a military-strategic vacuum after the *Warsaw Pact* was dismantled, and are now seeking shelter against mishaps under the NATO umbrella. Progress to date has been slow, although there have been discussions with the National Atlantic Assembly and North Atlantic Cooperation Council.

Above all, eastern Europeans have viewed the collapse of the Soviet Union as both a challenge and a blessing, holding new prospects and new threats. Gone is the eastern colossus, whose shadow darkened half of Europe. There is a geographic belt of states situated between Russia and the former socialist countries. At the same time, there appeared new and serious reasons for anxiety, primarily associated with the massive destabilization of the Soviet Union's sphere of influence, including armed clashes, ethnic conflicts, economic crises, refugee movement, and the expansion of organized crime.

Moreover, given the lingering power and historical legacy of the Soviet Union in the region, the new states in the region, regardless of ideological and political preferences, cannot wholly separate themselves from the destiny of the post-Soviet Union. The desire to close the gap between East and West in Europe and to adhere to the all-European economic, political, legal, and cultural sphere does not signify a total reorientation of East toward West. As the initial euphoria over the development of something approximating a Marshall Plan for eastern Europe gives way to realism, serious statesmen are become increasingly convinced that a promising 'eastern policy' is needed to raise the authority of their respective countries in the European and world arena. To this end, central and eastern European countries can benefit immensely by their understanding of the post-Soviet mentality, knowledge of the eastern markets, their long-standing relations and contacts in all fields of endeavour, and can become a reliable transitional area between West and East.

As constituents of a single post-totalitarian entity, the former Soviet republics, the eastern and central European countries, are in a position to render an invaluable service to one another as they move along the difficult and thorny path towards individual freedom, political democracy, and economic efficiency. Over the long years spent in the socialist community, the nations of the region developed relationships and interdependencies which are impossible to break without inflicting major damages on all states within the region. In particular, central European countries which are most successful, in terms of achieving integration in the western European institutions, can serve as a locomotive in bringing the rest of the countries up to their levels of development. In broader terms, the successful development of interstate relations in the East can become a powerful force for stabilization in the postsocialist era, and a factor in reducing tensions in the transition to the new order.

References

European Bank for Reconstruction and Development (EBRD). 1992. *Annual Economic Review*.
International Migration Organization. 1993. Report (published in Russian) (4 April).

The Transformation of the Central and Eastern European Economies

Jan Adam

Introduction

In Poland and Hungary, the collapse of socialism was gradual and was primarily caused by internal factors. Of course, without changes in the Soviet Union, particularly the abandonment of Brezhnev's doctrine, neither the Polish nor the Hungarian opposition could have brought down the system. In the former Czechoslovakia (henceforth referred to simply as Czechoslovakia), the collapse of the socialist system was the result of a domino effect; internal opposition alone did not have the strength needed to bring down the regime.

In all three countries, regardless of the way the old system collapsed, the new, noncommunist governments committed themselves to transforming their economies into market economies based on private ownership. The question was how to do it and at what pace? In substance, two general strategies were available: a gradual pace and the so-called shock treatment. (When economists talk about these two strategies, privatization is usually not considered. This is the case here, too.) It was primarily the International Monetary Fund (IMF) which pushed for a radical and rapid transformation, for a transformation whose chief macroeconomic policy components would be instituted at the same time. This strategy is often called shock treatment. It seems that the IMF pushed for such a transformation strategy primarily for political reasons. It wanted to make sure that there would be no returning to the old system. Namely, it was afraid that politicians in the postsocialist countries would not have the perseverance to push through the needed reforms if they encountered great difficulties in realizing a gradual solution. The past experience with reforms in the socialist regime, where none of the reform blueprints were ever completed, might have encouraged the IMF to take such a position.

Of the three countries under review, first Poland (in 1990), and later Czechoslovakia (in 1991) adopted shock treatment (the latter in a more moderate form) as a transformation strategy. Hungary opted for a gradual transformation. There, most economists took the position that Hungary did not need such extreme methods, since economic reforms had brought a significant advancement in changing the economy into a market economy.[1] In addition, the Hungarians, in the course of time, have become accustomed to solving their problems gradually. A good example is a comparison of how Hungary and Poland tried to solve the problem of price distortions. Unlike Poland, which resorted to a one-shot strategy—huge price increases—which turned out to be unproductive, Hungary tried to change prices gradually.

Poland and Czechoslovakia were in different situations economically on the eve of the shock treatment application. Poland was suffering from galloping inflation combined with great shortages, and was heavily indebted; whereas in Czechoslovakia both open and hidden inflation were moderate, the country did not suffer from great shortages, and was only slightly indebted. One could argue that in the face of Polish problems, shock treatment was an adequate cure. Many Polish economists who argued this line of reasoning before the application of the cure have changed their views since witnessing the impact of the results of this strategy.

There was little impetus for Czechoslovakia to imitate Poland, all the more so because, when Czechoslovakia embarked on its shock treatment, the negative results of the Polish venture were already known. In Czechoslovakia the transformation package "was launched in a context of relative macroeconomic equilibrium . . . that is in a situation that apparently did not call for major *stabilization* surgery" (Koves 1992: 32). In this article I am going to elaborate on the strategies applied in the three countries, and discuss their effect on the economy.

The Transformation Strategy

On 1 January 1990, in Poland, and on 1 January 1991, in Czechoslovakia, a package of radical provisions was put into effect, whose purpose was to renew market equilibrium and pave the way to a market economy. In more

---

1. When J. Kornai came up with the idea of a kind of shock treatment in his book (1989), he was criticized by many well-known economists who showed the dangers such a policy hides within itself.

concrete terms, the objective of the package was to stabilize the economy, which meant not only restoring market equilibrium at home (this referred primarily to Poland; Czechoslovakia did not suffer from great market disequilibrium), but also achieving a surplus in the balance of payments in order to meet debt-servicing obligations. Another no less important objective, tied to the previous one, was to create a competitive environment where price signals would guide the activities of enterprise managers and thus effect a change in their behaviour toward promoting economic efficiency.

To this end, the restructuring package included restrictive monetary and fiscal policies, strict wage control, liberalization of prices with some exceptions, and elimination of subsidies on most goods. Furthermore, it allowed for the opening of the economy to the influence of the world economy by liberalizing foreign trade and introducing internal convertibility of the currencies. Privatization was to follow.

Restrictive monetary and fiscal policies and the strict wage control had a two-prong goal: to ensure stabilization of the economy, and to cope with the inflation which was the result of freeing prices under high monopolization of the economy, a massive elimination of government subsidies, and a huge devaluation of the currency.

The Hungarian program of transformation, which was often called the Kupa program (1991) after the former minister of finance, followed more or less the same objective as the Polish and Czechoslovak programs, but was based on the idea of gradualism. When it was approved in 1991, it promised a turnaround in the declining economy by 1993, the reduction of inflation to a single number by 1994, and the completion of trade liberalization by 1992. The convertibility of the *forint*, which was to complete the transformation process, was promised for 1994. No mention was made about prices, since they were more or less freed in the meantime. Finally, the programme promised rapid completion of the legal infrastructure.

The transformation packages produced positive results. In Poland, where a huge market disequilibrium existed, shortages were eliminated. In all three countries, consumers have a greater selection of products. A more rational price system has come into being. The private sector is rapidly expanding. The foundations for market economy have been laid down.

The successes mentioned were achieved at a very high social cost. Poland and Czechoslovakia were plunged into a deep recession combined with a considerable decline in the standard of living. Hungary, despite the choice of a gradual transformation, did not manage to avoid a deep recession, however, there were less drastic consequences on their standard of living.

Monetary and Fiscal Policy

Control of the money supply was central to shock therapy. The main instruments for gaining this control were the regulation of interest rates and the imposition of credit limits on banks. In practice, the credit limits turned out to be a more reliable instrument than interest rates. The interest rates were adjusted to the estimated inflation rates, but because the real inflation rates in Poland and Czechoslovakia were much higher than the estimated, the original goal of having positive interest rates, if not instantly then as soon as possible, could not be achieved. Therefore the authorities tried to curb the extension of credits by banks by imposing credit limits on them, and thus reducing the real stock of money.[2]

Mainly in Poland, the restrictive monetary policy had only a partial effect compared to market economies, one of the reasons being that it was combined with a very strict fiscal policy of increasing taxes and severe curbs on wage growth. Though these policies plunged the economies into a deep recession, they did not tackle inflation to the expected extent. It could not be otherwise, because neither Poland nor Czechoslovakia had, and still do not have, a real market economy with full-fledged market institutions and a market culture, and, in addition, they had a highly monopolized economy. The high interest rate and even higher taxes quickly changed inflation in Poland from a demand-pull to cost-push inflation. Excess demand, which existed before 1990 in Poland, was replaced by insufficient demand after shock treatment was applied, and inflation was fed by higher production costs.

These macroeconomic policies did not put forces in motion which would bring about a relatively quick turnaround in the economy. They did not force enterprises to rationalize production or bring about a restructuring, or a reduction of real unit costs and an increase in productivity. The best proof of this is that unemployment rose at a much slower pace than the decline in production (see table 1), and thus brought about a worsening of overemployment—a characteristic feature of the former socialist economy—and a considerable decline in productivity.

---

2. For example, Hrncir (1991) mentions that money supply in real terms declined by 27 percent in the first five months of the shock treatment in Czechoslovakia. In Poland, the money supply declined in nominal and real terms in the first two months of 1990, and in real terms in most months of 1990 (Dabrowski 1992).

Table 1. Important Indicators of Performance

	Poland			Czechoslovakia			Hungary		
	1990	1991	1992	1990	1991	1992	1990	1991	1992
Gross Domestic Product*	88.4	92.4	101.5	98.8	85.1	91.3	96.7	88.0	95.0
Industrial Output*	75.8	88.1	104.2	96.0	75.0	86.1	90.4	81.0	90.0
Gross Agricultural Output*	97.8	98.4	87.5	95.7	91.7	87.7	96.0	95.0	77.0
Investment*	89.9	95.6	88.8	106.1	72.7	109.1	90.2	88.0	92.0
Budget Situation**	0.4	-3.8	-6.0	0.0	-1.7	-1.6	-0.1	-5.0	-7.5
Balance of Trade#	150.3	96.0	---	90.4	103.2	92.9	110.8	89.3	96.1
Rate of Inflation*	685.8	170.3	143.0	110.0	157.9	110.8	129.0	135.0	123.0
Rate of Unemployment+	6.3	11.8	13.6	1.0	6.6	5.1	1.9	8.5	12.3
Real Wages*	75.6	99.7	97.5	94.6	77.2	107.4	95.0	91.0	97.0

Notes: * = previous year=100; ** = expressed in % of GDP; # = Exports in % of imports; + = End of the year. In Hungary in the beginning of the next year. Sources: Poland: Chroscicki and Misiak (1993) and Mujzel (1993). Bulletin (1992), no.4, Budapest, for balance of payment. Czechoslovakia: Statistical Yearbook of 1993, Prague. Hajek et al. (1993). Bulletin (1992), no.4, Budapest, for unemployment and balance of trade. Hungary-Koves (1993), based on Koping-Datorg data bank. Most of the figures for 1992 are preliminary. Bulletin 1992, no.4, Budapest, for balance of trade.

In Hungary, the situation was different. The government did not impose such a restrictive monetary policy. True, the interest rate was positive, but not excessively. On the other hand, the money supply grew faster than the nominal gross domestic product (GDP); in other words, in contrast to the situation in Poland and Czechoslovakia, the real stock of money in Hungary increased in 1990 and 1991 (in 1991 the money supply increased by 26–28 percent, whereas GDP in current prices went up by only 13–17 percent) (*Reports from Within the Tunnel* 1992: 15). As a result, the opportunities for businesses to borrow were not as tight as in the other two countries. In 1989, borrowing grew faster than the nominal GDP and grew proportionally in 1990 and 1991 (Valentinyi 1992).

In Hungary, taxes were increased, but not on enterprises. In 1988, in connection with the introduction of a value-added tax and income tax, the government shifted the burden of taxation to the population, to the benefit of enterprises. Taxes on population, which were at 27.7 percent in 1987, increased to an estimated 36.8 percent in 1992 (Murakozy 1992). Thus, it is not so much the monetary policy, but rather the fiscal policy and other factors which caused the recession in Hungary.

One of the objectives of the new fiscal policy was to bring about a balanced budget and thus contribute to the fight against inflation. This was to be achieved, on the one hand, by considerably reducing subsidies and government investments, and, on the other hand, by increasing taxes.[3] Despite these measures, all three countries, although to a lesser extent in Czechoslovakia, grappled with budget deficits. Compared to the budget deficit in the United States or Canada, their budget deficits in 1991 were not really severe; however, in 1992, the situation worsened. The IMF is exerting great pressure on the countries to hold the line on the budget deficit to a maximum of 5 percent of GDP.

---

3. In Czechoslovakia, taxes were increased in 1990, a year before the application of shock treatment, whereas in 1991 taxes were even decreased slightly. In Poland, in January 1990, when the Balcerowicz program was put into effect, taxes were increased considerably. There was an increase in the turnover tax (from 15 percent to 20 percent on average), but what was perhaps no less important was the increase in tax on assets, on the average of four to five times (Maj 1991). This tax, as well as the tax on wage growth, was not paid by the private sector.

There were several reasons why countries had difficulty balancing their state budgets, the most important being the recession. The imposition of tremendous taxes on enterprises, when there was declining demand and production, primarily in Poland and Czechoslovakia, had the opposite effect to the one intended; the taxes had substantially reduced the profits of enterprises and, as a result, government revenues from enterprises declined in real terms. In 1992, in all three countries, revenues from the turnover tax (in Hungary, value-added tax) remained far below expectations, the main reasons being the decline in demand, a shift in consumption to food where the tax rate is lower, and, also, tax evasion, primarily by the private sector. The latter is a great problem. Corruption is quite widespread, enabling many firms to circumvent tax laws (which have many loopholes anyhow), including customs regulations (see Czarny and Czarny 1992).

Increasing unemployment, which entails growing amounts paid out for unemployment compensation benefits, was, and is, a significant drain on state expenditures, primarily in Poland and Hungary. The growing number of pensioners has a similar effect.

Wage Policy

It is understandable that if a country applies shock treatment, wage control is unavoidable. And indeed, in Poland and Czechoslovakia, strict wage control was imposed. In Czechoslovakia, it had the approval of the trade unions (apparently involuntary) and of the representatives of employers. The wage control was made up of two components: allowable wage increases and heavy taxes for exceeding them. In Poland, the allowable wage increase was set in the form of a partial indexation; for the first month of the reform it was 0.3 (which meant that wages could increase by 24 percent in January 1990 at the monthly inflation rate of 78.6 percent) and during 1990 by 0.5 percent on the average (see Kolodko, Gotz-Kozierkiewicz and Skrzewska-Paczek 1991).

In Czechoslovakia, the 1990 basic wage bill could grow by an increasing percentage in each quarter of 1991. (In the first quarter it was 5 percent and in the fourth 32 percent.) In June 1992, average wage increases were linked to the annual increase in profit (Cervenkova 1992).

In both countries, exceeding the allowed wage increase was penalized by very high taxes. In Czechoslovakia, the taxes were paid only if wage increases exceeded the 3 percent level allowed. In Poland, the taxes were first linked to a wage bill;[4] in 1991, the tax changed into a tax on average wages (Fiszer 1991).

The linkage of the tax to the wage bill in Poland was probably made in an attempt not only to fight inflation, but also to encourage enterprises to reduce the work force and the unit costs. However, this tax had a negative effect on production and productivity and thus made the recession worse. It discouraged enterprises from expanding production if this necessitated an increase in their work force, since they had to pay the aforementioned tax. In addition, enterprises could not reward workers who worked more productively if they could not at the same time reduce the work force. The negative effects on production and productivity could have been avoided had the authorities imposed the tax on average wages from the beginning, and had they used a special tax to regulate employment.

In Hungary, the old quest for wage regulation, which would both prevent wages from becoming an inflationary factor and give enterprises enough room for making wage decisions which would promote economic efficiency, continued after the collapse of the socialist system. The Hungarian wage regulation system was also characterized by limits on wage growth and the payments of taxes when the limits were exceeded. However, the taxes were much smaller than in the other two countries. (Herczog 1989; Popper 1991; *Munkaugyi Szemle* 1992: 1-2). As of 1993, there is no more wage control. Hungary can afford such a provision since the trade unions are weak, and unemployment is high.

Enterprise Behavior

As already mentioned, the transformation process in these countries brought about a recession. The decline in GDP, but even more in industrial production, was dramatic in Poland and Czechoslovakia in the year when the shock treatment was put into effect. In Poland, the GDP declined by 11.6 percent and industrial production by 24.2 percent, and in Czechoslovakia by 14.9 percent and 25.0 percent respectively. In Hungary, the greatest decline in industrial production was 19.0 percent, in 1991 (see table 1). There were several factors which brought down production. No doubt, the most im-

---

4. In Poland, enterprises which exceeded the wage bill paid 200 percent in taxes on the first 3 percent, and an additional 500 percent in taxes on each additional percentage point (Krencik 1991).

portant was the decline in domestic demand for consumer goods and investment goods as a result of restrictive monetary and fiscal policies and drastic curbs on real wage growth.[5]

The applied policy *vis-à-vis* state enterprises, which Kolodko (1992) characterizes as mismanagement of the state sector, undoubtedly played a very important role. The imposition of high taxes (in Poland, this was combined with tax discrimination against the state sector), the failure to devote proper care to enterprises, such as, among other things, introducing an effective system of management evaluation, and underestimating the need for a rapid decrease in monopolization, all contributed to a decline in production (for further details, see Kolodko 1992).

The dramatic decline in trade with the former Council of Mutual Economic Assistance (CMEA) countries, mainly with the former Union of Soviet Socialist Republics (USSR), in 1991, was also an important factor contributing to the recession. Its impact on the total decline in output is, however, controversial. Naturally, supporters of shock treatment attach greater weight to it than it deserves and vice versa. All three countries have managed to offset, to different degrees, the loss of trade with the former CMEA countries by increasing trade with the Organization for Economic Cooperation and Development (OECD) countries. It seems that some adherents of shock treatment do not take this fully into consideration.

It is often argued that all three countries had an overgrown heavy industry, and its decline was one of the reasons for the decline in industrial production. It is true that heavy industry was overgrown, but it is ironic that this type of production, on the whole, fell less in the first year of shock treatment than production in other industries.

Soon after the application of shock treatment, enterprises in Poland and Czechoslovakia made huge profits. The freeing of prices and the huge currency devaluation allowed enterprise to sell their products far over their costs, which in many cases were low because of the use of inputs purchased at the old low prices. Soon the conditions for making huge profits changed. Prices for inputs and interest rates, as well as taxes, increased, and demand and productivity declined. Many formerly profitable enterprises became un-

---

5. In Czechoslovakia and Poland, the decline in production in the first year following the application of shock treatment was also caused, to some extent, by huge hoarding before the transformation process was put into effect, in the anticipation of price increases, which was followed by a decline in demand after prices increased (Bruno 1992).

profitable. In Poland in 1990, enterprises taken as a whole still made a profit, but in 1991 they experienced a loss (Misiak 1992).

Many enterprises tried to compensate for the lower demand on domestic markets by increasing their exports. For example, Czechoslovak metallurgy, which suffered a 50 percent decline in domestic demand, managed, due to the huge devaluation of the crown, to increase its exports considerably (Vintrova 1992; Zima 1992).

The worsening of enterprise finances plunged many enterprises into a state of temporary or permanent insolvency. In all three countries, under the old regime, enterprises were indebted; but, the indebtedness ballooned in the transitional period. There are several reasons for this phenomenon in Poland and Czechoslovakia; knowing that the transformation provisions would bring about a huge increase in prices, many enterprises increased their inventories before the freeing of prices, without taking into proper consideration the impact inflation would have on demand. The decline in sales, along with the stockpiling by many enterprises—in order to avoid dismissing workers—was another reason for the increase in indebtedness and insolvency. Enterprise indebtedness is a major headache for all three countries since it endangers the solvency of banks (Ehrlich and Revesz 1992: 110-14; Groszek and Rak 1992; Kouba 1992). The matter is complicated by the circumstance that insolvency in itself is not a reliable gauge of the viability of enterprises. There may be enterprises which are indebted and if they are helped to get rid of indebtedness, they may become profitable units, and vice versa.

The architects of fiscal reform based their strategy on the idea that governments should undertake certain transformation measures, carry out privatization, and adopt proper legislation for a market economy, leaving the rest to market forces. This approach was especially characteristic of countries such as Poland and Czechoslovakia, where neoliberals occupied the economic portfolios. This policy was supported by the IMF which felt that interference in the economy might only hurt the economy.[6] The IMF also discouraged the application of an industrial policy, though there are many historical examples which show that the opposite was needed, especially during the transitional period. A study sponsored by Oxford University (*Historical Precedents* 1990: 32) warns that "past experience shows that even when the

---

6. For example, the representative of IMF discouraged the use of public works as a method of easing unemployment (see *Economic Transformation and Employment in Hungary* 1992: 80).

primary objective is the creation of a market economy, it is necessary for the state to play a substantial role for many years. Following the collapse of the command economies, euphoria among some advocates of free markets and deregulation may engender an exaggerated belief in the powers of market mechanism." (See also Bruno 1992).

When designing their transformation strategy, little attention was given to the old value system and how it might influence the behaviour of managers and workers in the transformation process. Most workers and managers detested the old system and wished for its demise; nevertheless, they identified themselves with some of its values, mainly with those connected with social programs, full employment, and more equal distribution of income. The decline in the standard of living and the threat of unemployment, which for many had already turned into reality, made the needed adjustment to the market economy and the internalization of a market culture difficult.

Foreign Trade

At present, Poland and Hungary are quite indebted and, therefore, servicing of the debt has been a great concern. Debt servicing requires an adequate surplus in the balance of trade or in the trade in services. The former depends to a great degree on the level of exchange rate, all the more if convertibility is an integral part of the transformation package, as was the case in Poland and Czechoslovakia. In setting the exchange rate one must also see to it that its stability can be maintained for some time at least.

These are not the only aspects which should be considered when setting the level of the exchange rate. There is also an impact on the general price level and demand, and therefore there is a need to balance the different aspects properly.

In setting the exchange rate, the Czechoslovak architects of the reform, even more than the Polish, took more of these factors into consideration. This meant a huge devaluation of the currency with all its adverse consequences: it contributed to the generation of inflation and, in the final analysis, to Czechoslovakia's recession.[7]

---

7. Gomulka (1991) argues that the devaluation of the Polish *zloty* was not a recessional factor since huge holdings of foreign currency made up a great portion of the money supply in 1989, and this percentage increased considerably as a result of devaluation.

Hungary followed a different policy; it decided to achieve currency convertibility gradually, and could therefore afford to adjust the exchange rate slowly and moderately to adapt to the needs of the economy. The gradual adjustment of the exchange rate has prevented inflation from being fuelled from this source, and has perhaps made the flight of capital more difficult (than from the other two countries, mainly from Poland), at a time when the domestic economy urgently needs it.

It is usually argued that the introduction of currency convertibility promotes foreign trade and makes it easier to attract foreign investment. As to the first point, it is difficult to say whether Hungarian foreign trade suffered as a result of not having convertibility, but foreign investment did not suffer; it has been higher than in the other two countries (*Nepszabadsag* 1 September 1993).

Foreign trade liberalization was an integral part of the transformation strategy. In order to be useful to the economy, foreign trade must be balanced; it must, on the one hand, contribute to the strengthening of the competitive environment, thus forcing domestic firms to achieve higher productivity, and, on the other, it should not endanger the existence of domestic branches of production which are not competitive, but which the state wants to preserve for social or political reasons.

The three countries did not follow the same policy. Poland went the furthest in its liberalization; it removed almost all import restrictions and reduced customs tariffs. The adverse effects of this policy were not instantly felt. For some time, Poland was protected by the highly undervalued *zloty*. Once this protection wore off, imports of consumer goods grew fast and Poland resorted to increases in tariffs (Rosati 1991: 213; Dziewulski 1992; Toth 1992).[8]

Czechoslovakia was more careful. It eliminated import restrictions and did not change the low tariffs, but imposed a 20 percent surcharge on tariffs, which was later reduced to 15 percent. But soon Czechoslovakia doubled its customs tariffs on some agricultural products and foodstuffs, and introduced some transitional quantitative restrictions with regard to some agricultural products (*Finance a uver* 1992: 59–60; Toth 1992).

---

8. Lech Walesa complained that Western countries were flooding the Polish market with consumer goods and ruining Polish industry. In my opinion he should primarily blame the customs policy of his own country. Bruno (1992) argues in favour of a gradual elimination of tariffs.

Hungary started to liberalize its imports earlier than the other two countries, as early as January 1989 (with engineering products), a process which was to be finished in 1991, by which time, tariffs were to be cut (Gacs 1991; Koves 1992: 51). For the time being Hungary has import quotas for various industrial consumer goods and for a few foodstuffs. In 1991, the quotas amounted to approximately 5 percent of imports (*Figyelo* 1992: 1 and 16).

Social Cost of Transformation

Agenda '92 (1992), a collective study initiated by the Austrian Academy of Sciences with the cooperation of many European scientific institutes, states "In a strategy for socio-economic reconstruction, private consumption levels and sectoral output levels in key areas . . . should be established as targets and the market forces, as well as the monetary devices used as instruments in achieving them" (7). With some exaggeration, it is possible to argue that the architects of the transformation in all three countries did the opposite in the hope that the establishment of market economy would soon bring prosperity.

Several years have elapsed since shock treatment and gradualism, respectively, were applied, and prosperity is yet to come. True, a small segment of the population has made fortunes, legally and illegally; but the majority is much worse off; it must bear the burden of the transformation. In none of the countries under review are the ruling elites much concerned about this development since they see the unequal distribution of the transformation burden as a way to create a prosperous middle class.

As a result of the transformation process, all three countries have experienced a decline in the standard of living. Figures on real wages give us a good indication of the impact of the transformation on the standard of living, though not a complete one. In Poland and Czechoslovakia, the decline in real wages in the year of the application of the shock treatment was quite similar, 24.2 percent and 22.8 percent respectively. In Hungary, the decline was the smallest; in 1990, 5.0 percent, and in 1991, 9.0 percent (see table 1). The recession brought about an increase in the number of people living below the poverty line. For example, in Poland, this number increased from 14.8 percent in 1989 to 31.2 percent in 1991 (Deniszczuk and Zukowska 1992).

The huge budget deficits in Poland and Hungary threaten health care and the educational system, and negatively affect the social security system. The standard of living has also been affected by the government's interest rate policy toward the population's bank deposits. In Czechoslovakia and Poland, in the years when shock treatment was applied, great losses in the purchasing power of savings occurred: in the former it was 40 percent (see Kohoutek 1991) and in the latter at least 30 percent, but probably much more.[9] Hungarians also suffered losses, in all likelihood smaller than the other two countries, since the difference between the inflation rate and the interest rate on deposits in 1990-91 seemed to be smaller in Hungary than in Poland and Czechoslovakia.

When talking about the standard of living, one should not forget unemployment. In Poland and Hungary at the end of 1992, it was 13.6 percent and 12.3 percent respectively. In Czechoslovakia, it was much lower; at the end of 1992, it was only 5.1 percent.[10] In all three countries, women and unskilled workers are more affected by unemployment than men and skilled workers.

Political Consequences of the Transition

All three countries under review committed themselves to carrying out not only a transformation of the economic system, but also a substantial change in the political structure. The path to a market economy was to be combined with the path to democracy. In all three countries, democratic elections were carried out, and forces came to power which were in opposition to the communist regime.

There is a close interrelationship between the transformation of the political and the economic systems. A smooth transformation of the economy, meaning without great shocks and a decline in the standard of living, has a beneficial effect on political stability and democratization. A transformation which entails a deep recession combined with a considerable decline in the standard of living may have the opposite effect, as will be shown below.

Some believe that under democratic conditions it is difficult to carry out a radical change in the economic system, since the change is necessarily combined with hardship, and in a democratic system it is difficult to make people accept hardship. Some even argue, though not publicly, in favour of an authoritarian regime. They allude to the historical experiences of Taiwan,

---

9. Rosati has used the figure 80 percent (1991: 228).
10. It is generally accepted that the Czech Republic will not be able to avoid high rates of unemployment once privatization is complete.

South Korea, and Hong Kong, which managed to achieve remarkable progress in the development of their economies in a short time under authoritarian regimes (see *Historical Precedents* 1990: 32). It is questionable to what extent the experiences of the Asian countries are valid for the European countries under review. In addition, it would be very difficult to want to impose an authoritarian regime on the three countries so soon after the collapse of the communist regime; after all, the fight against the communist regime was also carried out for political reasons.

The deep recession has perhaps had the greatest destabilizing effect on the Polish political system. In that country, the opposition to the communist regime was the strongest and was carried out by a workers' movement, Solidarity, which managed to gain the support of the majority of the population in a short time. In the second half of the 1980s, Solidarity gradually adopted the idea of a market economy and capitalism and, when it took over political power, it embarked on a radical transformation of the economy. As has been shown, this has plunged the economy into a deep recession combined with a decline in the standard of living. The architects of the transformation strategy promised a quick turnaround, and since it has not come, workers gradually lost confidence in Solidarity as a political movement.[11] This became clear during the presidential elections in 1991, when the prime minister of the day got less votes than a Polish Canadian who returned home to make a political career. The disapproval of the transformation strategy by most of the population manifested itself in the September 1993 parliamentary elections when the Democratic Left Alliance, the successor to the hated Communist Party, became the strongest political party, and when Walesa's political party won only the 5 percent needed to enter parliament.

In Czechoslovakia, the shock treatment and the accompanying deep recession has contributed to the split of the federation into two countries. The recession affected Slovakia much more than the Czech lands, and therefore the Slovaks called for a slowdown of the reform, a request which fell on deaf ears in Prague. In addition, the Czech government made it clear that Slovakia would have to live from what it produced, or, in other words, it could not expect help from the Czech lands, at a time when many in Slovakia saw the reform as a Czech venture. All this fed nationalism, and supported separatist forces in Slovakia. When in the Czech lands, V. Klaus's right-wing party, and, in Slovakia, Meciar's left-leaning populist party won a relative majority,

---

11. It is necessary to distinguish between Solidarity as a political party and as a trade union.

the two leaders decided to split the country, which they managed to do by applying manipulation and pressure and disregarding the will of the people. Of the three countries, Hungary is the most politically stable. It can be assumed that the gradualist strategy has something to do with it.

Does the Transformation Strategy Used Matter?

In all the countries under review, more than three or four years have elapsed from the start of the transformation process. One could argue that enough time has gone by to allow at least a provisional evaluation of the strategies applied.

All the countries, regardless of the transformation strategy, have fared more or less similarly as to output decline. Poland is, however, the first country where recovery has started. It is not yet known whether this will develop into a sustained growth.

In all other important aspects of performance, the countries differ. Poland and Hungary are suffering from a high rate of unemployment. The Czech Republic can still boast a low rate of unemployment; however, Slovakia is in the same league as Poland and Hungary. Poland and Hungary, mainly the latter, have a huge budget deficit, whereas the Czech Republic has managed to avoid this. The great foreign indebtedness of Poland and Hungary is one of the reasons for their deficits. Inflation in Poland and Hungary is still high; it seems that, in the Czech Republic, after a huge decline in 1992, inflation in 1993 was not much behind the Hungarian level.[12]

As for social costs, measured here in real wage decline and real savings losses, Hungary fared the best and Poland the worst. The Czech Republic is somewhere in the middle; there, real wages are climbing upwards.

The supporters of shock treatment use the fact that output decline was more or less the same in all the countries under review as proof that the gradualist strategy is not more effective than shock treatment. In my opinion, this is not a convincing argument, since the transformation strategy alone does not determine the performance of the economy. There are many other factors which have an important impact on performance. No doubt, other economic policy measures—besides the macroeconomic policies applied as an integral part of the transformation strategy—which are supposed to fur-

---

12. According to reliable estimates, the inflation rate in 1993 was 36 percent in Poland, 22 percent in Hungary, and 20 percent in the Czech Republic.

ther the transition to a market economy are the most important. The dosage used in individual components of the strategy is also of importance. Last but not least, the economic and political situation before the reform and the extent of indebtedness have an impact on the economy. It could even be argued that the concept of gradualism itself must be examined. To be more specific, does the Hungarian transformation process correspond to the demand for gradualism? It is also necessary to consider whether the gradualist strategy means that the same methods are used as in shock treatment. Was the pace of the reforms appropriate? Was it not too quick?

There have primarily been three economic policy measures which have negatively affected the performance of the Hungarian economy compared to other countries discussed in this paper, and thus weakened the effect of the gradualist strategy. I have in mind the treatment of agriculture, the introduction of a strict bankruptcy law, and the slow adjustment of the exchange rate to the needs of exports.

Hungarian agriculture was a success story. In 1989, agricultural output was almost twice as high as in 1938. Hungary made more progress in equipping agriculture with modern technology than other countries. A considerable portion of output was exported and the domestic market was well supplied. Average incomes of farmers were not much behind those of industrial workers. Agriculture is now in a deep crisis. Gross production output in 1992 was 32 percent lower than in 1989, more of a decrease than in other countries. One of the reasons for this decline is the decrease in domestic consumption. Though many have left agriculture, unemployment in agriculture is high. Incomes of the agricultural sector have been the most affected; they are no more than approximately three quarters of those in the "material sphere" (Meszaros 1993).

The crisis is primarily the result of three factors: compensation policy for the land taken to the collective farms, privatization, and other agricultural policy. Unlike Czechoslovakia, Hungary did not adopt a policy of restitution in kind; instead, compensation for property lost during the communist regime has been given in the form of vouchers. In agriculture, due to the pressure of one of the coalition partners, compensation has in fact been given in kind. As a result, a significant portion of land has gone into private hands, but only a small percentage of the new owners are interested in cultivating the land. According to the privatization law, collective farms are obliged to return land to their members if they wish this to happen.

The two policies have brought about a huge fragmentation of the land, created impediments to large-scale production, and introduced into the reorganized collective farms a feeling of uncertainty, which has manifested itself in a decline in arable land and lower economic efficiency. In addition, and here I am already discussing the third factor, the government has dramatically reduced subsidies at a time when agricultural prices are depressed (Keseru 1993; Meszaros 1993).

Poland had a minuscule cooperative sector in agriculture, and, therefore, privatization was not a problem. In the final analysis, Czechoslovakia took a similar route to Hungary's with regard to privatization. However, it seems that it was more generous with subsidies for agriculture (Divila and Sokol 1993; Silar 1993). Yet, what makes the decisive difference between the situation in agriculture in both countries is that, in the Hungarian economy, agriculture plays a much greater role than in Czechoslovakia.

In 1992, a new bankruptcy law came into effect in Hungary. Briefly, the law consists of reorganisation and liquidation procedures. According to the original provisions, a firm (banks are exempt) was obliged to file for reorganization if it could not meet its due payments within ninety days. If the creditors unanimously agreed to approve the firm's solvency plan, the firm could get a maximum ninety days moratorium for financial restructuring. If the creditors could not agree, or the restructuring could not be achieved, liquidation had to follow (see Kalal 1993; Gray 1993).

The law put into motion a mass of bankruptcy filings and overwhelmed the judiciary system. According to an official of the ministry of finance, firms which filed from April up to the end of September 1992—when the filing fever was the greatest—had been producing approximately one quarter of the GDP, contributed 35 percent to exports, and employed 18 percent of the total labour force (see *Figyelo* 1992: 25 n. 50). Most of the firms filing for bankruptcy procedures in 1992 were organizations which had limited liability (44.8 percent), but state enterprises were also well represented (12.8 percent). All firms, regardless of size, were affected; of the total number of firms which employed more than 300 people, 11.85 percent filed for bankruptcy, and 11.1 percent of firms declaring bankruptcy employed 51-300 workers (Kalal 1993).

Needless to say, the bankruptcy law was too strict, which was also the view of foreign experts invited to a conference in Budapest, in October 1992, in order to pass judgment on the law. The experts suggested several changes, some of which had already been approved by the government (Zsubori 1993). But the damage to the economy was already done. According to Mizsei (1993), the consequences of the bankruptcy law might have been "the most important single reason for the fall in GDP by 3-5% in 1992." Needless to say, employment was also negatively affected. What is no less important is that the above-mentioned official of the ministry of finance expressed fears that reorganization procedures would contribute little to the restructuring of the economy.

Neither Poland nor Czechoslovakia followed the Hungarian example. Both have bankruptcy laws, but they have not enforced them. The Czechoslovakian approach is interesting. The Czechoslovakian parliament passed such a law in 1991, but the government has postponed putting it into effect several times.

One important reason why the Czech Republic suffers less unemployment than Hungary has already been mentioned. Another factor is that, for some time, the Czech Republic has deviated from its former policy. Last year, it bailed out Skoda-Plzen, a heavy industry giant (and more bailouts are expected to follow), reintroduced wage controls, and continued rent control.[13] It has an additional advantage in that the growth rate of working age people is growing more slowly than in Poland and Slovakia. In addition, it is going to intensify its active employment policy (see *Hospodarske noviny* 22 February 1944). Finally, the Czech employment picture has been positively influenced by a huge influx of tourists, substantially higher than in other countries.

It has already been mentioned that, unlike Poland and Czechoslovakia, where huge devaluations of the exchange rates were an integral part of the shock treatment, Hungary only devalued its exchange rate by a minimal amount. Despite this, and the collapse of trade with the former CMEA countries, it managed to avoid a huge decline in exports. In the years 1991-92, there was even a revaluation of the *forint* in order to fight inflation. Only in 1993, did the value of the *forint* start to decline faster, but still its revaluation continued, though at a slower pace than before. The revaluation was one of the most important reasons that the balance of trade started to worsen in the second half of 1992 and continued to spiral downward in 1993 and negatively affected the GDP and employment. For the period January to September 1993, the balance-of-trade deficit amounted to 2,270 million dollars (*Figyelo* 1994). There were other reasons for the deficit: a de-

---

13. *Business Central Europe* (1993-1994, December January), in writing about Klaus, the present prime minister, who, in his capacity as finance minister was instrumental in the introduction of shock treatment in 1991, said: "His policy record shows him to be closer to Keynes than to Milton Friedman, his professed idol."

cline in agricultural exports due to drought and the general unsatisfactory situation in agriculture, the embargo on Yugoslavia, and the consequences of the bankruptcy law, etc. (Csermely and Oblath 1993; Lanyi 1993).

In Poland, there was also a deficit in the balance of trade, but to a smaller extent than in Hungary. Only the Czech Republic managed to avoid a decline; in fact, it managed to increase it exports in 1993. The trade turnover with Slovakia is disregarded here (see the *Bulletin* of the Czech Republic, October 1993).

I have mentioned several reasons why the Hungarian economy did not perform well, or, to put it in other words, why the gradualist strategy did not produce better results than shock treatment with regard to output and unemployment. In addition, it should be borne in mind that the Hungarians applied a restrictive monetary (though in a more moderate form than the other countries) and fiscal policy.

In comparing the two strategies, we should not confine ourselves to output and unemployment. Social costs other than unemployment should also be taken into account. It has already been shown that real wages, and probably real savings, declined less in Hungary than in the other countries. How the strategies contribute to political stability is also of great importance. In Poland, the deep recession destabilized the political system to some extent and generated great social tensions, and, in Czechoslovakia, contributed to the split of the federation.

In addition, there are advantages to a gradual solution. The scope of the paper does not allow me to go into great detail, and therefore I must limit myself to a few arguments. There is sufficient knowledge about how a market economy works, but this in itself is not a sufficient answer to the question about how best to achieve a market economy. The quest for transition is somewhat like groping around in the dark and hides multiple possibilities of mistakes. Shock treatment, which covers most components of the transformation at the same time, is more exposed to possible mistakes than the gradual solution. In addition, the gradual system has the advantage of allowing errors to be corrected more easily than shock treatment does, as Murrell notes:

> fast reforms do not have the potential for reversibility possessed by more gradual reform processes. Since there is a lag between implementation and effect, fast reforms offer no mechanism for stopping a measure during implementation. . . . (1992: 89)

As the Polish application of shock treatment has shown, the reformers applied some of the measures excessively in order to have a sufficient margin of safety (Rosati 1991) (the same was true of Czechoslovakia), and, as a result, the hardship on the population was even greater than expected and still persists. Gradualism enables such an overshoot, and unnecessary social costs can be avoided. In addition, it enables social costs to be stretched out over a longer period.

The transition is also very difficult because workers and managers alike lack a market culture and are still in the grip of the old value system, to some degree. To internalize a market culture takes a long time. This is another argument in favour of a gradualist strategy.

References

I would like to thank Social Sciences and Humanities Research Council, Ottawa for the extended research grant which enabled me to work on this study. I am also obliged to Professors K. Csoori, E. Ehrlich, H. Flakierski, H. Herwig, G. Kovari and G. Revesz for their valuable comments. I have already written separate papers on the transformation in Czechoslovakia and Poland (see Adam 1993a and 1993b).

Adam, J. 1993a. "Transformation to a Market Economy in the Former Czechoslovakia," *Europe-Asia Studies* 4:627-45. A modified version was also published in 1993, in Hungarian in *Kulgazdasag* 3:30-46.

Adam, J. 1993b. " What went Wrong with Polish Shock Treatment?" In *Politicka ekonomie* (in Czech) 4: 525-38, and in Hungarian in *Europa Forum* 1993. (December): 20-36.

Agenda '92 for Socio-Economic Reconstruction of Central and Eastern Europe. 1992. Austrian Academy of Sciences, a collective study from scientists of several countries.

Bruno, M. 1992. "Stabilization and Reform in Eastern Europe," *IMF Staff Papers* 4:742-77.

Business Central Europe. 1993-94. (December-January). Published by *The Economist*.

Cervenkova, A. 1992. "Mzdova regulace, letos naposled," *Ekonom* 25:24-25.

Chroscicki, T., and M. Misiak. 1993. "Nie za rozowo," *Zycie Gospodarcze* 45:11.

Csermely, A., and G. Oblath. 1993. "A magyar kulkereskedelem 1993-ban," *Nepszabadsag* (25 October).

Czarny, E. and B. Czarny. 1992. "Die Auswirkungen des wirtschaftlichen Umbaus auf den Lebenstandard in Polen (1990-1991)," *Osteuropa Wirtschaft* 3:237-54.

Dabrowski, M. 1992. "Az 1990-1991-es lengyel stabilizacio," *Kulgazdasag* 10:26-41.

Deniszczuk, L., and I. Zukowska. 1992. "Sytuacja materialna gospodarstw domowych w okresie wprowadzania programu stabilizacji gospodarki," *Ekonomista* 4:563-79.

Divila, E., and Z. Sokol. 1993. "Formovani novych podnikatelskych subjektu v ceskem zemedelstvi," *Politicka ekonomie* 5:579-88.

Dziewulski, K. 1992. "Kogo protegowac," *Zycie Gospodarcze* 5:6.

Economic Transformation and Employment in Hungary. 1992. Geneva: International Labour Office.

Ehrlich E., and G. Revesz. 1992. *Valsagos gazdasag, bizonytalan megujulas Kelet-Kozep Europaban,* Budapest: Institute for World Economics of the Academy of Sciences.
Fiszer, J. 1991. "Tax Reform in Poland." In *Economic and Social Policy Series, Volume 9.* Poland: Friedrich Ebert Foundation.
Gacs, J. 1991. "Foreign Trade Liberalization." In *Foreign Economic Liberalization, Transformations in Socialist and Market Economies,* edited by A. Koves and P. Marer. Boulder: Westview Press.
Gomulka, S. 1991. "Tworcza destrukcja," *Zycie Gospodarcze* 18:6-7.
Gray, C. 1993. "Bankruptcy Law and Enterprise Restructuring in Central Europe," *Transition* 5:1-4.
Groszek, M., and J. Rak. 1992. "Oddluzeniowy pejzaz," *Zycie Gospodarcze* 48:1 and 4-6.
Hajek, M., et al. 1993. "Ceskoslovenska ekonomika v zaveru roku 1992," *Politicka Ekonomie* 3:333-55.
Herczog, L. 1989. "Az erdekegyeztetes szerepe a berrendszerben," *Munkaugyi Szemle* 3:1-4.
Historical Precedents for Economic Change in Central Europe and the USSR. 1990. Produced by Oxford Analytica, group study led by Ch. Fernstein.
Hrncir, M. 1991. "Monetary and Credit Policies for Transition to a Market Economy," *Politicka ekonomie* 11-12:865-80.
Kalal, K. 1993. "Jednorocne skusenosti z bankrotov v Madarsku," *Narodni hospodarstvi* 7-8:37-39 and 30-34.
Keseru, J. 1993. "Rendszervaltas az agraragazatban," *Tarsadalmi Szemle* 3:14-25.
Kohoutek, M. 1991. "Tendence ve vyvoji usporovych vkladu obyvatelstva v letech (1990-1991)," *Finance a uver* 11:511-20.
Kolodko, G. 1992. "From Output Collapse to Sustainable Growth in Transition Economies." International Monetary Fund, mimeo.
Kolodko, G., D. Gotz-Kozierkiewicz, and E. Skrezsewska-Paczek. 1991. *Hyperinflation and Stabilization in Post-Socialist Economies.* Warsaw: Institute of Finance.
Kornai, J. 1989. *Indulatos ropirat a gazdasagi atmenet ugyeben.* Budapest: Heti Vilaggazdasag Kiado. This book was published in modified form in English entitled *The Road to a Free Economy, Shifting from a Socialist System: The Example of Hungary,* New York: W. W. Norton and Company.
Kouba, K. 1992. Interview conducted by E. Klvacova, *Ekonom* 46.
Koves, A. 1992. *Central and East European Economies in Transition.* Boulder: Westview Press.
Krencik, W. 1991. "Sprawa popiwku," *Praca i Zabezpieczenie Spoleczne* 8-9:1-7.
Kupa program. 1991. Official document of the Hungarian Ministry of Finance (March).
Lanyi, K. 1993. "Kulkereskedelmi folyamatok," *Figyelo* 33:22.
Maj, H. 1991. "Do wimiany," *Zycie Gospodarcze* 14:6.
Meszaros, G. 1993. "Az agrargazdasag valsaga es a mezogazdasagi kormanyzat felelossege," *Nepszabadsag* (5 November).
Mizsei, K. 1993. "Instituting Bankruptcy in the Post-Communist Economies of East Central Europe." Paper published by the Institute for East-West Studies, New York.
Misiak, M. 1992. "Na granici wytrzymalnosci," *Zycie Gospodarcze* 13:1 and 4.
Mujzel, J. 1993. "Privatization in Poland: Its Achievements, Weaknesses and Dilemmas." Paper presented at an International Workshop in Budapest.
Munkaugyi Szemle. 1992. Number 2.

Murakozy, L. 1992. "Az allamhaztartas a kilencvenenes evek Magyarorszagan," *Kozgazdasagi Szemle* 11:1050-66.

Murrell, P. 1992. "Evolutionary and Radical Approaches to Economic Reform," *Economics of Planning* 25: 79-95.

Reports from Within the Tunnel, Report on the Hungarian Economy in 1991. 1992. Budapest: Penzugykutato Reszvenytarsasag.

Popper, L. 1991. "Berszabalyozas! Berszabalyozas?" *Munkaugyi Szemle* 3:2-6.

Rosati, D. K. 1991. "Sequencing the Reforms in Poland." In *The Transition to a Market Economy*, edited by P. Marer and S. Zecchini. Paris: OECD.

Silar, J. 1993. "K problemum subvencovani zemedelstvi na zaklade zkusenosti let 1990-1992," *Finance a uver* 10:456-67.

Toth, G. L. 1992. "A kulgazdasag liberalizalasa. Tapasztalok Lengyelorszagban es a Cseh es Szlovak Koztarsasagban," *Tarsadalmi Szemle* 12:46-57.

Valentinyi, A. 1992. "Monetary Policy and Stabilization," *Soviet Studies* 6:985-95.

Vintrova, R. 1992. "Vseobecna recese a strukturalni adaptacni krize," *Politicka ekonomie* 1:39-50.

Zima, Z. 1992. "Pozadavky na adaptaci ekonomiky v nejblizsich letech," *Narodni hospodarstvi* 5:20-26.

Zsubori, E. 1993. "Valtozik a csodtorveny," *Figyelo* 26:18-19.

COMMENTARY

Whither Europe? Or is There Life After the Bipolar World: A Commentary

Holger Herwig

"The Future of Federalism" conference struggled for two days to come to grips with the reality of life after the collapse of the Soviet Union. In the process, it tackled a broad spectrum of issues and problems ranging georaphically from Canada to Russia, Yugoslavia to India. The cogent question raised of "Whither Europe?" could perhaps best be stated as the German writer Hans Magnus Enzensberger put it in his best-seller, *Europe Europe* (1989); if, in Winston Churchill's memorable phrase, Russia was "a riddle wrapped in a mystery inside an enigma," perhaps this conference permitted us at least to appreciate the complexity of the issue (see Evans 1968: 602).

The papers in this section addressed the basic question of future federations, whether economic or political, facing Europe in the 1990s. Jan Adam, an economist at The University of Calgary, and Viktor Kuvaldin, an associate of the Gorbachev Foundation in Moscow, key in on the post-1990 economic transformation of command economies into market economies in Poland, Czechoslovakia, and Hungary. They come to radically different conclusions. Gretchen MacMillan, a political scientist at The University of Calgary, sought answers to the European Community's (EC) most likely future course: development in depth or in breadth.

Professor Adam poses the problem simply and powerfully: were the International Monetary Fund (IMF) and the World Bank correct in pushing for radical and rapid transformation—so-called shock treatment—of the Polish (1990) and Czech (1991) socialist economies, or would a more gradualist approach, such as that tried in Hungary, have been better suited to local needs? Part of the problem lay in the realm of politics: neither the IMF nor the World Bank wished to see a return to the old system, and hence both demanded shock treatment in order to make sure that there could be no going back. Yet, there also existed very real economic problems. In 1990, inflation ran 558 percent in Poland and 58 percent in Czechoslovakia. Industrial production in Poland declined by 32 percent; in Czechoslovakia and Hungary, by 27 percent. Trade fell off sharply as all three countries were denied their former Council of Mutual Economic Assistance (COMECON) markets, especially the Soviet Union.

Radical reform brought immediate declines in social programs, standards of living, and real wages (12 percent in Hungary to 32 percent in Poland and Czechoslovakia), as well as a concomitant rise in unemployment (5 percent in Czechoslovakia and 11 to 13 percent in Poland and Hungary). Right-wing governments in Poland, Hungary, and the Czech lands (after 1992) have accepted recession as the price of reform. For the moment, trade unions and viable democratic socialist parties are without the prospect of success or power.

Adam argues that while most Western economists favour shock treatment, gradualism may perhaps have been a better strategy. Above all, it would have permitted the regimes in Warsaw, Prague, and Budapest time to identify and correct reform errors, allowed these cradle-to-grave socialist states time to adjust their extensive (and extremely costly) social security systems, and protected the majority from the ravages of radical and drastic reform. In short, Adam provided a rather bleak picture of the social and human cost of both shock treatment in Poland and the Czech Republic, and of the more gradualist reforms in Hungary.

Dr Kuvaldin disagrees. The "leading group" of reform states (Czechoslovakia, Hungary, and Poland), he notes, "have passed through the lowest point of the crisis and entered a stage of stabilization." The rate of decline in their gross domestic product (GDP) has been cut in half between 1991 and 1992; the rate of growth in prices has been slashed 300 percent; and the unemployment rate has declined 100 percent. Especially in the Czech lands, the key to success has been the rapid rate of privatization. Obviously, Alice-in-Wonderland's law is hard at work here: where one stands on an issue depends on where one sits; shock therapy in central Europe may seem costly in social and human terms from the perspective of Calgary, yet it may be mild from the vantage point of Moscow!

Kuvaldin's brilliant paper raises critical political points regarding future federative structures. He defines a basic north-south split between the central European trio of Poland, Czechoslovakia, and Hungary, dominated by right-wing or centrist politicians, and the southern tier of Slovakia, Romania, Bulgaria, and Serbia, still in the hands of what he terms the former communist "nomenclatura." Additionally, Kuvaldin detects the development of subregional forms of cooperation, that is, Alps-Adriatic, Balkan community, Baltic forum, and the Vysehrad triangle, perhaps as a "preparatory school" for the eventual implementation of a single Europe "metaproject." Finally, he sees alternatives to the European Community (EC) perhaps in two potential blocks: a "mini-COMECON" consisting of Poland, Hungary, and Czechoslovakia; and a Venetian "hexagon" of Italy, former Yugoslavia, Austria, the Czech lands, Hungary, and Poland.

Dr MacMillan would demur. For, regardless of how pesky the Danes and how devious the British may be on the Treaty on European Political Union negotiated at Maastricht in December 1991, she argues that the EC is the only game in town. Her real concern is over the federalistic future of Europe in general and the resolution of issues such as subsidiarity, democratic deficit, and citizenship (twelve states and nine languages) in particular.

Is the European Community a supranational state in the making? Mac-Millan argues "both yes and no." Since 1957, the founders of the erstwhile European Economic Community have struggled for economic and even political integration, but what has been accomplished has largely been brought about by the political elite and, more specifically, the executive leadership of the member states. Thus, MacMillan argues, if the supranational organization of the EC is to become a true supranational state, it will have to "acquire more wide-based sovereignty" and more institutional "legitimacy among the citizens of the member-states." Above all, Europeans will have to forgo a single political community and transfer their allegiance from national states to the European Community. To date, many have refused to do that. As in the case of the Polish, Czech, and Hungarian economic shock treatment, the jury is also still out regarding full European political integration.

In conclusion, I suggest that the last decade of the twentieth century in many ways reflects the problems and concerns of its second decade. The period following World War I was one of general economic recession, inflation, reduced budgets, and unemployment. Nascent democracies in eastern Europe were stamped out of the former Austro-Hungarian, Russian, and Ottoman empires. A strategic-political power vacuum existed in Europe, where Bolshevik Russia and Weimar Germany were momentarily stripped of power and consumed by internal chaos. In short, a period of multiple challenges and boundless opportunities.

Dr Kuvaldin alludes to a parallelism to the present decade. In terms familiar to the historian, he speaks of a contemporary "geopolitical power vacuum between the new Russia and united Germany, a vacuum which will be filled in this way or that." Much will depend on "this way or that." German unification will be completed by the end of this decade. Will a German government at Berlin be as willing in 2000 as it is in 1991 to push for European integration—perhaps at the cost of emasculating the powerful *Bundesbank* and *Deutschmark*?

Both Kuvaldin and Adam raise concerns that the vast majority of democracies created in eastern and central Europe at the urging of U.S. President Woodrow Wilson failed—with the notable exception of Czechoslovakia. And yet, that state could not survive the heady freedom of Václav Havel's so-called velvet revolution of late 1989. Will pluralistic regimes in Hungary and Poland, Romania and Bulgaria, Slovakia, and Albania fare any better? Will they be able to overcome the lost half century of imposed socialism and develop democratic institutions? Can the north-south economic and political divisions in Europe that Kuvaldin refers to be healed? And will Havel's central European tripartite alliance of Czechoslovakia, Poland, and Hungary, or the so-called Venetian hexagon of Italy, former Yugoslavia, Austria, the Czech lands, Hungary, and Poland, emerge as alternatives to the European Community? Kuvaldin, in fact, suggests that the emerging Rome-Warsaw axis perhaps reflects the ancient invisible border between western and eastern Christianity!

Finally, as Dr MacMillan queries, will the EC deepen integration among its existing members or broaden integration to include current associate members (under Article 238 of the Treaty of Rome), such as Hungary, the Czech Republic, Slovakia, Poland, Romania, and Bulgaria? There are few signs that the EC will embrace the "prodigal sons" from the east. There exist no serious plans to implement an eastern European Marshall Plan. Many western Europeans fear that incorporation of eastern Europe into the European Community, no matter how deeply citizens in Warsaw, Budapest, and Prague may regard themselves as Europeans, will lower their standards of living. Nor are western Europeans comfortable yet with the notion of embracing their former "enemies" within the protective umbrella of the NATO security system. Many are worried. Instead of a new *cordon sanitaire* having been created in eastern Europe by the collapse of the Soviet Union, there now exists a bewildering plethora of unstable ethnic and national states, all armed with nuclear weapons. The dark shadow of ethnic cleansing in former Yugoslavia hangs heavy over Europe.

In the American think tanks planted along Washington's Beltway, there currently exists the notion that the next decade will mirror the 1920s. If that evaluation is accurate, then the time has come to turn to the more positive developments of that period: a supranational League of Nations, the absence of a German problem, and the earnest attempts at disarmament undertaken at the Washington Conference of 1921 and the London Naval Conference of 1930. Surely, no one wishes a repeat of the 1930s.

References

Enzensberger, Hans Magnus. 1989. *Europe Europe*. New York: Pantheon.
Evans, Bergen. 1968. *Dictionary of Quotations*. New York: Delacorte.

Notes on Contributors

Jan Adam, Professor Emeritus, Department of Economics, University of Calgary, was born in Malcov, Czechoslavakia in 1920, and educated at the Prague School of Political and Social Studies. In 1951 he was removed from the Czech foreign service because of the prevailing political climate. In 1953 he received his doctorate in social science. He defended his Candidate of Economic Science (CSc) dissertation in 1963. Before emigrating to Canada in 1968, Professor Adam lectured at the Faculty of Philosophy at Charles University in Prague. He is the author of many books and articles since arriving in Canada. Among those publications are: *Wage, Price and Taxation Policy in Czechoslovakia, 1948-1970* (1974); *Employment and Wage Policies in Poland, Czechoslovakia and Hungary Since 1950* (1980); *Wage Control and Inflation in the Soviet Bloc Countries* (1980); *Economic Reforms in the Soviet Union and Eastern Europe Since the 1960s* (1989).

Alan C. Cairns is a Professor of Political Science, University of British Columbia. Professor Cairns received his BA and MA degrees from the University of Toronto and his Doctorate of Philosophy from Oxford. He has been a member of the Political Science Department at the University of British Columbia since 1960 and served as Head of the department from 1973 to 1980. Professor Cairns was the research director for the Royal Commission on the Economic Union and Development Prospects for Canada (1983-85). Three recently published collections of his essays are: *Constitution, Government and Society in Canada* (1988); *Disruptions: Constitutional Struggles from the Charter to Meech Lake* (1991) (both edited by Douglas E. Williams), and *The Charter v. Federalism* (1992).

Joyotpaul Chaudhuri is a Professor of Political Science at Arizona State University. Professor Chaudhuri was educated at Central State University in Calcutta, and at the University of Oklahoma. He was a postdoctoral visiting scholar at Yale University. From 1985 to 1990, Professor Chaudhuri was Associate Dean of the College of Liberal Arts and Sciences at Arizona State University. His main research interests are in the field of political theory, with particular reference to problems of democratic theory and jurisprudence. He is the author of several works, including: *India's Beleaguered Federalism: The Pluralist Challenge* (1992); *Founding America: The Political Legacy of Rights, Religion, Commerce and Diversity* (1992).

W. Harriet Critchley, Professor of Political Science and Director of the Strategic Studies Program, University of Calgary, received her doctoral degree from Columbia University in 1974, with a dissertation on ethnicity and political development in Yugoslavia, 1921-28. Since then, her research has concentrated on aspects of Canadian defence and arms control. Professor Critchley was a member of the Canadian delegation to all three United Nations Special Sessions on Disarmament.

Alain-G. Gagnon is a Professor of Political Science, McGill University. Prior to joining the Faculty of McGill University in 1989, Professor Gagnon was a member of the Political Science Department at Carleton University and at Queen's University. He is the author or editor of several books on a range of political themes, including: *Québec: State and Society* (1984); *Le développement régional. L'Etat et les groupes populaires* (1985); *Intellectuals in Liberal Democracies* (1987); *Social Scientists and Politics in Canada: Between Clerisy and Vanguard* (1988); *Canadian Parties in Transition: Discourse, Organization, Representation* (1989).

Brian Galligan is a Professor in the Division of Politics and Economics and Acting Director of the Federalism Research Centre in the Research School of Social Sciences at the Australian National University (ANU). He holds his doctorate in Political Science from the University of Toronto. He has written extensively on Australian politics, recently publishing (with Ann Capling) *Beyond the Protective State* (1992). Other books include: *Politics of the High Court* (1987); *Utah and Queensland Coal* (1989); and as editor or co-editor of: *Australian Federalism* (1989); *Intergovernmental Relations and Public Policy* (1991); *Comparative Political Studies: Australia and Canada* (1992). Professor Galligan is a member of the Constitutional Centenary Foundation and coordinator of the Constitutional Systems stream of the ANU's decade project on "Reshaping Australian Institutions: Towards 2001 and Beyond."

Roger Gibbins, Professor and Chair, Department of Political Science, University of Calgary, has written extensively on Canadian politics and society. His books include: *Prairie Politics and Society: Regionalism in Decline* (1980); *Out of Irrelevance: A Socio-political Introduction to Indian Affairs* *in Canada* (with J.R. Ponting, 1980); *Regionalism: Territorial Politics in Canada and the United States* (1982); *Conflict and Unity: An Introduction to Canadian Political Life* (1985); *New Elites in Old States: Ideologies in the Anglo-American Dominions* (with Neil Nevitte, 1990). He has also served as policy advisor with the Strategic Planning Unit of the Federal-Provincial Relations Office.

Mikhail S. Gorbachev is the President of the Foundation for Social and Economic Reform, and former president of the Union of Soviet Socialist Republics, and recipient of the Nobel Peace Prize. Mr Gorbachev was born into a peasant family in the Caucasus region of Russia. He studied at Moscow State University and the Stavropol Agricultural Institute. By 1978, he had become Secretary of the Communist Party Central Committee. In 1979, he was named a full member of the Politburo. He was the first elected president of the Soviet Union. For almost seven years, Mr Gorbachev brought a ray of light to East-West relations, initiating reforms at home that contributed to the beginnings of a free-market economy and political democratization. Abroad, he pursued policies that included withdrawal of Soviet troops from a fruitless war in Afghanistan. He sought an accommodation with the West that was essential to reducing the nuclear arms race; his policies toward the Germanies made possible the dismantling of the Berlin Wall and the ending of the Cold War. In August 1991, he survived an attempted *coup d'état* that caught the world's attention. At the end of December 1991, he resigned as president but has since continued to assume a prominent role as commentator on world affairs.

Bhodan Harasymiw, Professor in the Department of Political Science, University of Calgary, was trained at Queen's University, the University of Alberta, and the University of Toronto, and also attended Moscow State University in 1967–68. He is currently conducting research on processes of democratization in the former Soviet republics, particularly Ukraine. He is the author of *Political Elite Recruitment in the Soviet Union* (1984) and numerous scholarly articles. He has been political science editor of the *Encyclopedia of Ukraine* (1993) and assistant editor, *Canadian Journal of Political Science*, 1992-93.

Holger Herwig is a Professor and Chair in the Department of History, University of Calgary. Educated in German history at the University of British Columbia and the State University of New York (Stony Brook), where he received his PhD in 1971, Professor Herwig taught at Vanderbilt University until joining the faculty at the University of Calgary in 1989. A specialist in German diplomatic and military history, Professor Herwig has published widely in the field. Among his many books are: *Politics of Frustration: The United States in German Strategic Planning, 1888-1941* (1976); *Luxury Fleet: the Imperial German Navy, 1888-1918* (1980); *Germany's Vision of Empire in Venezuela, 1871-1914* (1986).

Yuri A. Krasin is Director of Social Programmes, the Foundation for Social and Economic Reform (the Gorbachev Foundation). An influential Communist Party theorist, Mr Krasin was trained at Leningrad University. In 1957, he joined the CPSU, from 1963 onward was an official in the International Department of the Central Committee, and in 1975 moved to the Institute of Social Sciences of the Central Committee. In 1987, he was appointed rector of that institution. Mr Krasin was a cautious advocate of reform in the Brezhnev period and received promotion under Mr Gorbachev. He came to prominence among scholars following the publication of *Revolution and the World* (1971), which was one of the first books to inform Soviet readers about western theories of the Russian Revolution.

Victor V. Kuvaldin is a staff member of The Foundation for Social and Economic Reform (the Gorbachev Foundation) and expert on the economic and political developments of the Soviet Union.

Guy Laforest is an Associate Professor of Political Science at Laval University, in Québec City and a former member of the Department of Political Science at the University of Calgary. He has written extensively on Canadian and European political thought and has been a prominent commentator on, and participant in, the Canadian consitutional debate. He is the author of *Trudeau et la fin d'un rêve canadien* (1992).

Leroy Little Bear is the Director of the Department of Native American Studies at the University of Lethbridge. He holds a BA from the University of Lethbridge and a law degree from the University of Utah. A specialist in native rights, Professor Little Bear has been an advisor to Indian groups, provincial governments, and the Department of Indian Affairs and Northern Development; he is the contributing editor of a number of volumes, including: *Government in Conflict? Provinces and Indian Nations in Canada* (1988); *The Quest for Justice: Aboriginal Peoples and Aboriginal Justice*

(1985); and *Pathways to Self-determination: Canadian Indians and the Canadian State* (1984).

Georgina Lynch is a graduate in Politics and Law from the University of Tasmania and worked as a visiting scholar at the Federalism Research Centre at the Australian National University. She is currently working as a lawyer with large commercial firm in Sydney. She is the joint author of a number of articles and chapters on environmental law and federalism, including articles published in the *Environmental and Planning Law Journal*.

Gretchen M. MacMillan, Assistant Professor of Political Science, University of Calgary, is a specialist in comparative politics. Professor MacMillan received her BA and MA in Political Science from the University of Guelph, and her doctorate from University College (Dublin), the National University of Ireland in 1987. Her doctoral dissertation, "Legislative Authority, Sovereignty, Legitimacy and Political Development: The Constitutional Basis of the Irish Free State," led to her interest in the European Community. Her research in this area has centred on similar issues, such as the role of institutions, particularly that of the European Council as well as issues of integration between the member-states and the supranational institutions of the European Community.

The Honourable Mr. Justice James C. MacPherson was Dean, Osgoode Hall Law School, York University from 1988 to 1993. He is presently a judge with the Ontario Court of Justice. Professor MacPherson received his education at Acadia University, Dalhousie University, and the University of Cambridge (LLM 1976), diploma in Comparative Legal Studies (1977). In 1981, he became director of Constitutional Law for the Government of Saskatchewan. In 1985, he became executive legal officer to the Rt. Hon. Brian Dickson, Chief Justice of Canada. He subsequently served as counsel to the Royal Commission into the Donald Marshall, Jr. prosecution.

Stephen J. Randall holds the Imperial Oil-Lincoln McKay Chair in American Studies at the University of Calgary, is Dean of the Faculty of Social Sciences, and was the organizer and chair of the Gorbachev Foundation-University of Calgary Symposium on the Future of Federalism, March 1993. He is author or editor of, among other works: *The Diplomacy of Modernization* (1977); *United States Foreign Oil Policy* (1985); *Hegemony and Interdependence* (1992); *Canada and Latin America* (1991, with Mark O.

Dickerson); *North America Without Borders* (1992, with Herman Konrad and Sheldon Silverman).

Linda Trimble is a Professor in the Department of Political Science, University of Alberta. Professor Trimble received her PhD in Political Studies from Queen's University. Her areas of specialization are Canadian politics and women and politics. She has written on gender politics in contemporary Alberta (in Allan Tupper and Roger Gibbins, eds., *Government and Politics in Alberta*), constitutional reform, and the CRTC policy on sex-stereotyping. She is currently writing a book with Dr Margaret Royal of St. Mary's University, entitled *Towards Transformations: Gender Politics and Public Policy in Canada*.

David G. Whitefield is an Associate Professor, Department of History, University of Calgary, where he has taught since 1967. Previously he was a lecturer in the Department of Economic History in the University of Edinburgh, Scotland. His academic work is mostly related to the theory of history and, in particular, to theories of historical materialism. His writings include works on the meaning of "class struggle," on the nature of intermediary social systems, and on the process of transformation from tribal to feudal society, and from feudalism to capitalism. For ten years, he was an academic consultant at the Academy of Sciences in Berlin, where he was engaged in the translation of *The Collected Works of Karl Marx and Frederick Engels*.

Mathew Zachariah is a Professor in the Department of Educational Policy and Administrative Studies, Faculty of Education, University of Calgary. Professor Zachariah holds a BA in Economics (Madras), a BEd (New Delhi), MS in Education (SUNY, New Paltz), and PhD in Comparative Sociology of Education (Colorado). He is the author of several publications, including *Revolution Through Reform* (1988). One of his major research interests is the comparative study of educational policy.

Index

Aboriginal peoples xix, 11, 44, 80–82, 123–24
Albania 102, 124, 117, 108, 241–42
Australia: and environment, xv–xvi, 141, 142, 149–151, 153–55; constitution of, 141–47, 150–57
Austria-Hungary 50, 100–101
Azerbaijan 110, 171, 173, 180

Balkans xv, xx, 52, 100
Baltic Republics 63, 177
Belanger-Campeau Commission; Québec, 113
Byelorussia 57, 170, 242–43
Bosnia-Hercegovina 51, 99, 100–102, 104–105
British North America Act (1867) 113, 125
Brundtland Report 25, 34, 151
Bulgaria xx, 100, 241–42, 245

Canada xiii, xiv, xviii, xix, 9–12, 17, 48, 54, 73–74, 113–130, 135–136, 192–94
Capitalism xvi–xvii, 54
Charlottetown constitutional accord xviii, xix, 113, 120, 126–27, 194, 202, 206
Charter of Rights and Freedoms: Canada, 12, 118–20, 127
Civil liberties 77, 85, 92–94
Cold War xvi, 3

Comecon xx, 239–44
Commonwealth of Independent States (CIS) xiv, 61–62, 64, 170–71, 172
Communism 12, 49, 61–62, 108
Confederation 170
Congress of People's Deputies: USSR, 65
Constitution Act (1982): Canada, 108, 122–23, 125, 193, 195, 199, 202
Croatia 51, 99–100, 102, 104–107
Czechoslovakia: economic reforms in, xx, 237–38, 240–41, 244–45, 250–69

Debt 257–60
Democratization 20, 59, 63, 66–69, 208, 226–28, 231–33, 238–41, 262–64
Denmark 223, 225, 228, 232

Eastern Orthodox Church 51, 100–101
Economic reforms xx, 4, 46–48, 59, 63, 66, 86, 222–23, 240–43, 249–269
Environment xiv, xvi, 17–39, 71, 74, 205, 207
Estonia 169–70, 178
Ethnic relations 4–5, 7, 59–60, 62–69, 71–75, 87–89, 99–111, 133, 176, 237–44

European Bank for Reconstruction and Development 240–41
European Coal and Steel Community 217
European Community xiv, xx–xi, 171, 216–35
European Parliament 219–29

Federal Treaty of Russia 175, 176
Federalists: United States, xiii, xvii, 47
Feminism xvii, 17–21, 23, 27, 204–209
Foreign investment 242–46, 260–61
Foreign policy 79–81, 84, 86–89, 94–95, 229–30
Foreign trade 251, 259–61
France 46–47, 128

Gandhi, Indira 85, 89, 96
Georgia 110, 171, 173, 177
Germany xv, 9, 48–49, 51, 225, 228
Gorbachev, Mikhail S. xi, xii, xix–xx, 13, 60–62, 170–71; August coup against, xi, 4–5, 169
Greece 48, 50, 82, 222

Hobsbawm, Eric J. xviii, 43, 47, 129
Hamilton, Alexander xvii, 46, 48, 77, 82
Hindus xvii–xviii, 85–86, 90–95
Human rights 22, 72, 111, 205
Hungary: economic reforms in, xx, 240–41, 244, 250–69

India vvii, 77–96, 133–35
Indian Act: Canada, 192–95

Industrial production 4, 46, 250–69
Inflation 252–53
International Monetary Fund (IMF) 249, 253, 258 n. 6, 273
Ireland 48, 51, 223, 229
Islam xvii, 51, 85–86, 89–95, 100–102, 102
Italy 9, 45, 48, 225, 232

Jefferson, Thomas 77–81, 83, 85, 89, 91–92, 96

Kashmir xviii, 87–93
Kazakhstan 64, 170, 242–43
Kravchuk, Leonid 171

Language: and nationalism, 7–8, 46, 48, 84, 90, 120, 185–86, 203–204
Latvia 169–70
Laurendeau, André 115–16
Lenin, Vladimir I. 5, 50, 58
Lévesque, René 113–30 passim
Lithuania 169–70

Macedonia 99–101, 104
Market economy xiv, 59, 240–41, 249–269 passim
Maastricht Treaty (Treaty of European Union) 216–19, 222–30
Marxism xvii–xviii, 4, 20, 31, 49–50, 58, 61–62, 72, 83–84
Meech Lake constitutional accord xviii–xix, 113, 118, 126, 199, 202
Moldova 110, 171–73, 177, 179
Moscow 61–62, 64

Muslims: in India, xvii; in Yugoslavia, xv, 51, 100-102, 104

Nationalism xvi, 11, 27, 34, 38, 49, 59-60, 63-65, 68, 71-75, 113-18, 123-24, 128-29, 199-201, 203-204, 238-39
Nation state: idea of, xiv, xviii, 7-8, 38, 44-54 passim, 60, 62-69, 206-209, 217-18, 225-26, 230-31, 237-38
Native Americans. *See* Aboriginal peoples
National security 246
North Atlantic Treaty Organization (NATO) 219, 246
New politics xvi, xix, 6, 17-39, 142, 205-207, 239-47
Nixon, Richard 77

Ottoman Empire 50, 100-101

Pakistan 89
Poland: economic reforms in, xx, 240-41, 244-45, 250-69
Portugal 222
Privatization 249, 258, 266
Punjab xviii, 87-93

Québec xviii, xix 11, 46, 73, 113-30, 199-204

Regionalism xiv, 11-12, 22, 34, 63-68, 85, 87-88, 91, 199-204, 237-38, 243-44
Religion xiv, xvii-xviii, 20-22, 50, 62, 84-85, 90, 100-101
Roman Catholicism 44, 51, 100-101
Royal Commission on Bilingualism and Biculturalism; Canada, 115
Russia xv, 6, 57-58, 60, 63-68, 174-75, 177, 242-43. *See also* Union of Soviet Socialist Republics.

Self-government: aboriginal, 81-83, 183-95, 205, 208
Serbia xx, 51, 100-102, 104-107
Slav 5, 51, 100-102, 104-106
Siberia 68, 176
Smith, Adam 31 n. 11, 46
Socialism 49
Solidarity 263
Sovereignty 4-8, 23, 26-27, 36, 47, 83, 143-45, 226-35
Spain 9, 83, 222, 225, 232
Sri Lanka 89
Stalin, Josef 5, 50, 59
State enterprise 4, 50, 256-59
Sustainable development, 20, 34-35, 151

Tatarstan 65, 176-178
Tito, Josip Broz 99, 104, 106-107, 133
Treaty of European Union. *See* Maastricht Treaty
Treaty of Rome 219, 245
Trudeau, Pierre Elliott 114-21
Turkmenistan 171-73

Ukraine 6, 57, 63, 170, 173, 177-179, 240-42
Unemployment 241, 252, 255, 262, 267
Union of Soviet Socialist Republics (USSR) xiv-xv, 4, 6, 57, 59-65, 165-70, 237-42. *See also* Russia.
United Kingdom 46-48, 83-85,

128, 225, 227, 232
United Nations Conference on the Environment xvi, 150
United States of America xiii, 9, 25-26, 33-34, 47-48, 52, 66, 80-84 90-91, 94

Wage controls 53, 251, 255-56, 261
Warsaw Pact 239, 246

Women: and economic reforms, xviii-xix, 19
World Bank 273

Yeltsin, Boris 52, 177
Yugoslavia: 1974 constitution, 99, 102, 104-110 passim, 133; economic conditions, 101, 106, 108-109, 133, 237-38; civil war, xv, 4, 101-102, 106, 109-110